D0871942

Love in the Time of Victoria

306.70942
B275

Love in the
Time of Victoria,

Sexuality, Class and Gender in
Nineteenth-Century London

◆

FRANÇOISE BARRET-DUCROCQ

Translated by John Howe

WITHDRAWN

VERSO
London · New York

LIBRARY ST. MARY'S COLLEGE
193818

First published as *L'Amour sous Victoria* by Plon, Paris 1989
This translation first published by Verso 1991
© Plon 1989
Translation © John Howe 1991
All rights reserved

Verso
UK: 6 Meard Street, London W1V 3HR
USA: 29 West 35th Street, New York, NY 10001-2291

Verso is the imprint of New Left Books

British Library Cataloguing in Publication Data

Barret-Ducrocq, Françoise
Love in the time of Victoria : sexuality, class and gender
in nineteenth-century London.
1. London (England). Sexual relationships, history
I. Title II. [L'Amour sous Victoria]. *English*
306.70941

ISBN 0-86091-325-2

US Library of Congress Cataloguing-in-Publication Data

Barret-Ducrocq, Françoise.
[L'amour sous Victoria, English]
Love in the time of Victoria : sexuality, class, and gender in
nineteenth-century London / Françoise Barret-Ducrocq : translated by
John Howe.
p.   cm.
Translation of: L'amour sous Victoria.
Includes bibliographical references (p.   ) and index.
ISBN 0-86091-325-2
1. Sex Customs—England—London—History—19th century.
2. Working class—England—London—Sexual behavior—History—19th
century. 3. London (England)—Moral conditions. I. Title.
HO18.G7B27   1991
306'.09421'2—dc20

Typeset in Bembo by York House Typographic Ltd
Printed in Great Britain by Bookcraft (Bath) Ltd

$27.85 HW 4-14-93 (SW)

To Philippe

To Marie-Claire

Contents

Introduction

There was once a society which is still held above all others to be the paradigm of sexual hypocrisy. An ostensibly, even ostentatiously virtuous society which furtively broke its own rules of conduct; a society which had nothing to say on sexual matters but left them to the professionals: medical specialist, pornographer and prostitute.

This summary image of Victorian society is extraordinarily tenacious. Its origins are to be found in the aesthetic and ideological revolution which swept through the British liberal bourgeoisie from about the end of the nineteenth century: Oscar Wilde to George Moore, Edward Carpenter to D.H. Lawrence. The arrival of 'sexual liberation' in the mid twentieth century revived this critique of sexual puritanism in Europe and America. Once again, past generations were censured for making a taboo of sexuality and dissimulating behaviour thought to have been quite licentious in private.[1] It was believed that to choose this version of reality was to align oneself with radicalism against conservatism, with liberated morals against narrow rigidity, with modernity and progress against the archaism of earlier centuries.

In reality, a glance at the moralizing literature of the nineteenth century shows that proposals for moral reform were accompanied by demands for ever more open discussion of sex. In 1884, only two years after it was formed, the Moral Reform Union expressed satisfaction at the partial ending of the 'conspiracy of silence' covering up male sexual depravity and the scandal of child prostitution. Forty years earlier, in 1843, an Anglican minister writing an introduction to William Logan's[2] book on prostitution attacked 'the false and affected delicacy which betrays the cause of virtue' and called for exposure of

I

the 'atrocities' and 'acts of debauchery' being committed on all sides. There are many other such examples, dating back to the Society for the Suppression of Vice at the beginning of the nineteenth century.

The fact is that alongside the Victorian period's undeniable modesty in matters of speech, gesture and clothing, there is at all times a public, respectable discussion on sexuality, an explicit and prolix discourse from which sensual enjoyment is absent, erotic excitement perhaps less so. This ambiguous road is thronged with a gallery of contrasting portraits: ruling-class debauchee, masturbating adolescent, frigid middle-class housewife, precocious and depraved slum-child; the factory girl with her easy morals, the prostitute, the violated virgin, the lubricious working-class housewife, the incestuous alcoholic, the mother pimping for her daughters; and more idealized types: fulfilled wife, attentive husband, chaste and informed student, innocent child. Each has his or her moment in the limelight.

What is the purpose of this insistent discursive tide? It stems partly from the growing scientific interest in their own bodies being shown by the dominant classes. Doctors, reformers, Christians, educators, developed in a wealth of detail, and often with great freedom of expression, their analysis of sexual behaviour considered to be patho-logical; they proposed harsh cures and tried to gain acceptance for their theories on, for example, the ideal number of coitions per month. In corollary, especially after the 1870s, there was increasing pressure for sexual education of the young, considered a rampart against immora-lity and a precondition for conjugal sexual happiness.[3]

But the most consistent, the most resounding sexual references are to be found in the immense literature dealing with the condition of the labouring classes, especially in the metropolis. Victorians saw the sexual depravity of the majority of Londoners as a threat to the moral and, potentially, the political order. The nation must be made aware of this situation – so unworthy of a great Christian country – and alerted to its dangers. The 'condition of the workers' and the question of working-class morality in the capital were seen as early signs of malfunction in a healthy social body.

Seen with difficulty through the mists of time, hidden behind screens of contemporary *pudeur*, the landscape wavers before the eyes of anyone trying to discern the truth about codes of sexual behaviour and morality in the Victorian period. In fact our knowledge of these matters varies considerably with the social class under examination. In recent years, a succession of historians and literary critics have striven with talent and imagination to retrieve the role of sensual delight and sexual love – hitherto kept firmly implicit – in the daily experience of the upper classes.[4]

But the sexual life of the people is hardly ever mentioned, being locked into a world made opaque by poverty, wordlessness and a crucial penury of first-hand documents. The little that *is* said on this subject bears an astonishing resemblance to the findings of Victorian bour-geois explorers. To maintain the necessary critical distance, twentieth-century observers treat with caution those commentaries that seem too ouvrierist, too moralizing or too supercilious; but in the end they are compelled, *faute de mieux*, to use again the Victorian accounts while discarding their ideological trappings. It was already being predicted, even before the end of Victoria's reign, that this people would vanish without leaving intelligible traces:

> That no voice will pass to posterity from the million-peopled ghetto of London will assuredly appear to the future historian a more inexplicable mystery. . . . What motives impelled their continual striving? What aspirations did they cherish? What temptations did they wrestle with? What hope sustained them through the unchang-ing monotonous days? These are questions that will remain for ever unanswered.[5]

After years of stubborn searching for whispers in that stony silence, the fortuitous discovery of a mine of private archive material, briefly opened and almost immediately closed again,[6] enables me today to extract from the past this image – certainly incomplete but, I believe, authentic and alive – of the sexual and moral behaviour of the London poor.

Comparison of this archive material with the indirect sources already available does hold some surprises. In the nineteenth century the populace was normally seen as amoral by reformers and philanthro-pists, and as libertarian by economic definition (until the bourgeoisie's ideological police could bring it into line) by political theorists who counted on the masses to change society.

The voices recorded in the Foundling Hospital's faded blue files, the voices of the women applicants and their associates, sound with an entirely different resonance. This is not to say that they deny the facts of their cases or the deeds of which, so to speak, they stand accused. Indecent flirtations, extra-marital sexual relations, concubinage, prostitution, adultery, bigamy, do indeed seem to have been the common experience of the women and men who recount their lives in these pages.

What differs from the conventional picture is the motivation and logic of the transgressions described, the evident perception of a specific moral code. I have tried to reconstitute this logic – often expressed with great naivety – and the detail of amorous encounters, to emancipate these couples from the label of brutal animality behind which they have habitually been confined.

The records enable us to visualize the subjects of this history in terms of their class and sexual relations. They throw a sobering light on the study of nineteenth- and early twentieth-century morals, a light which discourages excesses and demands re-examination of certain beliefs long accepted as dogmas in the history of ideas.

Labouring Classes, Depraved Classes

THE SETTING

The population of London was five times greater at the end of the nineteenth century than at the beginning, and at its most explosive nearly tripled in two generations.[1] The town itself grew in proportion, sending out tentacles decade after decade to devour the surrounding countryside. But population density remained extremely high throughout. The absence of transport, and later its cost, trapped the bulk of the working population in the middle of London, around the City.

The great public works undertaken in the 1820s,[2] the sanitary demolition programmes which began in the 1840s, the economic development of different areas, squeezed even more inhabitants into every dwelling and overwhelmed the inadequate urban services.

For most Londoners, the demographic and economic evolution of their capital meant forced movements of population, insufficient numbers of new houses (which in any case were inappropriate to most people's financial means and way of life) and prohibitive rents for existing property. Because London, like other European capitals, consisted of a rich town and a poor town.

The rich town was in the west, inside a perimeter bounded by Kensington, Hanover Square and the Thames.[3] Here were fine neo-classical mansions with gleaming white columns, tall houses of brick and stone with innumerable sash windows behind black-painted railings, hung inside with silk and cashmere draperies, their doorways carved from exotic hardwoods, their floors covered with carpets from

Smyrna and Madras; set around parks planted with lilac, gold-flowering laburnum, cherry trees dusted with pale pink. Here were wide streets, monumental buildings, sumptuous apartments, large quiet squares enclosing harmonious little gardens.

All around was Povertyopolis, Miserytown, its shape evolving with urban development. Initially coiled around the Rookeries in the heart of the town, its outlines stretched to the east of the City under successive demolition schemes, creating the East End which long retained the doubtful privilege of being the main centre of poverty and distress. Later it expanded across the river into Lambeth, Walworth and Southwark, and at the same time northwards into Kentish Town; pockets of poverty appeared in the west too – Soho, St George's. To contemporaries, certain districts were a byword for vice and desti-tution: Orchard Street, Devil's Acre, Seven Dials; St Giles's, notor-ious for criminality, was sought out by foreign visitors like Flora Tristan or Jules Vallès. Later in the century the lower depths drifted towards Wapping, the Isle of Dogs, the docks where the depravity of sailors on shore leave mingled profitably with that of the inhabitants.

Traffic between these two worlds was very unequal. All day and every day the working people came and went, busy with a thousand and one tasks of logistics, supply and maintenance in the prosperous parts of the capital; but rare indeed were the well-off Londoners who visited the poor quarters. Only an occasional philanthropist or eccen-tric would venture into this barbarian territory.

London at that time had very few large factories, being primarily a port, a centre of consumption, a seat of administration and culture. So most members of the better-off classes – businessmen, financiers, merchants, *rentiers*, civil servants and members of the liberal pro-fessions – had only the most tenuous direct economic links with the working-class population. It was inevitable that inhabitants of the rich town would see the popular districts as festering dens of filth, crime and debauchery.

A VAST HOTHOUSE OF SEXUAL IMMORALITY

Nineteenth-century London thus had the twin faces of Janus: one facing forward, the sumptuous display window of the Empire; the other half-hidden, a stinking backyard swarming with restless, impoverished masses. An assortment of commentators, social reporters, moral and religious crusaders, economic analysts, strove with increasing eloquence to describe this extraordinary and obscure arrangement, producing a whole literature of the picturesque, the infamous, the sensational and the threatening. This miserable and depraved mob living in the heart of the metropolis was, they feared, liable to compromise the civilizing mission of the whole Empire:

> The condition of the poor of the City cries shame on our boasted civilization and our indeniable opulence, and demands immediate reformation.[4]

And as the century advanced, the clamour of the moralists grew ever stronger. The list of these Cassandras, predicting the direst results from the barbarism of the masses, is a long and varied one. They fall into three groups, variously positioned in society and variously informed on the populations under discussion. The most numerous group consisted of philanthropists attached to charitable organizations. The others were made up of agents of the state – health officers, Poor Law officials,[5] inspectors of the educational commissions – and social observers like novelists, essayists, sociologists and journalists.

It will doubtless be pointed out that descriptions of this foreign society, this town-within-the-town, are not all the same, and that the writer's aims and political ideas, as well as the date of the work, modify its angle and tone. This is true, but only up to a point.

The signs of immorality

All contemporary observers were agreed on one thing at least: the universe they were discovering was a universe of vice and misery.

> On a sudden there comes a stench of rotting rags, of fermented filth; we are passing a lane or court, some squalid passage swarming with a whole tribe of poor ruffians. One can see them from the pavement without entering, like bugs lurking in the chink of a bedstead,[6]

writes Jules Vallès. In the working-class world, aesthetic criteria and rules of conduct are inverted, an anamorphosis all the more hateful for being perceived as a sign of bottomless ethical decay.

7

For these observers, clearly, external appearance was an exact reflection of internal reality: both a sign and a consequence of the moral condition. This handy correspondence between vice and ugliness enabled the phenomenon and its inner essence to be discerned at a glance. And a good thing too: the unalterable link between the physical and the moral meant that people wore their souls, so to speak, on their sleeves.

Thus the dark, tangled alleys in which our Victorian heroes wandered came to suggest furtiveness and sin. The meaningless swarming of unknown beings in the rooms and courtyards evoked images of the irrational and the animal kingdom, while the mephitic stenches of rubbish and unwashed bodies could only indicate obscenity. In the moral symbolism of the nineteenth century foul air and evil blended together, impartially polluting bodies and souls.

It may justly be said of the Mint, that the inhabitants breathe a polluted moral atmosphere, and impart it, like a contagious disease, to others . . .[7]

In Victorian society, with its shifting frontiers, external signs comprised a code enabling interlocutors to be placed almost on sight. In a society where a bourgeois morality shot through with puritan principles played a determining role, first appearance was inevitably identified with essence. As the century advanced, the aristocracy was increasingly compelled to hide its libertine tendencies under a chasuble of public virtue. By the same token the respectability of working men – and even more of working women – was measured by a set of easily seen qualities: sobriety, cleanliness and modesty of dress, institutionalization of sexuality, religious observance, regularity of employment, prudence and seriousness of distractions. The novelist Robert Roberts notes, with a certain bitter humour, that in poor areas the situation of a household was advertised by the quality of its curtains:

Window curtaining with us had high significance; the full drape, if possible in lace, being a necessity for any family with pretensions to class. No one scorned the clean modest half curtain, but a newspaper across the panes showed all too clearly that still another household had been forced to hoist the grey flag of poverty.[8]

But bourgeois observers were insensitive to these nuances of respectability; indeed, they saw the working-class world as being regulated by a system of counter-values:

Vice and wretchedness exist in their most appalling and hideous forms, stalking about with bold front, unblushingly, as though vice were virtue.[9]

The behaviour of the poor, seen as a whole, blatantly violated the principles of the dominant moral order. The labouring classes must therefore be immoral. The outward appearance, the manners, customs and culture of the people, were unequivocal signs of this immorality.

USE OF THE STREETS

Most European towns in the nineteenth century maintained avenues, boulevards or *ramblas* where people could take the air, meet one another, see and be seen. London high society, for example, would walk, ride or drive in Hyde Park, Rotten Row or the Mall. This use of urban space was subject to strictly defined rules governing times of day, seasons, escorts, and so forth. Outside these few times and places, respectable citizens used the streets only for getting to work, to the park, to church or (in a few places like the Brompton Road) for shopping. Anyone loitering in the street, especially in the evening, was liable to be taken for a debauchee in quest of amorous encounters. Streets in popular districts, by contrast, astonished visitors with their general activity, their noise, smells, lighting and insalubriousness, and their perpetually busy population, a human traffic apparently unaffected by climate or convention. Day and night, in the rain and mud of winter and the heat of summer, there bustled a confused throng of men and women, old folk and children. Many trades and professions were followed in the street: pedlar and knife-grinder, performer and tumbler, dustman and sweep, carter and prostitute . . . the London streets served as an annexe to cramped dwellings and a substitute for the village green whose memory was still fresh in many minds. Nursery and playground of the very young, the street served adolescents and adults as a place for eating, getting drunk, entertainment, discussion, courting and caressing, fighting and, for those seriously down on their luck, sleeping.

Social explorers were always ready to see the street, the 'drawing-room of the poor',[10] as a setting for all kinds of outrageous and depraved conduct. They were seldom disappointed. The swearing and

9

lewd jokes of the men, the obscene games of children and the physical freedom of the young of both sexes were the subjects of many an indignant commentary, like this one about Whitechapel:

> It is a dismal, dreary scene, presented here in the misty gloom of this November evening, and it is all the more gruesome and depressing from the revolting conversations of many of the people, especially of a line of rough-looking fellows who stand with their backs against the wall opposite the end of Miller's Court, smoking short pipes, chaffing the crowd, and bandying unseemly jests . . . [11]

As for women, they were the object of more or less permanent disapproval, first for the irritation and affront occasioned by their very presence. Of course nobody minded seeing a busy housewife hurrying to the shops, a hard-working seamstress on the way to deliver her finished work and pick up a new consignment of shirts, or women who followed the innumerable petty trades which flourished in those days. So long as she was in a hurry, obviously busy, the woman of the people was playing her proper role; her brisk passage through the streets was the gauge of her honesty. Loitering in the street, on the other hand, hanging about for too long or without an obvious errand, was seen as unnatural, since female activity was firmly centred on the world of the interior, indoors. So any wandering about which could not be explained by shopping or some other necessary activity came to be perceived as a factor or sign of doubtful morality. Suspicion was aroused by nothing more than a dawdling gait and the absence of any obvious errand:

> At quite the beginning of the month of June, about four o'clock in the afternoon, I saw a woman walking along Pall Mall dressed in the nicest and neatest way. I could scarcely make up my mind whether she was gay or not, but at length saw the quiet invitation in her eye . . . [12]

The gradual withdrawal of middle-class women from active life, a movement started in the eighteenth century and accentuated in the nineteenth, ended with the virtual seclusion of bourgeois women, whose expeditions to the outside world came to be surrounded by a precise code of decorous conduct. Hearth and home were 'the outermost garments of the soul', clothing at all times any wife worthy of the name.[13] Of course this shutting-in of women was only prescriptive.

But the custom which allowed working-class women and girls to wander the urban spaces at will invited a presumption of guilt.

> *Indeed, the state of the young girls in this district is truly dreadful, for it is quite common to see from a dozen to a score of them, of ages varying from twelve to seventeen, standing together at the corner of the street till one or two o'clock in the morning. They work in factories or make match-boxes, and seem to have no one to care for them.[14]*

The immorality of women could also be discerned in their apparel. Clothing that was too conspicuous or too scanty could never conform to the prevailing criteria of decency. As Michelle Perrot notes, in the similar context of nineteenth-century Paris,

> *The 'genteel woman' described by Balzac, a fascinated and nostalgic observer of the patterns of urban conduct established by bourgeois convention, is elaborately rigid in her turnout and tightly channelled in her itinerary. She clothes her body according to a strict code which laces, corsets, veils and gloves her from head to toe.[15]*

Most working-class women had an entirely different appearance. Their style seemed to express a vulgarity and carelessness implying the worst sort of sensuality: women 'half-naked', without corsets; matrons with their breasts unrestrained, their armpits damp with sweat; women with 'their hair all over the place', blouses dirty or torn, stained skirts; girls in extravagant hats and loud-coloured bodices:

> *They may be continually seen in their rooms pursuing their ordinary work without shoes or stockings, and with only a single garment on, secured by a petticoat tied round their hips . . . and in the same state they even continually walk through the streets in the middle of the day . . . [16]*

> *Some have a gay taste; and after being out all day on the heap, in the wet, will spend the evening in dancing and drinking. These frequently sleep away their Sabbath days; and are of the number who, on one or two holidays in the year, such as Whitsuntide, will be seen in flaunting ribbons and bright dresses, which on their return from their frolics, will go to the pawnshop, to remain till a similar occasion shall call for their use.[17]*

Others were brutal, drunken fishwives who embodied a negative image of the feminine ideal:

Women, who seem as if they had known rough usage; whose faces look as if they had once been in the school of the fist and the stick, and who, perhaps have often deserved it . . . [18]

The street was a shop window in which were displayed, without disguise or shame, the moral faults of working women: their vanity and laziness:

Lazy, dirty women are exhibiting to one another some article of shabby finery, newly revived, which they have just bought . . . [19]

their taste for base sentiments and impure emotions:

. . . Many may be seen of an evening, sitting along the edges of the pavement, with penny periodicals in their hands, the character of which is of every varied shade of good and evil; [20]

and above all their noisy vivacity and insolent verve: bold girls with bright, impudent glances and full-throated laughter, shrews insulting one another across the street, women far gone in drink, shrieking milliners' apprentices, urchin girls teasing the missionaries, adolescents arm in arm with their friends or hanging round the necks of their suitors. Such freedom of speech and action could only mean licentiousness:

Brazen, ragged women scream and shout ribald repartees from window to window. [21]

The mother is either lolling out of the window, screaming to the fighting women below, in the court, or sitting, dirty and dishevelled, her elbow on her knee, her chin on her hand, on the dusty, low door-step, side by side with a drunken woman who comments with foul oaths on all who pass . . . the big boy and girl 'larking' in vulgarest play by the corner . . . [22]

London's moralists hardly ever mentioned the factory or workplace – those other public settings for working-class life – in support of their contention that the lower classes were immoral. During the first half of the century, members of parliamentary commissions on factories and mines had written many fine passages on the horrors of naked bodies in promiscuous juxtaposition and the abuse of working women[23] by their colleagues or superiors. Doubtless these observations were so well known that it was thought there was no need to repeat them. Another reason why the harmful effects of factory life are treated as secondary may have been the difficulty experienced by social explorers in spending enough time in a workshop to measure anything at all.

PLACES OF AMUSEMENT

In any case, a much harsher light was thrown on the activities and behaviour of the working classes by the sinister glitter of the places where they went for amusement. If the reformers thought it reprehensible merely to frequent establishments where drink was sold, what were they to say about the scenes that took place there under the malign influence of gin or beer? The gratuitous oaths, the obscene jokes, the abandonment of restraint, the violence: all were vehemently condemned.

Andrew Mearns underlines the contrast between the dark, dreary slums and the excitement and bright lights of the gin palaces and public houses:

> Look into one of these glittering saloons, with its motley, miserable crowd, and you may be horrified as you think of the evil that is nightly wrought there . . . [24]

The struggle against alcoholism was spearheaded by the London City Mission,[25] and later the Salvation Army, both of which believed that intemperance and prostitution were indissolubly linked. One report contains this exchange between a young streetwalker and an officer:

> Drink? I should think so! Do you imagine we could live this life without drink? . . . The drink drowns all feelings of sorrow and shame, deadens the conscience, and hundreds could not lead the life they do if it were not for the excitement of alcohol . . . [26]

Among other favoured targets of charitable associations were 'Sunday taverns' and pleasure gardens. These very popular establishments, large gardens which could entertain hundreds of people at a time, offered a variety of amusements: dancing, concerts, plays, bars and restaurants.[27] They included the Royal Eastern at Vauxhall, Copenhagen

House, the Royal Standard Tavern and the Red House, among many others.

The moralists – whose opinion campaigns eventually succeeded in getting many of them closed down – believed these 'dens of iniquity' to be centres for prostitution and sexual licence. Thus in the Eagle Tavern, City Road,

> The smell of the liquor, the smoke of the cigar . . . the crowds of young persons, and chiefly in pairs, the nameless liberties given and taken, all exercise a fearful influence in banishing sober reflection from the mind.[28]

Another missionary sent to observe the state of morals in a pleasure garden reported:

> I myself, counted seventy-four young men, chiefly under twenty years of age, pair off during one hour with as many females; and from the character, dress and public habits of the females, there cannot be much doubt as to the purpose for which they left.[29]

Another group of missionaries, doing similar research at the Red House near Vauxhall Bridge, testified after lurking in an arbour for a couple of hours:

> [There was] a company of young persons of both sexes: their conduct and conversation was disgusting.[30]

Also perceived as both causes and symptoms of immorality were weekly markets and annual fairs, music halls, concert rooms, tea gardens, penny theatres, cockfights and rat-baiting,[31] boxing tournaments, national holidays, horse-races, travelling fairs at which, it was said, passions ran riot, and the sort of quasi-holidays offered to working-class Londoners by the Kent hop-picking season.

Finally, it was thought, only dedicated and ceaseless effort could protect the popular classes against their own propensity for all forms of lewdness. The Victorian ideal held that life should be organized around work for the greater glory of God: it should be a life of toil, from which the virtuous take repose only in the form of Sunday prayer and meditation, their only distractions the joys of family life.

It is implicitly by this standard that the sexual morality of the working classes was measured. Their chosen recreations, usually spiced with alcohol, were seen as further evidence of disorderliness and licence. Even the most ordinary distractions, music halls and penny-gaffs, were represented as occasions of debauch and prostitution. Greenwood says of the music hall:

> There is not a single music-hall – from the vast 'Alhambra' in Leicester Square, to the unaristocratic establishment in the neighbourhood of Leather Lane, originally christened the 'Raglan' – that I have not visited. And I am bound to confess that the same damning elements are discoverable in one and all.[32]

Penny-gaffs, very fashionable in the 1860s, were small rudimentary theatres in which, for a penny, people could listen to saucy songs and watch pantomimes. The shows were often broadly comic, poking fun at temperance leagues and the police. Every evening, between six and eleven, they attracted a mixture of housewives with babies in their arms, adolescents, cab-drivers, coalmen, dustmen, sailors, prostitutes and 'respectable persons'.[33]

Even the most improvised entertainments, like the famous Kiss-in-the-Ring described with amused indulgence by Munby, seemed to the moralists to indicate a total absence of modesty and self-respect, mingled with a taste for pagan pleasures.

> . . . The rule is, that when a girl has chosen you and you have pursued and caught her, you acquire the right to choose another and be pursued and caught. . . . It is interesting to see how far things that would in a higher class be counted 'liberties' are tolerated here and even expected, without suspicion of evil. . . . Again, when this romping has ended in her submission, you place your arm round her waist, and lead her tenderly back to the ring: and when you get there, your kisses may be numerous, your embrace somewhat fervent; and if she is pretty, interlopers very likely rush in and snatch a kiss from her . . . in passing, as she rests on your arm.[34]

LIVING CONDITIONS: ONE-ROOM DWELLINGS AND SEXUAL LICENCE

Contemporary observers of working-class morals inevitably drew a third conclusion: that there was a close link between living conditions and the development of sexual licence:

The grossest immorality is the necessary result of their promiscuously crowded habitations . . . [35]

This diagnosis, dating from 1845, was taken up by the great urban housing reformers (Lord Shaftesbury, John Simon, Octavia Hill, Beatrice Webb). It was to become one of the central themes of pamphlets on public health and the condition of Londoners in the nineteenth century.

In fact, the idea that promiscuous slum living conditions were the major cause of depraved conduct became the centrepiece of the discourse on popular sexuality. Nowhere else is the observer's rather ambiguous pleasure (identified by Michel Foucault in his *History of Sexuality*) in 'exercising a power that questions, monitors, watches, spies, searches out, palpates, brings to light',[36] made so apparent.

We know that some investigators went so far as to dress in rags and, thus disguised, spend nights in common lodging-houses or work-houses, to hear the rumours and chatter of the people at first hand.[37] For obvious reasons, social researchers[38] often interrogated people who had come down in the world, whose basic attitudes would have been very similar to their own. What could not be seen could at least be deduced or imagined: in stifling summer or feverish winter, nothing but lubricious rustlings, perverse movements, unnatural touchings.

There was, in fact, much that visitors found shocking about the living conditions of the London working classes. Apart from the homeless who slept in the streets or in the parks, apart from the considerable numbers living in municipal lodging-houses and dormitories, a large proportion of families had but a single room at their disposal.

The 1901 census reveals that 45.2 per cent of households in Finsbury lived in one or two rooms, and that a third of the inhabitants of Stepney, Shoreditch, St Pancras, St Marylebone and Holborn lived in the same situation.[39] For some categories the proportion was higher still: 50 per cent of dockers and 46 per cent of pedlars lived in one-room dwellings.[40] The room would be shared by many occupants, large families being the rule in Victorian society, especially among the workers.[41] High rents, the indebtedness young people felt towards those who had raised them, the ups and downs of domestic service and seasonal labour, all help to explain the presence of large numbers of young adults in these family cells. Bereavements and separations meant that the children swarming underfoot were often the issue of several beds.

The dissonance between two conceptions of communal life was especially profound during this period of history. The poor, doubtless through force of circumstances, maintained the old custom of living together in one or two rooms, while the privileged had developed a new sense of privacy, of modesty, and regarded bodily promiscuity with increasing distaste. Philippe Ariès, Peter Laslett, Jean-Louis Flandrin and Lawrence Stone have all underlined the recent origins of this attitude to space. In the 'great houses' of France under the *ancien régime* the sense of conviviality, the spirit of patronage, meant that visitors – friends or relatives – were often invited to stay the night, sharing rooms of undifferentiated function:[42] trestles would be set up for meals, beds for the night. This custom survived long after the appearance of bedrooms. Few tales of adventure or the picaresque are without a scene in which the traveller is forced to share a room with strangers at some overbooked coaching inn.

> *Imagine the promiscuity of life in these rooms in which it was impossible to be alone, which had to be crossed to get to the other rooms in the suite, in which several households, several sets of boys or girls, slept side by side (without counting the servants, at least some of whom had to sleep close to their masters) . . .* [43]

In the eighteenth century, however, the ruling classes began to develop hitherto unknown notions of propriety: privacy of the couple, of the nuclear family, of the individual. New taboos, a new sense of politeness, came to privatize most of the natural bodily functions – belching, farting, defecation, childbirth and above all, sexual activity – in the name of modesty, morality, and eventually hygiene. In earlier times, Ariès points out,

> *The traditional ceremonies which accompanied marriage, and counted more than religious ceremonies which only later acquired any degree of solemnity; the blessing of the marriage bed, the guests' visit to the newly-weds ensconced in it, the wedding-night rowdiness and so forth, all stake society's claim on the couple's privacy. Why should anyone object when in fact there existed virtually no privacy, when people lived mixed together, masters and servants, children and adults, in houses open at all hours to the intrusion of visitors?* [44]

The new sociability soon modified displays of nudity, tolerated at other times and according to fashion, in the boudoir and other parts of the domestic space. During the 1851 Great Exhibition at the Crystal Palace, hundreds of thousands of spectators of all classes filed past the buxom forms of nude statues. On the beaches, whose attraction had recently been discovered, limbs and even bodies were laid bare; but during the same period, an ankle glimpsed in a drawing-room would occasion confused blushes.[45]

The use of modern technical inventions to eliminate smells and noises was still some distance in the future. It is amusing to reflect on the limits primitive technology placed, for example, on the ethereal image of the Victorian lady. Walter recalls in his pornographic auto-biography that as a child, sharing a bedroom with an unknown couple on the occasion of a ball given by his parents, he heard

a rattling in the pot, then a rest, then again a rattle and knew the sound of piddling.[46]

Practical reality sometimes obliged these worthy creatures to urinate noisily into a chamber pot, thus giving manifest proof of their carnal essence to the rest of the household, including the servants.

Generally speaking, however, only exceptional circumstances could authorize sharing a bed or a room. Segregation of the sexes was regarded as a *sine qua non;* where this rule had to be broken, a multitude of precautions and admonitions was employed to discourage peeping. In the example just quoted, Walter's mother closes the bed-curtains hermetically and forbids him to get up or manifest his presence in any way. This new concern was especially strong in relation to children.[47] They were increasingly isolated from the adult sexual world,[48] and protected with remorseless vigilance from the twin dangers of solitary pleasure and the bad example likely to be set by nurses and housemaids.

These anxieties remained entirely foreign to the poorer classes until much later. It was normal to sleep in the same room, and quite often parents, children and outsiders slept higgledy-piggledy in the same bed. Dicky Perrot, in *A Child of the Jago*, sleeps curled up across his parents' bed.[49] In his invaluable account of an East End upbringing during the last decade of the century, Arthur Harding recalls:

I remember, this is a strange thing, even so late as when I come out of Borstal, I was sixteen, seventeen years of age, my sister was twenty. And we both slept in the same narrow bed. She slept at the top and I slept at the bottom, and the two kids, my sister Mary and George slept with my mother in the big bed.[50]

The material reasons – shortage of housing, harsh climate, insecurity – are obvious enough. So are cultural and ideological reasons: the lack of refined behaviour, fondness for communal life, gregariousness during work and leisure, all combined to resist the individualism on which the new society was based.

This is why, in the minds of contemporary observers, over-population of the slums was indissolubly linked to sexual licence. Either they considered that the state of the slums produced immorality in itself, or they believed that the popular masses were demoralized by enforced promiscuity. The argument about the reciprocal relationship between these two phenomena died down in the middle of the century, at about the same time that the environmentalist theory arose. Few contemporary texts neglect to mention

. . . the demoralizing influence of the indiscriminate mixing together, in families, of all ages and both sexes.[51]

The higher the ratio of inhabitants to a room, the more manifest the resulting corruption appeared to be. Here, seven families lived in one room; there, a couple with nine children. Overcrowding in a dwelling can be measured by the volume of air per inhabitant. In one district, a whole family occupied between 15 and 46 cubic metres of air space, when the established minimum for health was thought to be 107 cubic metres for each individual over the age of twelve.[52]

Whether the point of view was scientific or moralistic, the conclusions were always the same: there were too many people in too little space, and this crowding of individuals was equally damaging to physical and moral health.

The reasoning seems to be of theological type, supported by an adaptation of the dogma of original sin: to approach too close to the forbidden fruit is to run the risk of gathering it. Temptation is held to spring from proximity alone. It is easy to understand that by contrast with the ideal image of the Victorian family – the essence of order and discipline, where everyone has a place to occupy, a role to fulfil, a room to live in – such proximity was seen as bruising to the

sensibilities and disturbing to the mind. In consequence, the promiscuity of working-class families was thought pathogenic *in itself.*

Evil stemmed from the incitement implicit in the proximity of the
other, from the unnatural confusion of the sexes and ages. Hence a
moral plague every bit as contagious as a disease epidemic:

> *All this proceeds not from any unwonted or extraordinary depravity in the character
> of these victims of licentiousness, but from the almost irresistible nature of the
> temptations to which the poor are exposed. . . . The progress of vice in such
> circumstances is almost as certain and often nearly as rapid as that of physical
> contagion.*[53]

A priori, one might think, there was nothing in these conditions to
encourage sexual dalliance:[54] the dwellings were cramped, uncomfort-
able, malodorous, and often contained a sick person, squalling infants,
restless children. But the inhabitants of these places of infamy hardly
seemed to be human; animal metaphors here take on a new fullness of
meaning. Looked upon as pigs, as rats, as rabbits and all kinds of other
species, the poor came immediately to react by instinct, obeying their
senses. Promiscuity produced, so to speak, an excitation of the senses
that people could no more resist than a cat on heat can resist the male's
scent. In the darkness of the nights, the body of the other was
permanently present, touched, scented, heard. The most private acts
were displayed:

> *Of these inmates it is nearly superfluous to observe, that in all offices of nature they
> are gregarious and public; that every instinct of personal or sexual decency is stifled;
> that every nakedness of life is uncovered there.*[55]

A number of observers criticized the promiscuity which often pre-
vailed around women in labour, and a Paddington Medical Officer of
Health described, in veiled terms, the embarrassment felt by some
women during menstrual periods.[56]

Debauchery was also thought to be incited by what visitors saw as
bodily nakedness. On the face of it, given the geographical latitude,
there is something surprising about this allegation. All the visitors
meant, however, were things like the immodest exposure of shoulders
and upper arms, over which the strap of a camisole was sometimes
seen to slip; bodily hair seen under the armpits or on a man's chest; a

skirt lifted to show the calf; and above all, for women, absence of the complicated and voluminous undergarments (corsets or pants), shawls, artful draperies and elaborate coiffures then in fashion. Lacking these fineries, which hid the body and exhibited prosperity, the working classes seemed quite simply naked.

People were naked at work:

> We went to another, where husband and wife were working together making some kind of springs used in gas factories . . . the room was very dirty, there was a baby almost naked lying on the floor, crying, while the mother was only dressed in her chemise and one or two petticoats, the neck and shoulders quite bare.[57]

They slept naked:

> Men, women and children, the young and the old, families, acquaintances and strangers lie down in common nakedness together. There is no form or show of propriety, decency or morality; but, at times, a vitiating and disgusting bestiality unknown to savages.[58]

And of course they were naked while washing or changing their clothes, always in the presence of others:

> Now that his own nature was becoming steadily more refined, he was increasingly disgusted by the promiscuity of life in the village. Were they just cattle, then, to be herded together like this in the fields, so on top of each other that nobody could change his shirt without showing his behind to his neighbours! How wonderful it was for health, and how inevitably the boys and girls grew up together in filth and corruption![59]

The very children went naked – a sign of misfortune mingled with neglect and indecency – like this boy encountered in Bethnal Green:

> We asked an intelligent, half-naked lad, lounging at one of the doors, what he did with himself all day long in the streets. . .[60]

and this young family in Limehouse Fields:

> The very young children running about the room quite naked, the elder ones with merely a rag pinned round them . . .[61]

Social explorers may have had very limited access to what went on at night in the homes of the poor; but they could easily enter 'common lodging-houses', which seemed to them the ultimate in licentious promiscuity, and even take up residence there. The confusion in these places was extreme, because they sheltered many households at once, individuals of all ages and conditions jumbled together. A one-room apartment, with a family of eight or ten persons packed in for the night, was a haven of peace compared to

> . . . the common lodging-rooms, where each of the four corners is occupied by a family; and as many as sixteen persons, men, women, and children, some of them drunken and quarrelsome, have been found crowded into a small dormitory.[62]

These lodgings had originally been established to give shelter at night to the travellers, mainly single men, who flooded into London during the great migratory movement which affected the whole British Isles at the end of the eighteenth century. They also resulted, as Stone[63] points out, from the growing inclination of some social classes to protect their own family privacy: during this period large numbers of apprentices and artisans, no longer welcome in the homes of the shopkeepers and craftsmen who employed them, were obliged to rent a room or space with other workers, find digs with a family or move into a common lodging-house. During the nineteenth century these establishments became the normal refuge[64] of all those – families, solitary women, children, the elderly – who were too poor[65] to pay a weekly rent, but not yet so destitute as to seek shelter with a charitable society, in a workhouse (where men would be segregated from women and children) or in the appalling penny hangs[66] which were really the last stop before the street, park or Embankment. Common lodging-houses were usually mixed, unsegregated, and contained all aspects of misfortune: unemployed labourers, sacked domestics, beggars, jailbirds, tarts. This heterogeneity, which only reflected the usual mixture to be found in a street or even a house, terrified social observers.

> But remember that dozens of really respectable families do have to frequent these places now, and mix with malefactors day and night, because there are no other places open to them.[67]

The free association of all these people in the bedrooms, or in the communal living-room where they gathered to keep warm, prepare improvised meals and get drunk together, suggested the very antithesis of the Victorian home: a caricature of a household, without authority, governed by no religious or secular principle. The passing in 1851 of the Common Lodging House Act failed to introduce even the most rudimentary principles of hygiene.

Common lodging-houses offered the spectacle of total moral turpitude. Nobody bothered to ascertain whether client couples were legally married,[68] and these houses appear to have been widely used for illicit sexual activities. Young girls and boys were subject to all sorts of pressures from older guests. Calls of nature were answered in the sight and hearing of fellow-guests; people dressed and undressed without the slightest show of modesty. Every moment of this tiresome cohabitation seems to have been marked by violence and indecency. Recreation often degenerated into scenes which appeared unspeakably foul:

> There are dances at some of these lodging houses especially on Sunday evenings . . . one penny is charged for each dance to each person. These dances are often scenes of great evil. Boys entice the girls to dance with them and afterwards to sleep with them. One missionary knocked in the middle of the day . . . a voice directed him to enter, when he saw two young men and two young women dancing together, all in an entire state of nudity, a fiddler playing in another part of the room, while they danced.[69]

On this occasion the missionary made the young people put their clothes back on, and delivered a severe reprimand. Henry Mayhew notes several times that there were many who preferred the street to this oppressive promiscuity:

> I have known decent people, those that are driven to such places from destitution perhaps for the first time, shocked and disgusted at what they saw. I have seen a decent married pair so shocked and disgusted that they have insisted on leaving the place, and have left it.[70]

William Acton records this statement by a prostitute:

> During this time I used to see boys and girls from ten and twelve years old sleeping together, but understood nothing wrong. I had never heard of such places before I ran away. . . . I saw things between almost children that I can't describe to you – very often I saw them, and that shocked me.[71]

And according to a City missionary:

In some of them, both sexes sleep together indiscriminately, and such acts are practised and witnessed that married persons, who are in other respects awfully depraved, have been so shocked as to be compelled to get up in the night and leave the house. [72]

Observers were not unaware that common lodging-houses sheltered only the very poorest people – pedlars and especially casual labourers and migrants. [73] But they referred to them often, because moral laxity was much easier to spot in these places than in private dwellings.

So it is in the description of living conditions that we find the most specific and abundant references to the sexual immorality of the labouring classes. Every time the observer refocused his binoculars, as it were, they revealed a new scene more disgracefully immoral than the last. Seen from outside, from a distance, the world of the poor looked perverse, but still in a vague, undefined sort of way. People's public behaviour, the overall physical texture, hinted at the existence of vice. Closer observation in theatres and other places of pleasure did indeed reveal depraved conduct. And the study of living conditions confirmed with even greater clarity the existence of widespread immodesty and forbidden sexual practices.

The reasoning is extremely straightforward. The poor lived in permanent enforced intimacy; hence, they could not have even the most elementary sense of moral decorum; therefore they engaged without restraint in all sorts of prohibited sexual practices. The description of these material conditions is certainly articulated with the general ideological deviancy in which the popular classes were said to be steeped – atheism, republicanism or socialism, intemperance, crime. But although the balance between these elements varies with different observers and periods, and although causal connections are assessed in different ways, in the final analysis the immorality of the labouring classes is always linked to mixing of the sexes, which in turn is always imposed by living conditions.

Characters in the family drama

Sexual licence was indicated, finally, by the form of the working-class family and the type of relations engendered by it. We have noted that it hardly conformed to the ideal image of the Victorian family. It was perceived and represented in dramatic fashion as a source of difficulty both for its own members and for the rest of society. Industrialization and urbanization, it was thought, had destroyed stable and harmonious traditional structures; hence there were too few landmarks for determining identities and roles within the family.[74] Sexual transgressions – concubinage and incest in particular – often confused the expected image. And philanthropists, social explorers and the courts kept uncovering situations which appeared to be of 'frightful depravity'[75].

Nothing could be taken for granted in the chaotic aggregate the family group seemed to have become. That man sitting over the cold ashes in the fireplace: was he the 'lawful' husband? A lover? A man passing through? Might he not also be the lover of this adolescent girl, his daughter perhaps, perhaps also his daughter-in-law or niece? Was he the father of *any* of these children? Who supported the family: the man, the wife or the children? This baby in the arms of a young girl, still almost a child herself: was he her little brother, as she claimed, or had she come home between domestic jobs to 'hide her shame'? How did this woman earn her bread: might she not supplement her tiny earnings as a seamstress with 'wages of sin'? And the little girls and boys, who knew what games they got up to in the corners of the room, in the dark courtyards . . . and how many more children would there be, if none had been done away with by abortion or infanticide? Might not others have been abandoned?

Everything discovered or suspected, every confession, every piece of spiteful gossip, seemed to confirm a distortion of the ideal family image. Confronted with these grotesque situations, disorientated by what seemed total chaos and confusion, observers worked out a typology of the characters in the family drama, while oscillating helplessly between indignation and compassion.

THE HEAD OF THE FAMILY

In place of the authority and dignity of the *paterfamilias* who was nowhere to be found, the observers sketched in a sort of double image: that of a man of violence, an alcoholic brawler, most probably atheist and republican, superimposed on that of an unhappy father crushed by fate, reduced to total impotence by the combined effects of his own weak character and the social and economic circumstances. This unnatural father kept the bulk of his wages for himself, spending them in taverns and on games of chance; took no responsibility for raising and educating his children; and, drunk with fatigue, stupidity and alcohol, committed or allowed to be committed the most depraved sexual acts upon the persons of his wife and children. Sometimes, driven by circumstances or passions, he disappeared, never to be seen again; but was replaced almost immediately by a very similar sort of being:

> This 'father' was evidently a better fellow than most of the nomadic husbands who wander about from family circle to family circle, ready to replace its absent head at a moment's notice,[76]

comments George Sims. Arthur St John Adcock's character Mr Guffin, a print worker, is a remarkable synthesis of the way the image of the husband and father was perceived in this working-class context:

> In Melia's simple philosophy, which was compact of her own and neighbours' experiences, fathers bulked as a troublesome and vicious species of human animals that went to work with more or less regularity of mornings and came home very drunk at night. If they were allowed to gain the upper hand it became their habit to thrash the family at frequent intervals, and to yield for its maintenance but a small surplus of the Saturday's wages. When, however, the feminine head of a family had sense and spirit to assert herself as Melia's mother had done, it was quite possible to keep a father in subjection, and, by sheer, dogged nagging and brow-beating, to inspire him with wholesome fears and reduce him to something approaching tractability.[77]

This duality is usually represented in the literature by sketching two contrasting characters. Among the unequivocally bad, one man was described by a City missionary as a 'monster of iniquity' who drank, used 'frightfully profane' language, led a dissolute life and abandoned the family home when he felt like it.[78] Another unnatural father, recently bereaved, seduced his eighteen-year-old stepdaughter. Brutal and depraved, he soon brought into the house another young woman with whom 'he lived as man and wife'.[79]

But almost as much severity was reserved for men who did not play the correct role of a head of family. One example is the Bethnal Green weaver, seen peeling potatoes beside a basket of shellfish he would later hawk in the street, while his wife nearby was weaving a piece of 'rich black satin'. Should not the husband be doing this work, worried the missionary, and should he not leave such unmanly tasks to his wife?[80] Engels, too, was made hot under the collar by the reversal of sex roles sometimes imposed by circumstances:

> . . . *poor Jack was sitting by the fire, and what do you think he was doing? Why he sat and mended his wife's stocking with the bodkin; and as soon as he saw his old friend at the doorpost, he tried to hide them. But Joe, that is my friend's name, had seen it, and said: 'Jack, what the devil art thou doing? Where is the missus? Why, is that thy work?' and poor Jack was ashamed. . .*[81]

CHILDREN

Children were depicted in much the same way: either as impudent, vicious urchins or as innocent victims of general depravity and parental neglect. A well-known illustration shows two little girls of seven or eight with their mother.[82] The children are charming, intelligent, 'attractive and well-behaved', but have to share the 'den' to which their mother, cheeks and eyes painted, 'day and night entices her depraved prey'.

This image alternates with one of wild, insolent hooligans, great drinkers of alcohol and singers of rude songs. A *Quarterly Review* journalist surveyed the pupils of fifteen 'ragged schools' as follows:[83] 162 admitted they had been in prison; 116 had run away from home; 170 slept in common lodging-houses; 253 lived by begging; 216 were without shoes or socks; 280 had no hat or bonnet; 10 had no under-clothes; 249 had never slept in a bed; 68 were the children of convicted criminals; 125 had stepmothers; and 306 had lost one or both of their parents.

The eclecticism of these categories reveals how vague and imprecise the zone of actual immorality was. These 'stunted' children, their pale, drawn faces expressing 'the opposite of childish innocence', are subject to outbursts of 'savage violence' in school, throwing stones, breaking windows and lamp-glasses and giving shrill cries. Then the same writer, or another, introduces them in a different guise: the sad gaze, the mudcaked rags, the helpless babies covered in filth and vermin; or the sweet little red-haired girl, her features still childish and innocent, who has been violated by her employer and is playing with her baby as with a large doll:

> He vilely used his influence to put the child under a sort of slavery, binding her to silence with terrible threats of prison for her if she dared to tell of his actions.[84]

YOUNG PEOPLE

The typology continues with the description of young people. Few social explorers would disagree with George Gissing's literary version of two types of adolescent. Pennyloaf Candy is

> . . . a meagre, hollow-eyed, bloodless girl of seventeen yet her features had a certain charm – that dolorous kind of prettiness which is often enough seen in the London needle-slave.[85]

Indifferent to the horror of the slums, to the coarse conversation of her employers, to her mother's alcoholism and her father's brutality, even to the beating she gets from another girl which she does nothing to prevent, she is destined for an early marriage followed by a life of impoverished slavery. Gissing contrasts her with her neighbour Clem Peckover,

> . . . a girl of sixteen, tall, rather bony, rudely handsome; the hand with which she struck was large and coarse-fibred, the muscles that impelled it vigorous. Her dress was that of a work-girl, unsubstantial, ill-fitting, but of ambitious cut. . . . The exquisite satisfaction with which she viewed Jane's present misery . . . put her at once on a par with the noble savage running wild in the woods. Civilisation could bring no charge against this young woman; it and she had no common criterion.[86]

Clem lives on the edge of delinquency, rather like this fourteen-year-old girl described by a missionary:[87] sacked from her job for theft, she spent her time with other adolescents in the King's Cross penny-gaff, wandered the streets late at night, played malicious practical jokes and engaged in all sorts of immodest horseplay, leavened with lavatorial humour. James Greenwood draws a similar portrait of the young workers in a factory making artificial flowers:

> Old and bold in petty wickedness, and with audacious pretensions to acquaintance

with vice of a graver sort, she entertains them with stories of 'sprees' and 'larks' she and her friends have indulged in. She has been to 'plays' and 'dancing rooms' . . .[88]

Observers believed that the promiscuity of the slums and the absence of parental and religious guidance encouraged precocious imitation of adult sexual licence. Even very young girls had their suitors, and often lovers too, acknowledged without shame and defended with adult ferocity. The sight of a suspected rival often led to fisticuffs:

He is considered her legitimate property by one lady, and the said lady has surprised him treating her rival to gin. Neither of the girls are more than seventeen, I should say, yet they are fighting and blaspheming and using words that make even myself and my collaborator shudder. . . 'Go it, Sal,' yells a female friend, and Sal goes it, and the boys and girls stand round and enjoy the spectacle, and add their chorus of blasphemy and indecency to the quarrel duet of the Madame Angots of the gutter.[89]

It is easy to understand why early marriages, following such a childhood and adolescence, were widely seen as one of the major causes of working-class misery. Without a planned common future, without savings, motivated only by sensuality and the wish to escape from the overcrowded slums, marriage 'between young boys and young girls' was generally thought 'the great curse of the East End', leading to adultery and inevitable separations.

We should note, however, that in the 1870s some people began to adopt a contrary view, recommending that early marriage be encouraged to stem the tide of pre-marital debauchery:

The second principle to be kept steadily in view is the encouragement of early marriage. A statesman writing a generation ago, on the causes in the past which have contributed to the prosperity of England, says: 'The lower and working classes are an early and universally marrying people; this sacred habit is one which, while it has secured the virtue and promoted the happiness of the country, has. . . constituted Britain the most powerful and prosperous empire of the world.'[90]

WOMEN

But the centrepiece and protagonist of the family drama was the woman in her triple role of housekeeper, wife and mother. The virtuous creature struggling gamely to defend her home against fire and flood is a strong and abiding image; that of the purity and innocence of childhood, on the other hand, is relatively recent, while the idea of a morally pure head of household is difficult to sustain. Only the struggle for equal rights for women might eventually smudge the ideal blueprint; but the violence of the suffragettes was still some way off.

This is why observers seeking

> *. . . what God meant a mother to be, full of kindness and calmness, and thought, and care for those whom He has given her to love – her husband and her children,*[91]

were scandalized when they found only bad mothers, bad wives and bad housekeepers. Two main types emerge from the ocean of distress and vice.

The first is the sacrificial victim, unknown, abused by circumstances and exploited by men: helpless mother, miserable wage-slave, prostitute driven to despair.

Attempts were often made to explain and excuse. It was because of the terrible one-room system that so many mothers gave up trying:

> *The woman, whose chief labour is in this one room, has little time to leave it for fresh air. She feels she cannot keep it straight, and she turns fretful and crusty, and sometimes cruel – loses her motherliness, gives her poor children no tender thoughts to remember with her name; if they drag up to manhood, they become 'roughs', and if the girls have known neither 'womanhood' nor 'motherhood', what can be looked for in the next generation, but fresh rooms full of un-mothered misery?*[92]

Through a single lapse of virtue they had been thrown into misfortune, perhaps into crime. A young woman of the Clerkenwell district survived with some difficulty, sharing her lodging with another woman and supporting her illegitimate child by making shirts and shoes. Despite her 'fall' there was nothing vulgar in her appearance or conduct. But she was 'bone-weary' with hard work, poverty and discomfort, so exhausted that one night, when her child would not stop crying, she was almost overwhelmed by the temptation to get rid of it. Might she not then obtain a warm and comfortable job as a domestic?

> *I felt . . . horribly tempted to destroy it. . . . It seemed to come so strong upon me, I was*

almost doing it; when one night I dreamed that I had done it, and the baby was laying dead in a little coffin. I felt dreadful . . .[93]

Another young woman lived in the most extreme indigence after being deserted by successive partners. Her four-year-old son had just died. The man she had married at the age of seventeen to escape from drunken parents had been transported for seven years for theft. The second had been a very young boy with whom she lived in concubinage, the son of a woman friend who shared her room.[94] It was said that victims of this sort formed the bulk of the battalions of prostitutes who haunted the London streets, selling themselves to add the 'wages of sin'[95] to their meagre earnings as seamstresses or milliners.

The image of woman-as-victim alternates with a different representation, in which women of the people are seen as hard, brutal and deeply depraved. Members of the first category are often said to be 'attractive', good-natured, modest; the second consists exclusively of women who are vile, ignorant, strangers to any idea of virtue or decorum.[96] These women are a disgrace to their sex, utterly base and degraded, the absolute dregs of the civilized world:

We see not in the streets of Paris or Geneva our poor drunken and distracted sisters dragged (to the degradation of all women who witness it) between two policemen to a court of justice, for having broken the peace. On the Continent it is certain that women do not, as in England, as a habit, forget their sex in the fumes of gin and beer, as do our poorer classes.[97]

What characterizes these women more than anything else is their wild defiance of the observer's code of morals. Their carelessness, their frivolity, their audacious impudence are tirelessly catalogued. These indomitable, intoxicated furies seem to fear nothing and nobody, least of all a moral and spiritual authority, or the representatives of the law.

Their loud voices and coarse insolence are deployed against everybody: husband, neighbours, visitors. Their virulent way with words is underlined in accounts of the innumerable domestic quarrels which broke out over division of the week's wages.

When words are lacking, blows are never far away, and accounts by investigators in poor districts are embellished with many fight scenes. The brawl between Liza and Mrs Blakeston in *Liza of Lambeth* is a model of its kind, and recalls the celebrated contest between Gervaise and Virginie in Zola's *L'Assommoir*,[98] from which Somerset Maugham may have drawn inspiration:

> 'Not done nothing ter me?' furiously repeated the woman. 'I'll tell yer what yer've done ter me – you've robbed me of my 'usbind, you 'ave. I never 'ad a word with my 'usbind until you took 'im from me. An' now it's all you with 'im. 'E's got no time for 'is wife an' family – it's all you. An' 'is money, too. . .
>
> 'I'll give it yer!' proceeded Mrs. Blakeston, getting more hot and excited, brandishing her fist, and speaking in a loud voice, hoarse with rage. 'Oh, I've been tryin' ter git 'old on yer this four weeks. Why, you're a prostitute – thet's wot you are!'
>
> 'I'm not!' answered Liza indignantly. . .
>
> Mrs. Blakeston stood close in front of her, her heavy jaw protruded and the frown of her eyebrows dark and stern. . .
>
> 'Yer dirty little bitch, you!' she said at last. 'Tike that!' and with her open hand she gave her a sharp smack on the cheek.
>
> Liza started back with a cry and put her hand up to her face. 'An' tike thet!' added Mrs. Blakeston, repeating the blow. Then, gathering up the spittle in her mouth, she spat in Liza's face. Liza sprang on her, and with her hands spread out like claws buried her nails in the woman's face and drew them down her cheeks. Mrs. Blakeston caught hold of her hair with both hands and tugged at it as hard as she could.[99]

The crowd separates the two women and urges them to 'fight fair'. Then they set to again. Sometimes in real life broken bottles were used, or a husband or neighbour would be felled with a length of wood:

> Waiting till the man who had given her offence was alone, his door being open as he sat asleep in his chair, she rushed upon him, and with a heavy door key inflicted a fearful gash upon the side of his head.[100]

An admirable example of the social observers' picture of the lifestyle and behaviour of a certain type of working woman is found in the report of a London City missionary who was trying to convert a woman living in Bethnal Green.[101]

In the familiar setting of total destitution – a single room furnished with a couch bare of covers, a sleeveless shirt stretched across the broken window to keep out the cold and light – were five dirty, naked children who seemed never to have heard the name of Jesus: 'Each inquiry was met but by the vacant stare of amazement and an unmeaning laugh.' The mother's face bore the marks of depravity and excess: she lived with a man who might not even have been the father of her children. The missionary had no difficulty in finding that the household did not seek solace in spiritual things but in a bit of 'bacca', a drop of beer or 'a glass of gin', all things which 'do nobody any harm' but were wonderfully restoring to poor people. Send the children to *school*? That's all very well for some! The woman retorted:

La! bless you, master, how can poor critturs the likes of us send children to school? Why, we can't get wittles for 'em to eat, let alone things to kiver 'em. You people an't got no feeling of the poor, or you would never ask such a thing.

The characteristic insolence of a certain type of working woman can also be seen in this exchange between an old woman and a municipal official who is trying to persuade her to leave her insalubrious slum:

'These places ain't fit to live in,' the Vestry Officer says. 'I told you before.'
    'Ain't fit to live in!' she snarled scornfully. 'Why, I've lived here all my life, master.'[102]

These male and female stereotypes, setting the tone of the working-class family, are broadly predominant in the literature of social exploration and in reformist theory. The figures, colourless or aggressive, and their attitudes, resigned or brutal and provocative, are exactly as would be expected, outside the dominant code of sexual conduct.

Thus, observation of characters and customs, confessions wheedled out of people to add to the illegitimacy statistics, paternity suits and prosecutions for sexual offences, built up a picture of working–class sexuality which was not just contrary to moral law, but outside all law. The dominant system of values made it impossible to discern anything other than a universe ruled by intemperance and disorder.

From this perspective, the sexual life of the labouring classes was illicit because it lacked the basic components of a code of sexual morality. Initiated under pressure of sensuality or passion, it was pursued with seeming indifference either within the institution of marriage, or outside it.

THE NATURAL HISTORY OF TRANSGRESSIONS

Profligacy

The excessive, undisciplined sexual behaviour of the working classes was seen as just one aspect of their general irresponsibility, their inability to resist their instincts and passions or to think ahead.

Every characteristic of the working-class world – its physical aspect, its lifestyle and culture – revealed this profligate wallowing in sins of the flesh and sensuality. The labouring classes seemed to be governed by their lowest instincts, at all ages and in all circumstances, as if (the more indulgent observers conceded) this was the only pleasure available to them.

THE REIGN OF THE IMPURE

Everything reinforced this image: the licentious character of conversations, the indecent gestures and improper games seen in the street, in workplaces, in places of amusement. The display of uncovered bodies suggested immodesty. It was realized, of course, that poverty was partly responsible for the presence of torn rags in the clothing of the poor; but surely the exposure of breast or thigh must be a product of lubricity, all this looseness and indecency a result of the taste for alcohol and sex?

The very filth which hygienists were campaigning to eradicate, the slime in drains and gutters, the ordure in the latrines, held an entire social group captive at an anal and immature stage of development. Dirt and foul odours were associated in the unconscious with an excessive and deviant sensuality which they were thought to reflect and encourage. Parent-Duchâtelet had earlier made the connection between sex and dirtiness in his work on prostitutes.

> One of the distinctive characteristics of prostitutes is a noticeable disregard for all aspects of cleanliness, either of the body or in dress; exceptions to this rule may be considered unusual: one could say that these women are perfectly happy to live in filth and ordure.[103]

Homosexuality was associated with the same repulsive bodily neglect.

And conversely, we are assured by contemporary medical manuals, the absence of intimate hygiene is an encouragement to onanism and sexual excesses. The entire working class thus appeared steeped in unbridled pagan sensuality whose material product, constantly visible, was the inexhaustible fecundity of couples and the existence of bastards. Medical treatises attested to an ambiguous correlation between pleasure and fertility. Precocious sexual relations and marriages between very young partners were interpreted as a response to irrepressible concupiscence.

A sour note in this unanimous discourse was sounded by the physiologist Harry Campbell, whose studies led him to believe that working women were even less interested in sex than women of the middle classes.[104] This conclusion, which in the nineteenth century ran counter to all the accepted arguments, naturally attracted the attention of the sexologist Havelock Ellis. Although he criticized the objectivity of his colleague's investigative method, Ellis at first supported his psychosociological interpretation:

> While the conditions of upper-class life may possibly be peculiarly favourable to the development of the sexual emotions, among the working classes in London, where the stress of the struggle for existence under bad hygienic conditions is so severe, they may be peculiarly unfavourable.[105]

Later he revised this view, coming round eventually to Löwenfeld's theories which held that, on the contrary, working-class women did not suffer from the same 'sexual anaesthesia' as those of the upper classes:

> In England most women of the working class appear to have had sexual intercourse at some time in their lives, notwithstanding the risk of pregnancy. . . 'Well, I couldn't help that,' I have heard a young widow remark when mildly reproached for the existence of her illegitimate child.[106]

In the depiction of this social group, condemned by its passions to an eternal saraband among the torments of hell, the prostitute, born of the people, incarnates the moral degeneracy of her class.

She represents the epitome of sexual excess: through her profession, of course, and because she enabled men of all classes to slake their illicit sexual passions. She made plain what was normally imagined and deduced, in a fashion which was all the more worrying because social observers knew that beside the prostitutes 'who do no work, but live entirely on the "wages of sin" ',[107] some of the women they met in the course of their researches were 'workers by day and prostitutes by night'.

It is certainly true that during the period we are considering, unlike earlier periods, systematic investigation into the reasons why some women take up prostitution had left little room for the idea that one of these reasons is a special propensity for sins of the flesh. The causes were thought to be essentially moral, economic and social. The phenomenon of prostitution – that 'great social evil' which troubled consciences, aroused the interest of scientists and politicians and divided public opinion – finally involved more than the moral state of the people. It has been seen as a 'symbol of the dislocation engendered by the new industrial age'.[108] This reading tends to minimize the individual responsibility of the prostitutes and emphasize instead the role of those privileged by the new economic order: men, the seducers and exploiters of this sexual system.

The idea that excessive sexual activity is caused by natural predispositions was also contradicted by contemporary medical theory.[109] The venereologist William Acton opened his book on prostitution by refuting the idea that it is caused by excessive sensuality on the part of the prostitutes.[110]

But setting aside 'uterine compulsion', and although economic conditions were now being taken into account, it was still the case that the aetiology of prostitution focused attention on the immoral environment in which the prostitutes had been brought up. Religious education was lacking, slum conditions were promiscuous, children and adults were given to obscene amusements; these degenerate surroundings were thought to anaesthetize decency and make anarchic sexual relations seem normal. Jabez Burns, for example, appears to believe that the working-class way of life is solely responsible for prostitution:

> Think of six, or eight persons living and sleeping in one room – the parents and sons and daughters – these daughters often growing into young women. Then, besides, their daily associations are with ignorant, depraved youths, with whom the evenings are spent in drinking places, or places of low amusement. Remember that these are living persons,

with strong animal instincts; and that their passions are uncontrolled, and that constant opportunities are presented for going astray. Is it any marvel that they fall – any marvel, that before they are out of their teens, they are conversant with every odious form of debased sensualism?[111]

Whatever the specific reasons thought to have led to prostitution, the environment was always there in the background, like a heap of compost, nourishing the lurid blossoms not just of streetwalkers but of the working classes in general.

ANIMALITY

Alongside the commentators influenced by evangelical doctrines, who emphasized the importance of the economic and moral environment, there existed a parallel, eugenicist current which held that the moral atrophy of the labouring classes was a product of their very nature. The bestiary from which many narrators derived their images vividly reflected the idea that primitive irrationality, the sensuality of an inferior species, was threatening to reverse humankind's progress towards civilization and cause a terrifying collapse into chaos. The return to a beastly, brute state, to animality in the lowest sense, as remote from humanity as it is possible to be: that, the eugenicists believed, was what marked the sexuality of the labouring classes, and lay behind the behaviour so loudly deplored by the social explorers.

The only identifiable principle seems to be that of unresisting abandonment to the most basic instincts, the blind drive to satisfy the senses: the coarse satiation of bellies already swollen with alcohol and copulation. It was feared that, with the passage of time, the vices of the ancients would be added to those of the parents, and that these degenerate appetites would grow stronger from generation to generation.

2

The Foundling Hospital

A tall, well-built woman with a shawl wrapped over her shoulders was walking briskly along Russell Street one luminous Saturday morning in June. She had come from her home in Westminster, near the river, where she earned a humble living by making artificial flowers for a Mayfair shopkeeper.

Clocks were striking seven. The woman was passing an enormous building site where masons were hard at work on the new British Museum. Through the half-demolished gateway of the old building she glimpsed the unreal-looking, tall, pale columns of a vast new structure climbing unevenly towards the sky. Her pace slackened. She had come a long way, and something cold and heavy was tightening about her heart. Having turned into Southampton Row she at length came to her destination, the gatehouse of a large building. In her arms a young baby slept.

Facing her at the other end of the immense formal courtyard was a chapel surmounted by a pediment; two parallel wings at right angles to it, each of two storeys, formed the sides of the rectangle. The walls were of pink brick, the roofs of grey-blue slate; pillared arcades ran the full length of the ground floor. It was a fine building, harmonious and austere; but the visitor felt a chill of fear. For she was standing in the gateway of the Foundling Hospital. Of all the innumerable institutions for the care of the London poor, this was the only one to welcome bastard children.

That is why the woman was there, and why she felt hope and fear. There were so few places. The admission procedures were so draconian.[1] Rejection would be a disaster; but success would entail an agonizing separation from the child.

39

Nevertheless, the Foundling Hospital had always been a symbol of enlightened benevolence. The best, the most generous and fraternal spirits in England had given money and patronage to rescue unwanted small children from a life of misery. Appalled by the number of abandoned brats in the ditches between Rotherhithe and the City, a sea-captain called Thomas Coram had been moved to do something about a situation he thought unworthy of a civilized nation. Following the example already set by Rome, Lisbon and Paris, the Foundling Hospital opened its doors in London on 25 March 1741. Georg Friedrich Handel donated a large organ for the chapel, where he put on an annual performance of his *Messiah*. The Hospital's large panelled reception hall, with its massive chimneypiece and heavily moulded ceilings, soon became London's leading art gallery: in it were hung works donated to the institution by William Hogarth, Thomas Gainsborough, Allan Ramsay, Sir Joshua Reynolds, Andrea Casali.

It did not take long for certain pious souls to become worried about the harmful effect such indulgence might be expected to have on morals. Joseph Massie, for example, wrote:

> People may now enjoy their natural Pleasures without bearing those consequential Charges which they ought to pay, and with an Exemption from Punishment and Shame, the Consequence will be, one Sort of Increase.[2]

The opinion campaign gathered force; the remedy, when it came, was sovereign. In 1760 funding to the Hospital was cut off, compelling the governors to suspend admissions. When it resumed a few years later, the admissions committee had changed its policy. First the number of admissions was reduced, then admission was restricted to war orphans and the children of deserted wives; finally, from 1801, only illegitimate children were accepted. Thomas Coram's hospital, which had been founded to save the lives of abandoned children and give them an education, now also assumed responsibility for shepherding their mothers back to the paths of 'hard work and virtue'.

For the applicants, the effect of these changes was to add new problems to their existing ones. But the questionnaires filled out in their names are a find of inestimable value to modern researchers.

When our sample visitor entered the Hospital, she was given a very detailed admission sheet. The internal rules of the establishment

required an unmarried mother wishing to place her child permanently, or for a limited period, to conform to certain criteria. She had
to be able to show that her good faith had been betrayed, that she had
given way to carnal passion only after a promise of marriage or against
her will; that she therefore had no other children; and that her conduct
had always been irreproachable in every other respect. She must also
be without any sort of material aid. Finally, the child had to be under
one year old.

This was thought the best way of ensuring that the children would
be brought up under good conditions and of promoting the moral
rehabilitation of single women deserted by their seducers.

The system was designed to avoid giving unwitting encouragement
to women who were selling their bodies. This meant obtaining an
ordered account of all the circumstances surrounding the birth of the
candidate child, and recording in detail everything that could be
gleaned on the woman's sexual relations with her partner. Each
applicant had to fill out a printed form detailing her own civil status
and those of the child and its father, their ages, her own and her lover's
occupations, and their addresses. The completed form was accompanied by a verbal statement relating in as much detail as possible the
story of the mother's life since her amorous encounter. This was
written on two or three sheets of thick blue paper.[3]

Do these accounts contain the truth about popular sexuality? Do
they confirm the views we have been examining, the interpretations of
contemporary social observers? It may be thought unwise to believe
the assertions of women in a state of desperate material and mental
distress, who were talking at all only because the hospital institution
required it. They were more than likely to feel acute shame when
asked to reveal all the circumstances of their 'fall' to questioners of the
opposite sex, and of different social class. It seems reasonable to
assume a whole mass of deliberate and involuntary distortions.

In fact, however, it is really quite easy to show how the truth came
through, how lies were tracked down and patiently exposed; and also,
happily, to see that the committee of governors, which made the final
decision in each case, was far from rigid in its judgement of the
petitioners' virtue.

Michel Foucault is worth quoting here for the insight he gives into
the confession ritual which, he says,

. . . is also a ritual that unfolds within a power relationship, for one does not confess without the presence (or virtual presence) of a partner who is not simply the interlocutor but the authority who requires the confession, prescribes and appreciates it, and intervenes in order to judge, punish, forgive, console, and reconcile; a ritual in which the truth is corroborated by the obstacles and resistances it has had to surmount in order to be formulated . . . [4]

To have her troubles comforted, in other words, the applicant had to supply a multitude of proofs: give the exact circumstances of her encounter with the child's father; bring the smallest memories to life – the intensity of her feelings, how long they lasted, where the act of love was performed; protest her innocence or admit her connivance and, sometimes, her own desire; give the names of relatives, employers, notables, family doctors, parsons, and ask for their corroboration. Finally, she had to produce any material evidence that would help pin down the truth about sex and amorous relations: letters arranging meetings, love letters, farewell letters, letters to and from friends and relatives. These handwritten, first-person statements[5] thus have the appearance of confessions made to an unchanging, ritual pattern. 'When I first met the Father . . . ', they begin, hundreds of them, time after time.

The administration was not content merely to listen: it made systematic and exhaustive inquiries. Like a priest in the confessional it was seeking repentance, catharsis. But like a court of law it required every suspicion, every assertion, to be supported by evidence; every decision, for or against, to be backed up by a report deemed to contain the final truth.

Our sample visitor was not expected to lay claim to any improbable moral perfection. She would have been aware that there was nothing to worry about on that score. But her resolution and skill were tested to the full by the task of recalling her experiences in these severe surroundings.

Case after case, year after year, couple after couple, the Foundling Hospital committee tried to grasp the truth of a sexual and love experience that was always the same, always a repetition of the last case, but somehow original each time. In pursuit of this aim, which was both ambitious and banal, the committee compiled a patient, methodical inventory whose originality will, I hope, become apparent. It contains much that is surprising, especially in comparison with traditional accounts by Victorian social explorers.

But is the full, literal truth about popular sexuality to be found in the tons of files accumulated by the Foundling Hospital during the nineteenth century? I am afraid not. The whole story may have been demanded, but what was supplied was limited by the petitioner's outlook and the committee's terms of reference. All the Hospital really wanted was sufficient evidence to justify the selection of children who had been conceived in highly specific circumstances.

So do these files just contain yet another slightly different representation? Are we left with two opposed, equally misleading images, with the truth hovering somewhere in the middle like the centre panel of an unfinished triptych?

No, not that either. What we find in this archive has the feel of a time-damaged fresco or an enormous, very faded snapshot, in which delicate fugitive details, luminous highlights of tenderness and tragedy, still trace the broken outlines of a vanished past.

3

Love and Marriage

In many ways, the women washed ashore on the steps of the London Foundling Hospital remind one of the valiant remnants of an army vanquished in a great battle. They emerge from it betrayed, dishonoured, sometimes despoiled, and always weighed down by the insupportable burden of an infant. Their enemy, the butcher of their feelings, is always the same: man.

Such, at least, is the conventional image offered by the petitioners to an institution which granted help only to those it believed to be victims of male cynicism and sexual immorality.

There can be no doubt that many of the applicants made instinctive use of words evoking the age-old battle of the sexes. Courts, police, family, employers, charitable institutions, all were urged to find against the male troublemakers who had laid waste their hitherto peaceful and blameless lives.

Of course there were profound differences between the interests and objectives of these men and these women. But to grasp the subtleties of relations between the sexes in working-class London, it may be helpful to put this conflict in parentheses for the time being.

'MY VILE SEDUCER HAS BEEN THE CAUSE OF FOUR OTHER YOUNG WOMEN'S RUIN'[1]

The archive contains several accounts of the most extreme form of sexual coercion: rape.[2] We are dealing here only with sexual violence, declared as such by the applicants, an act which had occurred only once, in the absence of emotional ties.

It may be questioned whether the facts were really as claimed by unmarried mothers who might have been trying to conceal illicit sexual adventures. Answering these doubts was precisely the task and *raison d'être* of the Foundling Hospital committee, which had access to all available means of checking the information given. Let us be content with its findings.

Relations of pure violence between the sexes are not exclusive to Victorian society, and there is no need to consult Deuteronomy to understand that in patriarchal societies the forcing of women is both forbidden and practised.

Nevertheless, although all the women in our sample who had been attacked in this way spontaneously expressed shame and disgust, few had reported the offence at the time. Most limited themselves to confiding in their mother or a workmate, until the day hospital regulations required them to reveal their 'misfortune'.

> *The Father of my child, on the 3rd April, being alone with him in the house, on a Sunday, he committed an act of violence upon me in the parlour. . . . On the following day I went to my mother to attend my sister's wedding and I told my mother what had happened.*

The petitioner's mother confirmed that

> *He forced her quite against her will that he tore her clothes and so on in the struggling. I did not know what to do as her father and I thought it too late to prosecute him.[3]*

These manifestations of a form of brutality which reifies women by denying or ignoring their free will can be attributed to the pathological behaviour of certain individuals. They also belong to the universal history of relations between the sexes. The acts described are not of a type committed only by nineteenth-century English males.

Philanthropic visitors were supported by workers' associations in condemning drunkenness for its damaging effects on efficiency at work, its devastation of fragile family budgets and the violence it caused in family and neighbourhood relations. Accounts of ferociously battered women and children are legion. Sexual violence by drunkards on their wives, daughters or women friends is very rarely mentioned, however. It will be claimed, perhaps, that it was accepted at the time that drinking causes sexual violence. This is by no means certain. In a society which believed in the principle of sexual inequality, which made constant allowance for the strength of sexual desire in men while questioning its very existence in women, drunkenness as a supplementary cause of violence would have passed more or less unnoticed. Packed into small, crowded rooms where each body was constantly exposed to the glance, the touch of every other, every member of the household seemed to be implicated, in a vague, general way, in the sexual immorality of the whole working class.

Close examination of the statements does reveal, however, that drunkenness was usually to blame for sexual attacks. The very young barmaid of a pub patronized by Fleet Street journalists spells out the context of one of these little-known incidents. The barman

> . . . came to my bed room at one o'clock in the morning in a drunken state and effected his purpose. My mistress was in the country. My master was below. I cried but was not heard . . . the morning after the occurrence he excused himself by saying he had had a drop too much.[4]

All the recorded evidence shows that these rapes were committed not in public places but in the workplace or at home.

Paradoxically, bourgeois houses were ideal locations for these attacks. In the attics, basements and backstairs of the Victorian home, that haven of peace and security, housemaids were in permanent contact with a male population whose intentions were often bad. Like the casual labourer who was hired for an afternoon to shift furniture from room to room: he had ample time to plan his move, and ample pretext for working out a route, surveying corridors, identifying bedrooms. So that when he had been paid, instead of vanishing into the evening streets, he climbed the backstairs one last time to the nurse's room, 'threw her on the bed and violated her'.

When their employers were away, or more commonly at the theatre or in church, maidservants were often left alone in large suburban houses isolated from each other by lawns, shrubberies and thick hedges. Not everyone had the relative good luck of Hannah M, maid-of-all-work for a butcher's family, who managed to get her story corroborated by a neighbour who had heard her screams.

> *One time when the family were all out, he seduced me. I resisted, screamed out and the next door neighbour Mrs. P heard and told Mrs. Z. directly she came home.*[5]

Of course this situation was also useful to masters and their male guests, whose social position gave them a large measure of impunity. Through shame or deference, and through fear of getting the sack, very few maids dared complain to their mistresses.

> *About August, my mistress left France for England and during her absence in September my master came to my bed at 2 o'clock in the morning and violated my person (there was no other servant in the house which was a cottage in a garden). My mistress returned a week or a fortnight afterwards when I quitted and came to England in the same boat as my master who promised to pay my wages, about £7 which he failed to do.*[6]

These unscrupulous employers had little to fear from the law, as those maids who tried to involve the courts usually discovered to their cost. One example is that of Lucy J, in service with a Colonel Z who shared a comfortable Marylebone apartment with a doctor of his acquaintance. One night as she passed his door on her way to bed, the doctor called Lucy and told her to go into the dining-room and extinguish the gas light that was still burning there. As soon as she was inside the room, he threw himself on her and raped her. The cook, who had heard sounds of struggle, agreed to give evidence in court, but in vain. Lucy J's complaint was dismissed, despite her colleague's evidence, despite the almost unheard-of intervention of the two gentlemen's wives, who stated that the girl's allegations were entirely plausible. That is why, as the applicant tried to get her six-month-old child admitted to the hospital in Red Lion Street, its father was pursuing his medical practice quite undisturbed a few streets away.

It is quite possible that some of the more complaisant wives saw their partners' ancillary love affairs as a means of lightening their own conjugal burden. This would seem to be the case with the story of Mary Ann, employed as maid-of-all-work in the home of a Camberwell wheelwright.

Before she had been there six weeks her master started taking what she called 'liberties' with her. Zola's realistic descriptions give us an idea of the real nature of these sexual advances, made furtively in passages, behind doors.[7]

She complained to her mistress, whose response was to call her a ninny, a flirt and a scatterbrain. A few months later, after a short struggle, she was raped by her master in the kitchen.

I struggled with him and ran out into the backyard but he caught me by the waist and brought me back into the house and seduced me by force. All this time we were alone in the house. Mrs. P was at the Queens Theatre and went home at night. I told Mrs. P the next morning but she pretended not to believe it. . . . It was repeated when Mrs. P was at Church, also by force and Father said he would give me some medicine if I fell in the family way. I left the P's and went to my mothers.[8]

At this point, accompanied by her mother, she made an official complaint, but they were told that nothing could be done before the birth of a child. By the time Mary Ann gave birth, the wheelwright and his wife had vanished without trace. It was only then that tongues began to loosen: the couple had a dubious reputation. She was not the first servant whom John P had 'got into trouble'.

In an age when the absence of means of contraception meant that sexual relations often resulted in pregnancy, when pregnancy and childbirth were themselves mortally dangerous to women,[9] when it was difficult to nourish an infant and its life was always under threat, it is easy to see how a cynical couple like the P's would have found it convenient to make sexual use of young domestics. The child born out of these social and sexual contradictions was conceived, carried, born and raised for six months by a twenty-one-year-old servant-girl literally standing in for Mrs P. While prostitution, so convenient in some ways for maintaining family peace, at least required a cash payment, the use of working girls by certain middle-class men, and sometimes their families or friends, recalls feudal serfdom and suggests that the professional duties of maids sometimes extended, unofficially, to the sexual servicing of another class.

The attitude of some of our petitioners' employers shows pretty clearly that certain masters regarded these practices as their due. Almost invariably, when forced to acknowledge what had happened, they offered compensation in money, showing at the very least that domestic service and sexual services had become confused in the master's mind.

On the servants' day off, while the mistress was at church or on a walk, the big houses of the rich murmured with illicit desires and furtive ambushes. The culprit might be a naval officer staying with friends, a brother visiting his sister's house, a nephew in residence for the holidays. The military cadet on leave was doing nothing much out of the ordinary when, soon after his arrival, he found his way into the cook's bedroom.

> *He secreted himself in my bed . . . I found him when I went to dress for dinner, he suddenly pounced upon me when I undressed, I threw a basin of water over him, and scratched his face and otherwise resisted him all I could. . . . He succeeded in effecting his purpose.*[10]

His aunt – the cook's employer – protected him against the girl and her family, and later against the law, by refusing to disclose his whereabouts for prosecution.

Despite the brutality of these confrontations, with our witnesses taken by surprise and unable either to defend themselves or to alert their colleagues, not one of these women mentions being afraid, or claims to have suffered any lasting trauma. The physical struggle is often described with great precision, but the emotions accompanying it are never mentioned. Was the act itself perhaps made less odious by the violence and exploitation, through a sort of numbing of sensibility? Did this make it easier to forget the attack with the passage of time? Or were words simply lacking in these young women, confronted as they were with so many trials in succession?

Some sort of answer is discernible in the story of one maker of artificial flowers.[11] A former Sunday-school teacher – thus indubitably pious – she met her seducer, a twenty-seven-year-old clerk, at a singing class given by the organist of Christchurch. He lured her to his rooms by persuading her to listen to the fine tone of his piano, raped her and allowed her to depart after offering her a glass of brandy and water. When her child was safely established at the Foundling Hospital, however, she married a widower older than herself, a jobbing jeweller, and brought two more infants into the world. Five years later, since luck had turned in her favour and she now lived in a comfortable home, she wrote to the Institution asking for the return of her daughter, as she wished to raise her with the other children and 'give her a name'.

CASUAL LOVES AND IMPOSSIBLE ROMANCES

It would be quite wrong to conclude from this, as others have done, that sexual relations between bourgeois men and working women inevitably involved physical violence.

The question has been much debated by bourgeois and proletarian moralists, but the Foundling Hospital's admission files contain testimony from the victims of these exogamous liaisons. The women who were obliged to recount their sexual adventures to the Hospital's staff did so in much the same spirit as penitents applying to church refuges, or the 'fallen women' patronized by social explorers: they strove to present themselves in a pathetic light in order to secure material help.

So meticulous were the Hospital's investigations, however, that the whole family and working environment comes to life before the reader's eyes. This helps expose fantasy and wishful thinking.[12]

'Female servants are far from being a virtuous class'[13]

Occasional or full-time recourse to prostitution by women of the working classes was a well-known nineteenth-century phenomenon, associated particularly with certain luxury trades. The girl assistants in glove and leather-goods shops, confectioners' and tobacconists', who were constantly brought into contact with rich customers and commercial travellers, often found it difficult to resist the temptation to take this route to an easier life. This theme is found in a variety of comic and knowing songs:

> Such a nice little cosy cigar divan
> Is the Piccadilly cigar divan . . .
> She says her name is Millicent, and that she comes from France,
> But well I know she comes from Bow – they used to call her Nance . . .
> To all but very wealthy men her prices would seem large,
> For instance an Havanna smoke would cost you one and four;
> But if Milly bit the end off she would charge a shilling more . . .[14]

Many a shop-girl listened giggling to a customer's compliments and allowed herself to be wooed with little presents and suggestive pleasantries.

Ours is mostly a ladies' shop: but sometimes a gentleman might come in for gloves or Hat. Yes if he asked me to put the gloves on for him, I should, of course; but not without. And if he wanted to joke me, I should say 'One of the young men'll attend to you Sir'. Our old gentleman is very particular about us joking with the young men, or the travellers. . . . We see a good many travellers and they like to have their joke with us when they can. One bought me (I forget what) once, and said 'Miss, will you accept this little present?' and I was very glad to have it . . .[15]

Makers and sellers of fancy goods and haberdashery, dressmakers, milliners, furriers, hat-binders, shoe-stitchers, embroiderers, piece-work seamstresses, all haunted the Foundling Hospital, for their occupations were both badly paid and subject to a long off-season, factors which encouraged mercenary sexual relations.[16]

Arthur J. Munby, so strangely fascinated by working women, so easily moved to indignation by his sharp eye for social injustice, gives an example of this situation in his Notebooks:

In Regent Street I was followed by two shabby furtive looking girls, and importuned in the usual manner. But they were not prostitutes – oh no! they were work-girls, working at Michell's the artificial florist in Oxford Street: and when work is slack, they turn out onto the streets for a living. Now Michell's is the fashionable shop to which I went, with Ned Anderson. . . & Fanny Meredith and other bridesmaids, to buy wreaths and veils for Ned's wedding.[17]

Some house-servants too, especially maids-of-all-work who had sole charge of a household, toil-weary, badly fed, poorly paid, used this expedient occasionally while in service, more often after being dismissed. Public houses and lodging-houses occupied by single men provided permanent opportunity.

Matilda T[18] worked in this last type of establishment. Her mistress rented out rooms in Upper Berkeley Street, not far from Piccadilly Circus and the Haymarket, which swarmed with prostitutes, and only a stone's throw from Curzon Street, Half Moon Street and Chesterfield Street where courtesans and demi-mondaines had their apartments. It could well be that this location influenced the young servant, or gave ideas to one of the tenants, an Egyptian gentleman called Ali Zahran. It seems in any case that the inquirer was interested, not in the respectability of the hotel where she worked, but in the lack of respectability of a young woman who had been born in a squalid slum not far away.[19] The Egyptian traveller, she explained, had turned up one night in the kitchen where she was sleeping and set about seducing her. He had started by promising to 'keep' her; later, he swore, they would get married. It did not take long for the Foundling Hospital interviewer to get her to admit something she had left out of her initial statement: she had been given a sovereign each night, 'so that I would not say anything'.

Part-time prostitution, certainly, but with the manifest hope of forming a real, more permanent liaison; a dream kept alive by the ostentatious lifestyle of the kept women one passed in the street.

> *She at least has all that she bargains for: fine clothes, rich food, plenty of money, a carriage to ride in, the slave-like obedience of her 'inferiors', and the fulsome adulation of those who deal with her for her worth. Very often. . . she finds a fool with money who is willing to marry her. . .[20]*

That this enviable destiny was reserved only for a few, that it was in fact far more difficult to arrange than it looked, is amply demonstrated by the stories of the Foundling Hospital's hundreds of little maid-servants; for a single Laura Bell holding court in Wilton Crescent, for one 'Skittles' queening it in Chesterfield Street, what regiments of girls like Matilda T tried their luck in vain! The inquirer, a Mr Twiddy, notes drily that in the opinion of her own people, Matilda had simply played and lost: that was all there was to it.

> *Petitioner's circumstances appear to be generally known to neighbours, who seem to sympathise in what they appear to consider more her misfortune than her fault.*

Another twenty-two-year-old, Sarah T, followed the same career with greater success, until pregnancy slowed her down at least for a time. She had been a domestic for a few months, but her lack of commitment was so evident that she was soon sacked:

> *A young woman. . . lived with us for two months in the spring of 1864. I have forgotten exactly what character I received with her, it was only a short one, and I fancy not very good, I engaged her more for charity than because I thought her a suitable person. I regret to say that her conduct while in my service was not good, and my impression was that she was not a respectable young woman or a fit companion for other servants. . .[21]*

wrote a former employer. She next took a room in Carey Street, in the shadow of the Law Courts, at the house of a Mrs H whose income as a landlady was most probably supplemented with procurer's fees.

From the character of the neighbourhood and from the cunning shown by Mrs H in her conversation with the inquirer respecting petitioner's mode of living while there. He is of opinion that petitioner was in bad hands while in that house.

Sarah stayed there for six months without working. She had kept alive, she assured the Hospital, by pawning her clothes – a fib which the inquirer chose not to investigate. No housemaid, especially one who had been employed so sporadically, would have been able to save enough out of her wages to live for six months without working; still less would she have possessed a wardrobe worth pawning. Eventually, however, by a stroke of good fortune, as she walked along the Strand – known for its prostitutes – in May 1865, the girl made the acquaintance of a lawyer on his way to the Chancery court. Her life changed immediately: she dined in restaurants, went to the theatre, and almost at once started a liaison which lasted six months. She received regular payments, she confessed, and relied on her friend for subsistence.

In this way the interviews build up a broad picture of the choices open to the daughters of the poor: difficult, convoluted, and often (as in this case) doomed to failure. As we shall see, the great majority of Foundling Hospital applicants confessed that they had surrendered to their suitors after a promise of marriage; Sarah's attempt to conform to this convention produced the claim that

When Crim. Con. occurred it was under his promise of protection.

The lawyer started to disentangle himself on the day she announced that she was expecting a child, or soon afterwards; Sarah herself could no longer remember. In any case, the magic had stopped working. It is one thing to go on seeing a girl who offers what you cannot get from the women of your own circle; to enjoy rustic charm, candour, simplicity, the vivacious manners and buxom flesh which Munby describes so well,[22] in surroundings of racy conviviality – music hall, pleasure garden – where adulterous sexuality comes easily; and something else altogether to abandon your class by setting up house and having a child, even if you stop short of marriage. So the lawyer, Charles S, broke it off. Sarah only ever saw him again on one occasion, four months later, at the Bedford Hotel, where she went to ask him for help. She got seven shillings, a quarter of the amount he had given her on their first evening together. Nothing could have illustrated more cruelly her abrupt loss of market value.

Not long afterwards, a member of the London Bible Women and Nurses Mission[23] knocked on her door and undertook to set her back on the straight path. As Sarah seemed receptive to the divine Word and repented loud and long, she was recommended to a supervisor who took her into service. Bible Women's reports often complain about the factitious character of some confessions. In Sarah's case, through fear of being once again abandoned to her own devices, she was careful not to admit her condition to her new mistress and 'persisted in denying it' until nature made it obvious. The response was immediate: she was sent straight to the Cleveland Street shelter for indigents, where she gave birth to her child and stayed six months. During her stay the Bible Women continued to visit her and dispense religious wisdom, hoping for a 'sincere repentance' and promising that if the child were adopted, she would once again be found a job as a domestic. This, it was hoped, might put a final stop to Sarah's attempts to build a career which seemed to her at least as desirable as that of a housemaid.

The blurred frontiers between domestic service and prostitution, respectability and dishonour, lying and sincere repentance, expose the limitations of the dogmatic analyses favoured by Victorian moralists and doctors, torn between the wish to redeem prostitutes and the conviction that their lives were ruined, that they were destined for an early end. It is precisely this uncertainty which justified the work of the Foundling Hospital's administrators in their own eyes.

'Nice life this, for a girl of three and twenty, my Kerristian friends'[24]

Many of the young domestics and artisans who applied to the Foundling Hospital lived in conditions of extreme physical and moral hardship. On the whole their living conditions were not as hard as those of the indigents who sought shelter in workhouses, nor was their work as back-breaking as the forced labour performed by brick-makers and rag-pickers; nor were they exposed to the elements in all seasons, like travelling pedlars.

Nevertheless, their lives were pretty demanding. To understand fully the situation of applicants to the Hospital, it may be useful to go over a few professional and pecuniary details.

To begin with, there were very considerable differences between the wages of maidservants in residential districts, who earned between £12 and £18 a year,[25] and those of 'slaveys', very young girls who toiled unaided in lower-middle-class houses for £5 or at most £7. Both categories in any case received only a small amount in cash, as the statistician W.T. Layton points out.[26]

They were housed, fed, and, in big houses, given beer and laundry allowances. When the cost of clothing had been deducted, however, they were left with very little pocket money, certainly not enough to pay the five to seven shillings a week it cost to place a child with a foster mother. This made some writers impatient with the flood of advice urging domestics to save their money and plan for the future:

> Some persons who lecture them on improvidence assume that out of £15 they might lay by £10, and so on; but any sensible housewife will say at once that this is absurd. The plainest and most economical style of dress, respectable enough for a middle-class kitchen, cannot, we are assured, be provided for less than £6 in the country and £7 in town. Then, is the maidservant never to do a kind thing to her own family or anybody else – never to pay postage – never to buy a book or anything that is wearable?[27]

A milliner employed in a factory earned nine shillings a week in 1861, and up to ten shillings in the busy season. A tailor's machinist earned sixteen shillings a week, but tackers and finishers in the same factory earned at most nine or ten shillings.

A few governesses, whose salaries were much larger, did manage to save hundreds of pounds, but at the cost of sacrifices which can only be imagined.

Those who were not specifically attached to the service of individuals earned their miserable wages through gruelling physical effort. In the nineteenth century, domestic tasks, still carried out with rudimentary equipment, were innumerable and generally unrewarding in themselves. Fires had to be made up, coal fetched, grates cleared and ashes disposed of daily. Streets awash with mud and refuse for a good part of the year, houses and factories belching thick smoke which mingled with the mists rising from the river, meant a continuous battle to keep floors, windows, walls and doors clean.[28]

On his way to dine one evening, Munby paused for a few moments outside the kitchens to watch a scullerymaid toiling alone in the steamy restaurant basement:

> She stood at a sink, behind a wooden dresser packed with choppers and stained with blood and grease, upon which were piles of coppers and saucepans which she had to scour, piles of dirty dishes that she had to wash; her frock and cap, her face and arms, were more or less wet, soiled, perspiring, and her apron was a piece of sacking, wet and filthy, tied around her with a cord. The den where she wrought was low, damp, illsmelling; windowless, lighted by a flaring gas-jet. . .[29]

Artisans doing home-based piecework or employed in factories worked sitting down, fingers and bodies bent to the same repeated tasks, to the limit of their strength. One woman, obliged to resume her former trade of dressmaker after the death of the man with whom she lived, confided her lassitude to Munby:

> So now she works as a tailor making waistcoats, at home. Lives by herself in a little room near Gray's Inn Road; earns 12/6 a week – pays 4/- for lodging, so keeps herself, living frugally. Finds it very dull, sitting alone all day at work, sitting alone all the evening because one can't afford to go out and amuse oneself, walking alone about the streets of an evening – very dull![30]

Living with her family would not necessarily have been any better. The work would have been just as hard, and she might also have had to face a mother's tyranny, the dangers of prostitution, satirically explained in a popular song:

> Come hither bring the scrubbing-brush, and chuck away the slops. . .
> Now go and pawn your father's boots – let's have a drop of gin;
> And if the tally-man should come, say I am not within:
> Tell him Father's very ill, and likely to die;
> But mind and hold the door ajar, and pretend to pipe your eye,
> You may tell him I shall be alone any night at nine,

These were my mother's customs, and so they shall be mine;
These were &c. . .[31]

Everyone worked interminable hours. The scullerymaid at Rouget's restaurant described by Munby was shut in her appalling cellar from noon until eleven at night. Servants and artisans alike started work in the very early morning and finished late in the evening: a twelve-hour working day, barely interrupted by a few minutes of relaxation.[32] Hours of rest and recreation were few. Domestics had only one full day off a month; some had in addition two afternoons or one evening a week.[33]

These painful working conditions were made worse by the desperate boredom of solitude and monotonous labour – not easily assuaged, for newly arrived provincials, by lonely walks through a town where everything cost too much.

Lest we should be accused of distorting the picture with slanted generalizations, it is worth noting that many Foundling Hospital applicants had jobs not far from their families; and that others found the bustle and variety, the street musicians, the whole swarming anthill of the capital, an endlessly fascinating spectacle.[34] Besides, gazing into shop windows, wandering through bazaars, buying small necessities, dawdling past street jugglers, strolling through parks, were all occasions on which one might be approached, accosted, diverted for a moment from the burdens of loneliness and disheartening drudgery.

It seems reasonable to suppose, therefore, that sexual adventures with men of a different social class were really attempts to escape from this life. Extra income might be sought through occasional or full-time prostitution. But other Foundling Hospital applicants had obviously believed they could secure the affections of – and perhaps even marry – a man able to offer them some of the comfort, luxury and leisure enjoyed by the inhabitants of wealthy neighbourhoods. Their statements indicate that domestics and workers in the clothing trade were especially susceptible to promises uttered by unknown seducers.[35] Daily contact with the middle classes had refined their tastes, swollen their ambitions, reinforced their wish to acquire nice clothes and accede to a vaguely pictured happiness. Penny romances, and the popular refrains heard on every street corner, kept the hope alive that love might just possibly conquer everything, and especially the barriers between social classes.

> *I said, lovely maid if you'll not be my bride,*
> *My life I will waste in some foreign land.*
> *What pleasure in treasure where love it is wanting,*
> *Your beauty upon me has now cast a spell,*
> *I'll marry you speedy, and make you a lady,*
> *If you will be mine dear factory girl.*[36]

Dreams of this kind are attributed by Mrs Gaskell to her eternally dissatisfied heroine Mary Barton:

> *So Mary dwelt upon and enjoyed the idea of some day being a lady, and doing all the elegant nothings appertaining to ladyhood. It was a comfort to her when scolded by Miss Simmonds, to think of the day when she would drive up to her door in her own carriage, to order her gowns from the hasty-tempered yet kind dressmaker.*[37]

And of course the town and its households swarmed with a mass of young bachelors, starved of feminine company and longing for romantic adventures. Apprentice painters, medical assistants, office workers, pharmacists' juniors, notaries' clerks, military cadets, medical and law students, haunt the accounts of Foundling Hospital applicants, just as they haunted the capital's fevered streets and quiet parks, forever on the lookout for a stroke of luck. After dinner in their lodgings, or a club or coffee house, their time was their own through the long evenings and the empty Sunday afternoons: what better way to spend some of it than by chasing dressmakers, milliners, little servant girls? It was an easy and inexpensive pastime, safer and more interesting than buying love from a professional.

> *I met Father* [a medical student] *whilst on an errand for my mistress. He spoke to me and walked with me. He appointed to call upon me a day or two after and we again walked out together and so on, once a week for twelve months. . .*

> *I first met Father* [a clerk] *at the Gardens whilst with my sister's children. He was with other young men but he was alone when he spoke to me. He walked part of the way home with me and we made an appointment to meet again the next night and so on in the same way.*[38]

> *I met Father first in the shop of his master Mr. J, where I was in the habit of going for medicine.*[39]

I met Father first in Oxford St in the Autumn of 1851. Father [a bank clerk]
followed me and ascertained my abode.[40]

Other women met their future lovers through their employers,
through friends or in the hotels or lodgings where they lived. The
housemaid of a pharmacist or surgeon might be seduced by her
master's assistant; a lodging-house maid by a student, commercial
traveller or officer; a barmaid or hotel servant by a regular guest; a
young clerk might seduce his parents' servant-girl; a model might
succumb to the advances of an artist.

Women of the middle classes were adopting grand, elaborate manners, withdrawing into creamy laces and brocades, wrapping themselves in heavy, silky materials and abstaining from all manual
activity; but some of their menfolk were still attracted by more robust
physical qualities and less mannered attitudes.

It would be going too far to attribute the taste of some Victorian
men for the daughters of the people solely to the freedom of working-
class sexual morals. Of course the women's relatively relaxed attitudes
did play a part, as did the social impunity which usually attended the
jilting of women who got 'caught'. But Arthur J. Munby, a man
literally obsessed with the physical aspect of women of the people,
conveys vividly the attraction that the strong rough hands and muscu-
lar forearms of working women possessed for some men. The combi-
nation in these girls of prettiness and clumsy awkwardness fascinates
him, but at the same time inspires a fairly obvious class repugnance.
An intelligent observer who walked endlessly about the streets, he one
day saw coming towards him

> . . . *a wellgrown servant girl of eighteen or so dressed in the usual frock and without*
> *bonnet or even cap, who had been sent on an errand and was coming back along the*
> *crowded street. Stooping and lurching from side to side, she shambled on in most*
> *ungainly fashion, munching an apple and looking at nothing. Her arms, which were*
> *bare and dirty, hung stiffly outwards from the shoulder like a pair of pump-handles;*
> *and her large coarse bony hands, with the clumsy fingers all aspread, fell dead and*
> *helpless from the wrists as she moved, like the paws of an ape. Thus she passed*
> *through the welldressed portly crew; a creature as awkward and as void of outward*
> *self-respect, as one could conceive. And yet she had a good figure, dark wellset hair,*
> *and a face young and delicately pretty. Such as would have become rather a trained*
> *milliner, or even a lady.*[41]

Munby seems to have found it deeply seductive to be served by these women of the people, to have them bring lunch up to his room, draw the curtains, carry his luggage or, like the shrimp-fisherwomen on the beach at Boulogne-sur-Mer, carry him on their backs to prevent his ankle-boots from getting wet in pools of seawater.

Munby, of course, was an extraordinary character, a man who carried his passion through to its conclusion by making a lady, eventually, of a woman who continued to address him as 'Massah' even after they were married. But there is more to his private diaries than the account of his own conflicts, his chaste admiration for the refined women of his own circle, his uncivilized penchant for women of the people whom he saw as an androgynous species, slaves at once masculine and maternal. They also help to illuminate the – necessarily illicit – attraction felt by some of his contemporaries for working-class women. When one reads in the Foundling Hospital files of the many seductions carried out in bedrooms while the chambermaid was attending to some task, what springs to mind is the image of a fantasized mother, a woman who satisfies every need. This expectation is amusingly expressed in an early twentieth-century song:

> He asked for a candle to light him in bed,
> Likewise for a napkin to tie round his head,
> She waited on me as a fair maid should do
> And I gave her the wink to jump in bed too.[42]

In fact the sexual desire of middle-class men for domestics was already perceived as a new social phenomenon in the nineteenth century. The sexologist Krafft-Ebing thought that the white apron worn by serving-maids suggested women's underclothing and the intimate parts of the body concealed by it. Some prostitutes dressed up in aprons to make themselves look like little maids.[43]

Apart from the working girls' ambition to move into a better world, and the pleasure men derived from succumbing to the ambiguous charm of young maidservants, these – necessarily furtive – love affairs were often imbued, for both parties, with beguilingly piquant romance. Munby once again provides an agreeable example, in this description of a flirtation with the pretty Laura, which passes unnoticed by the rest of the company.

As the young ladies crowd to the hall door and I am helping Grandmamma to her

*carriage, Laura, waiting in the background, says low 'Let me carry your bag, Sir' –
and I give it her; and in the dusk outside she holds the carriage door open for me – and
as she closes it and gives me the bag, somehow her thick broad hand comes in contact
with mine, and does not retreat. Oh ho! Here we have a scene for a novel: the hero
from his chariot bows farewell to the elegant imperial creature who thinks she has
him captive, but meanwhile his real adieus are given, in secret pressure of her
working hand, to the humble serving maid who hands him to the door.*[44]

And as one can see from correspondence still on file, it sometimes
happened that, for a while at least, one of these affairs would blossom
into an authentic love story.

Born in Westminster, newly in service with a rich doctor near Hyde
Park, Eleanor Q was nineteen when she met and fell for Thomas E.
She was introduced to the charming pharmacist's assistant by the
kitchenmaid. He courted her assiduously for nearly a year, then
proposed marriage. Once they were engaged she thought it permissible to visit him in his lodgings, and was soon pregnant. He urged her
to leave her job, move into a room which he would rent for her, and
start making preparations for marriage. He seemed so set on marrying
her! When he decided to leave for the North her pregnancy was very
advanced, but she was not worried: he had given her £20 to cover the
cost of travelling to Edinburgh where she was to join him. The
romance was abruptly shattered by a letter from Scotland, two
months before the birth of the child:

My dearest Eleanor,

*I arrived here quite safe last Saturday night and sit down to write to you as I
promised but I fear the contents will not be so welcome to you as you anticipated for I
must now tell you what I had not the courage or heart to do when I last said good bye
to you namely that after due consideration I feel convinced it would not be for the
happiness of either of us, if I was to carry out the promises I made you when I was
carried away by my [illegible], I cannot but acknowledge the wrong I have done
you, but as I have not the certain means of supporting myself much less a wife, I
should not only involve myself and you in further difficulties and my friends would
not acknowledge us if I married you. . . . As I find I cannot do anything in
England. . . I have determined on the advice of my friends and with their assistance,
to try my luck abroad. . . tomorrow the ship leaves and carries me from a land where
I have never done much good for myself or others but I hope to find a better state of
things abroad. . . . I must now, my dear Eleanor, say that hard word adieu, and*

with it, farewell to the many happy hours I have spent with you, Adieu my poor girl and forgive if your heart will let you. . .[45]

There follow a few admonitions to the girl to avoid bad company, and a promise to get in touch at the end of his travels.

Judging the reality of these sentiments is not as easy as it looks. They may be seen as trivial hypocrisy covering up a shabby confidence trick. At the same time it is impossible not to see the contradiction between the aspirations of a domestic hoping to escape her condition through marriage, and the hopes of a young man who aspires to rise socially. 'I can do nothing here,' he writes: nothing, in any case, within the power of a young man who has studied pharmacy and whose social model is the middle class. To marry a domestic would be to break with his family, lose their support, drag himself down. However deep his feelings for the girl, he has suddenly realized that starting life in London with a baby and an almost illiterate wife will be extremely trying, worse than the betrayal whose meanness he seeks to attenuate by persuading himself that it is as much in the young woman's interests as his own:

> *I do hope, after the first shock is over, you will think that this step may save us much future misery.*

But being let down by men in whom they had placed such hopes sent many girls off the rails. Look at one of the numberless life stories gleaned by Henry Mayhew from the alleys of Westminster, and try to imagine how else it might have ended.

The prostitute Mayhew questioned had been living in a 'house' for years. She too had been given what looked a generous sum of money when her man had left her. After working for a while as a dressmaker's machinist she had lost her job, and her child had subsequently died in a state of extreme destitution. That was when she had begun her venal way of life, she remarked, adding wistfully:

> *If there had been a foundling-hospital, I mean as I hear there is in foreign parts, I would have placed him there, and worked somehow, but there isn't, and a crying shame it is too.*[46]

In reality, as we know, the Foundling Hospital had been in existence for a considerable time. But the Hospital committee kept such examples in mind when judging the cases brought before it. That is why it sometimes broke its own internal rules by admitting the children of mothers it thought altogether culpable.

One is compelled to recognize that the credulity and blindness of some of these girls was matched only by the black-hearted villainy of knaves seeking a moment's diversion at someone else's expense. There can be no doubt that the youth of their victims played a part in the success of these neighbourhood Don Juans. Laura P was already working, although she was only fifteen, when she succumbed to a clerk's advances. She was not aware of what the inquiry would later reveal:

> He left in debt. He is said to be of dissipated habits and is believed to be capable of committing the fault attributed to him in this instance.[47]

In another case the inquirer underlined the total, friendless isolation of the young prey:

> Father's mother states that her own son had cruelly deceived Petitioner who is an orphan and without relatives.[48]

Usually, however, there is nothing specific to explain the reckless attitude of these girls.

Let us hypothesize, then, that the low value they placed on virginity, combined with a sharp and vital appetite for diversion, explain why these young women granted their favours so easily, at the first sign of a chance to interrupt the monotony of their lives and receive some immediate gratification. Walking in St James's or Regent's Park on the arm of a well-turned-out gentleman, getting love letters, being desired when really you were everyone's slave, being whisked to the intoxicating ozone of Ramsgate from a life of sewing hats twelve hours a day, might well have been thrilling enough to mask, for a time, the risk of a pregnancy whose costs would have to be borne by the girl alone.

Others were less easily misled. When Mary spent her days off walking about on the arm of a young medical assistant, her friends

> . . . viewed [their acquaintance] with much suspicion on account of the disparity of their positions in life.[49]

Harriet T was given a very similar warning. This time the voice of social reason spoke through her employers, owners of an Edgware Road pharmacy where her suitor worked as a dispenser. They criticized 'the impropriety of attaching herself to B, whom they represented to her as having no intention towards her'.[50]

Sometimes these social differences were even more extreme. A housemaid ran into a friend of her former employers, the son of a rich doctor who had already 'shown an interest' in her; he walked a few yards with her, took her to the theatre in Richmond a few days later, and made her his mistress. A dressmaker spent a year of idyllic happiness with a civil servant neighbour who then vanished to South America, leaving her £6 and the promise of a ticket to follow him. A shop-girl out walking with a friend met a medical student from St Bartholomew's Hospital; on learning of her pregnancy, after their affair had lasted a year, he told her that he could not marry her.

There is no doubt that some of these girls sought knowingly to compromise a wealthy man into marriage, or at least into providing some material advantage and compensation in the event of pregnancy. Munby was the wily intended victim of one of these manoeuvres, which he regarded with indulgent amusement.

After dining in the Strand one Saturday night in winter, he met a young dressmaker's machinist whom he knew slightly, Mary Ann Ireland. They talked for a moment. As it was eight o'clock and she was in a hurry to go home, her day's work finished, he accompanied her on her way to Mile End. She spoke of her life and her too-rare chances to go out. He left her in the miserable, rubbish-strewn street where she lived, said good night and turned towards home. A moment later he heard running footsteps behind him: it was Mary Ann, out of breath, inviting him in. Her mother had said it was outrageous not to ask 'the gentleman' to sit down for a minute. 'I hesitated for a moment,' Munby writes, 'but curiosity got the better of my suspicions.' He was introduced to the whole family and spent some time chatting to them. 'Curious!' he writes indulgently after taking his leave,

> I suppose my next visit would be that of an accepted suitor! But whatever their family aims may be, is there not an honest simplicity of manners and character in all this?[51]

In reality, middle-class families were well prepared to resist these attempts and seldom hesitated to respond brutally to demands from girls for reparation. The mother of Priscilla T – a girl who had been promised marriage by her employer's brother – got nothing but threats. The seducer's brother wrote menacingly:

> Mrs. T, I don't intend that [my wife] should be annoyed by your letter writing, so if you insist upon doing it, we shall have to do what we don't wish to do, you can do what you please but be careful.

> Mrs. T, I don't want to be bothered any more about my brother's affairs, so don't send me any more letters,[52]

another letter ends.

'Home, sweet home'

In the light of these documents, there is something ironic in the exhortations of those philanthropists, like Octavia Hill, who feared that society was in danger of splitting into two antagonistic groups and urged the formation of closer and more friendly links between rich and poor.

> You want to know them, to enter into their lives, their thoughts. . . . You might meet them face to face as friends. . . mere intercourse between rich and poor, if we can secure it without corrupting gifts, would civilize the poor more than anything.[53]

That there existed, in Victorian households, a measure of familiarity between maidservants and the males of the family is clearly indicated by the sort of advice ladies were offered on this aspect of prudent household management.

Too much emphasis is generally placed on coercive relationships between masters and young domestics, or between very small children and the nurses who sometimes initiated them into sensuality. Our sources refer repeatedly to more complex links, rooted in sensual friendship and power games, between maids and adolescent boys; often genuinely intimate relationships, formed over a period of time, unnoticed – or opposed in vain – by the young man's mother.

It was common practice for very young girls, even children, to be engaged to help in the nursery and lend a hand in the house. Frances H was ten years old when her aunt, at that time in service, began taking her regularly to play with the children of the Reeves family; when she was fourteen, she entered the family's service herself. Ann T, whose mother had died when she was a baby, went to work for a pharmacist after the death of her father; she was fifteen at the time. These little girls grew up among the children of the household and their employers' young apprentices.

Childhood and adolescent friendships flowered naturally between these young people of different social status. They played together, exchanged Christmas and birthday presents, borrowed one another's books. Similar friendships formed between young adults – for example the one between Ruth Y, a kitchenmaid, and the very young Captain David K, on sick leave after losing his right hand. When Ruth and the lady's maid withdrew to their room in the evening after work, the captain would often join them for innocent badinage and horseplay.

Although real up to a point, these friendships were seldom completely unreserved. The Foundling Hospital files make it clear that when difficulties arose everyone tried to claim the role of victim: the girls swore that they had been subjected to the boys' over familiarity, while the boys asserted, from the safety of the family ramparts, that they had been led on and enticed into a trap. In any case these relationships could be far from chaste, as Frances H complained:

> They were forward children and used to take liberties with me. I complained of the younger one to his mother but she said it was my own evil thoughts and would not attend to me. . . . Arthur R. after he had grown up had connections with me against my consent. . . it was afterwards repeated. . . he is the father of my child and this I would swear.[54]

In another case, a maid called Grace had come to be regarded as a sick-nurse attached to the person of the eldest son of the house, who was 'delicate' and frequently bedridden.

> After six months he took liberties with me. He took me by force to his bedroom and gave me Brandy and Water. Crim. Con. was repeated frequently.[55]

Ruth Y, who had so often chatted with Captain K in the company of her friend the lady's maid, was one night surprised to find him in her bed.

One night in December of last year he came to my bedroom and was admitted by the lady's maid who slept with me. I was asleep when he entered the room. The lady's maid left him with me and I saw nothing of her until the next morning. The Father came to bed to me and I resisted all I could but he succeeded. I think I must have been drugged for I was in a state of partial unconsciousness. On the next morning I remonstrated with the lady's maid, but she only laughed at me, and said it would be all right. . . . . He used to jeer me afterwards and say I was in the family way by the young man I then kept company.[56]

Provocative talk and sexual games seemed harmless enough to girls accustomed to the coarse gestures and smutty jokes of the servants' hall, but the situation could degenerate. In this permissive environment there grew the sort of conflicts one would expect: sexual rivalries, social jealousies, class-based contempt, all sharpened and intensified by being confined to the claustrophobic world of a household. It is not too difficult to imagine possible reasons for the lady's maid's mean and treacherous conduct towards Ruth Y.

Different motives are apparent in the story of Ann T. His employer's wife described William P, the presumed father, as

When a boy. . . frolicsome. . . he, she and the errand boy have played together. . . . Being an orphan she was shown more than usual kindness by us, which made kindness on the part of William P. to her reasonable.[57]

But after the pharmacist died, William took charge of the dispensary

and gave up former playfulness. This position filled Petitioner's mind with jealousy. Petitioner talked with anger about him to neighbours because he was so proud he wouldn't speak to her.

The appearance of an illegitimate pregnancy, or an adoption application from an unmarried mother, brought suddenly into the light things which had lain hidden for years: the unassailable condescension of the upper classes towards their servants, the rancour of girls who hitherto had always allowed themselves to be browbeaten without protest. Plus, of course, the natural irritation experienced when a family was upset by one of these unwanted pregnancies and the incrimination of a member of the household.[58] In the presence of the bastard infant, masks were dropped: compassion for orphans, pet schemes for educating the servants, affection born out of years of daily intimacy, could vanish abruptly.

A brutal ferocity on the employers' side, countered by desperate resistance from the unmarried mother and her friends, would cleave the former household into two warring groups before the eyes of the Hospital's inquirers. Each group would strive to demolish the honour and besmirch the respectability of the other. For the masters – despite the frequent claim that maidservants were treated as members of the family – the sexual transgression itself seemed less scandalous than the disturbance to the social hierarchy. Rubbing shoulders with the populace, making room for its representatives in your family through enlightened charity, was one thing; to put yourself on an equal footing with it would be (it went without saying) another thing entirely.

This is a clear example of an obstacle to moral regeneration. If the girls had been content to commit sins of the flesh with men of their own social class, it would have been sufficient to dismiss them. Under circumstances of this sort, however, it looked a good idea to throw doubt on their probity, and their other qualities too.

> *Mrs. P. always spoke in the highest terms of Petitioner until this affair and afterwards quite changed her tone,*[59]

comments one sympathetic, wholly unimpeachable witness. These situations meant that a girl who had been 'almost one of the family' would suddenly be represented as a sour, envious, insolent liar. Frances H, for example, who

> *received the same domestic treatment as the children of the home, and the education she has received was obtained there. She. . . has been confirmed by the Bishop and has received the sacrament,*[60]

became a lying trollop overnight:

> *She was not truthful, she was fond of romping and laughing with the men about the premises. It was insinuated that Petitioner with other girls of her own age and condition were known to talk and flirt with gentlemen visitors at the Isle of Wight during their promenade. . .*

However strong the presumption of paternity, and despite all previous ties of affection, the very fact of their application to the Foundling Hospital shows that servants in this situation could not count on the support of these families to help overcome their difficulties, even in exceptional circumstances.

Mrs R clearly thought herself immensely charitable for arranging to send the young mother – and the infant who was undoubtedly her own grandson – back to London after the confinement, which took place while the family was on holiday on the Isle of Wight:

> I will send a respectable person to bring her in the train if you will meet her in London. I do this entirely out of fluctuating emotion and because you have no means to support her and she has but little of her own.[61]

Captain David K, who so enjoyed the company of domestics, agreed to send five pounds to Ruth Y:

> As you are in such distress and have no friend to help you, I send something and I ask you to let us hear no more of this. But if I hear that you are in distress when I return to England, I shall take an opportunity of sending you something.[62]

But families were inclined to form their own ideas on the child's real paternity.

> Had I from the first known the truth, much as I should have blamed her conduct, I would have helped her to an honest living,[63]

claims the mother of young Arthur R. For although the youth admitted having sexual relations with the maid, his entire family got involved in the denial of paternity. As soon as she had given birth, his father made the young woman sign a statement swearing 'till the day of judgement' that she had only once had sexual intercourse with his son. In a letter to their mother, couched in astonishingly direct language, Arthur's brother Oliver attempts to prove the material impossibility of conception:

> Papa had just told me the dreadful news about Frances which I could have sworn were untrue until Papa asked Arthur, when he owned that he had been with her once; one afternoon in the nursery about a week after he came down last year. . . he says that she asked him saying there was no harm in it. He says he was not in her more than a minute and he could not have been 14 years old at that time.[64]

But the real task was to assemble evidence implicating a man of the same class as Frances:

She was very intimate with Price [a nineteen-year-old groom] *and always running after the* [illegible] *and farm-men. Was it not rather one of them. . . . I do not wish to cast it on any innocent person but it was rather suspicious for Price to say he did not want to come again when he had no place and had been treated so well by us; he was often boasting about girls especially Harriet G. . .*

In much the same way, Captain K's father answered the hospital's inquiry by naming

A coach named John P of Clapham who was in the habit of courting the woman. . . . I have since heard that she stayed out with him on several occasions without the knowledge of her mistress and I trust that Mr. P has deserted her and is the father of the child.[65]

The girls and their supporters, of course, indignantly dismissed these suspicions, pleaded not guilty. Their statements, and the attitude of their allies, anticipate the new moral sensibility which began to appear during the 1880s, urging mothers to take a more enlightened line on sexual education and run closer surveillance of their households, while denouncing the social and moral impunity which protected middle-class men and boys from the consequences of their actions. The campaign for the repeal of the Contagious Diseases Acts, and the work of the Moral Reform Union, William Thomas Stead and others, tend in the same direction.

In the first half of the century the author of a manual for housewives and mothers, Sarah Ellis Stickney, had been noticeably vague on matters relating to children's and servants' sexuality:

For the little thoughtless girl just entering beneath your roof – the young nursery-maid – she of whom nobody thinks, except to find fault when she has done wrong – she who perhaps never thinks herself, except to contrive how she shall manage to purchase a ribbon like that upon her mistress's cap – This very girl is gradually experiencing under your care, that great and important change of thought, feeling, and habit, which is not improperly called the formation of character; and this girl will consequently take away with her whatever bias she receives either from your neglect, or your attention. . .[66]

Forty years later there was less beating about the bush. Elizabeth Blackwell writes briskly that housewives and mothers who are sexually ignorant will be incompetent in bringing up children and keeping an eye on the morals of their elders. She ridicules the numerous manuals on family management available at the time, which were avidly read by the rising middle classes.

> In all the excellent treatises on physiology, domestic economy, and education. . . all knowledge is generally omitted which refers to the sexual functions. . . . A woman attempts to carry on her work blindfold, who tries to educate her children, guide her household, or take her proper part in society without this knowledge.[67]

She is highly critical of people who did not keep up to date on current medical practice, like the acquaintance who one day asked

> . . . if providing a mistress for her son would be very costly in Paris? She had accepted as a fact what she had been taught – viz. that no young man who could not marry early could remain healthy without resorting to vice.[68]

Domestics, for their part, were warned against the perils to be encountered in the dwellings of the rich. One manual for their instruction offers this advice:

> Before placing you in a house where there are grown-up sons, your parents ought to make very strict inquiries. Such situations are always dangerous, and perhaps altogether improper for a girl just entering service.[69]

And should a master become overfamiliar, the manual suggests,

> . . . You must instantly repair to your mistress, tell her that you would not willingly disturb her peace. . . that you grieve you cannot remain in her house, and hope she will approve your determination.[70]

The girls whose stories we are following were not unaware of all these things. But one cannot help suspecting that when faced with the Hospital committee they tended, like Dr Blackwell, to attribute all the carelessness and laxity to their employers.

Rose T was vigorously supported in this claim by the landlady of the flat rented by her former employers:

> The family consisted of Mr. and Mrs. I. and 4 children of which Arthur (the Father of petitioner's child) was the oldest and of about 18 years of age. . . . The children

were badly managed. . . the father of Petitioner's child was of a turbulent temper –
of unscrupulous habits, pampered and spoiled by his mother – that she (informant)
had learnt from her own private servant that petitioner was constrained by Mrs. I. to
remain alone with the father in his bedroom to watch and nurse him during his fits of
pretended illness. . .[71]

The culprit's father replied that

His boys may have behaved in a rough and unbecoming manner to petitioner
occasionally but when so, they were he believed, always chastised for the faults
complained of.

In judging this conflict, in which the middle classes exploited the
shameless reputation of working girls to escape their own responsibilities, and domestics accused their masters of failing to look after
them properly, or even of corrupting them, the Foundling Hospital
ultimately came down on the side of the servants, but without
pressing the employers to 'do their duty'. There was absolutely no
question of forcing them into marriage. In Queen Victoria's time,
every sensible person knew that

Servants are not fit companions for men born in a class much higher than themselves,
and therefore should stoutly refuse the offer, were it seriously made to them.[72]

TEMPTATIONS AND PRECAUTIONS

In the nineteenth century, very few working-class women made the
conscious decision to live on their own. The first women to choose
celibacy – and chastity – as a way of life came from the middle
classes.[73]

The majority of our petitioners were close to the ideal age for
marriage, as prescribed by those manuals intended to be read by the
working classes:

When she has been long enough in service to have formed her character, when she
has saved something to begin to keep house, and when she has had time to know the
state and character of her intended.[74]

Are we to deduce from this that apart from the cases examined above, most of the applicants were motivated solely by the wish to start a family? Perhaps, since many claimed that this was their intention. But what of the others? How did these working couples meet in London? Where did they pursue their amorous idylls? What obstacles stood in the way of their plans?

So far we have dealt only with case histories involving middle-class seducers. In fact, these are only a minority. The bulk of the statements in the archive describe lovers of much humbler social background, although the professional status of men and women was not always exactly the same: most of the men belonged to the class of junior clerks, artisans and skilled workers,[75] and were thus socially superior to the women, most of whom were labourers or unqualified white-collar workers. But the relatively low professional status of domestics was counterbalanced by housekeeping skills acquired in service, and often also by a small nest egg accumulated specifically with a view to getting married.

Measuring the compatibility of different professions is a difficult task in any case. There is no absolute scale of values in this area. A production-line worker in an advanced sector of industry might be better paid and enjoy higher social status than a foreman in a traditional sector. In our sample, a kitchenmaid in an aristocratic household had a job that was socially superior to that of housekeeper and maid-of-all-work in the home of a small retailer, although the latter would have had sole charge of the house.

The admission files are not sufficiently detailed to show how precisely matched the couples were in this respect, nor do they always give the man's age (information which might modify our understanding of some cases). Let us simply note, therefore, that the couples appear to be compatible socially and professionally, except of course in cases of rape or sexual liaison between master and servant.

**'As I was going to Chelsea one day
I met with a pretty girl on the way. . .'** [76]

sings the love-struck narrator of a contemporary ballad. From this fortuitous meeting, once he has overcome the beauty's reserve, are born a happy marriage and a bouncing baby boy.

Meetings between the sexes took place all the time in the streets of the metropolis, which pulsated with life and incident. A girl going about her work or returning home at the end of the day, on an errand for her employer or taking a Sunday stroll, would be walking alone. A young man would accost her. People still walked a great deal in Victorian London, and spoke freely to strangers. Munby was astonished by the naive and trusting way in which working girls confided in strangers:

> Long before we got there, however, we had become quite friends; she had told me half her history, and I had grown charmed with her artless frankness. . . . Ten minutes goes a great way to making friends with a servant maid. . .[77]

The streets in which all poor children played, and where some were brought up, were not seen as a hostile place. They were 'the drawing-room of the poor', where the world opened out for them.

> About a month after coming to London I met the Father in the street, whilst walking. He spoke to me and walked with me for an hour.[78]

> This was three years ago. I met him when I was going to my place and he helped me with my box.[79]

> I first met Father in the street as I went to the public house for beer.[80]

> I first met Father in June by meeting him casually in the street.[81]

In the street one routinely met the servants of neighbouring houses, and construction workers from nearby sites:

> Our acquaintance commenced by his passing the door of my master on his way, as he said, to and from work as a journey-man mason in the House of Lords,[82]

explains Ann, who worked as a domestic near Westminster Abbey. In central London, there were the Guards and other military whose presence could cause a condition known as 'scarlet fever':

> I saw him first on duty at Buckingham Palace, we used to walk out together in the Parks.[83]

And of course there were the representatives of law and order, whose uniforms and reassuring, familiar presence often made them irresistible:

He was a policeman on duty in the square, and used to speak to me.[84]

While at Petersham I met Father in the street. He was a policeman. This was two years ago.[85]

The policeman as suitor is a standard character of popular ballads and farces:

If your wife should want a friend,
Ask a policeman!
Who a watchful eye will lend
Ask a policeman!
Truth and honour you can trace
Written on his manly face;
When you're gone he'll mind your place.
Ask a policeman![86]

The same sarcastic tone is found in *The Area Belle*, a popular comedy in which Pitcher the policeman seduces Penelope the cook in the pantry:

What a proud thing it is to be entrusted with the duty of watching over the hearths and homes of one's native country – to be the guardian spirit which protects these scenes of peace and plenty from the foot of the spoiler.[87]

and in 'The Special Bobby':

To keep the peace, oh, what a hobby,
And to know the cooks all love the Bobby, . . .
And to trot out girls of all ages,
Help 'em to spend and borrow their wages,
Ain't it grand, ain't it grand, ain't it grand. . .[88]

Other couples met in parks and museums, in the gallery of the music hall, on the wooden seats of trains to Brighton or Gravesend and sometimes, more respectably, in church.

It was in one of the museums in South Kensington that Mary T fell into conversation with William A, a carpenter, one day in the summer of 1859. The well-maintained paths of Hyde Park and St James's Park often feature in the statements, but not as often as Hampstead Heath and Greenwich Park, with their vast rolling acres covered in soft, inviting grass. Crystal Palace, an immense dream in glass and iron built beside the Serpentine for the Great Exhibition of 1851, holds all the records. A six-month-long celebration of triumphant industrial power, art and free trade, which Queen Victoria thought 'the finest, most imposing and most moving spectacle . . . ever seen', the Exhibition was an unmitigated disaster for large numbers of dressmakers and cooks.

> *When first acquainted with the Father I was lodging with Mrs. E. at Clerkenwell, earning a livelihood with my sister at lacework. This was July 1851, I went to the Exhibition where I met Father who was polite and showed me the things.*[89]

The Crystal Palace was dismantled in 1854 and moved to Sydenham, where it remained a favoured Londoners' pleasure-ground until 1936. Its prehistoric animals, aquarium, grotto and orangery, more certainly still its merry-go-rounds and swings, its bars and fireworks, beckoned little servant-girls and their partners-to-be from all over the capital.

In the street or on the train, on the way home or to visit their families, young women were often alone and unaccompanied; but they never visited places of diversion except in a group, made secure by the presence of friends or relatives.

> *. . . I first became acquainted with the Father, by accidently meeting him in the Amphitheatre, where I had Gone with a Female friend, Eliza T. He spoke to me and walked home with me. . .*[90]

Idlers as well as devotees attended the open-air sermons where ecstatic evangelists tirelessly harangued multitudes of interested sinners; some contemporary observers insisted that prostitutes went along too in search of clients. Be that as it may, it was at London Fields, where she had gone to listen to one of these divinely inspired preachers, that the twenty-two-year-old housemaid Caroline M met her lover. Another girl, Maria G, met the mechanic James G at a night service in the Surrey Theatre. Traditional churches, chapels and other places of worship hardly seemed to protect their faithful any better. Esther D, a seamstress, met her seducer, one Joseph G, on a pew in a Greenwich church. The same thing later happened to Bertha Y and Susan C.

Warning working girls of the risks of speaking to strangers was one of the fundamentals of educational literature. *The Servant Girl in London*, a serious little book which ran to several reprints, does so repeatedly under evocative chapter headings:

> *Chapter II: On the journey Up to London, and on the Peril of Making Acquaintances on the Road.*
> *Chapter V: The Public House; a Remonstrance to Masters and Mistresses on the Cruel Custom of sending out Young Girls for Beer.*
> *Chapter VI: On going on Errands: the Baker's, the Grocer's, the Butcher's, carrying letters, &c.*
> *Chapter VII: The Streets; idle and vicious Marauders about Town. Asking one's way.*
> *Chapter IX: The Public Gardens, Parks, Exhibitions, Theatres, Masquerade, Cheap Ball-rooms, &c.*
> *Chapter X: The Fairs; Greenwich Fair, Bartholomew Fair. No decent Girl should go to a Fair even with her own Family.[91]*

'Nothing can be more ridiculous than for any young woman to expect to find a husband in the streets,' warns the anonymous author. Judging by the applicants to the Foundling Hospital, this advice was not always heeded. We should note, however, that these recalcitrants constitute only 24 per cent of our sample, and that they nearly always tried to compensate for the discreditable circumstances of the first meeting by introducing their new friend to their families:

> When first acquainted with the Father I was living with my mother at Milton Street, Dorset Square, earning my livelihood as a dress maker, assisted by my mother. I met the Father in Kensington in January last when he accosted me and we met several times in the same manner. . . . A fortnight after, I introduced him to my mother and my sisters and he visited me accordingly.[92]

As a general rule, then, the couples came from very similar – at any rate compatible – professional and family backgrounds. Introductions were effected in natural ways, by friends common to both parties, or through working together or living in neighbouring rooms. One would expect introductions of this kind, which are everywhere the most usual, to provide broad protection against the cynical schemes of passing adventurers or, worse still, pimps on the lookout for new merchandise.

Hundreds of people in this wicked town make it their business to wander about the streets of London in search of credulous young women, in order to sell their honour to other wealthy villains by whom they are employed.[93]

Warnings of this sort were constantly repeated in melodramas and penny novels, and by defenders of virtue of every stripe. This is surely one reason for the prudent and unromantic way in which the young women whose life stories we are examining usually chose their suitors.

Domestic servants – the innumerable chambermaids, the cooks on whose skill the social reputation of great houses rested – most often took up with people they saw daily below stairs: footmen peacocking around in handsome livery, tough and wily coachmen who knew the town by heart. Opulent establishments with numerous domestic staff were of course especially propitious to these encounters. Sophia E surrendered to the entreaties of James Y six months after going into service at the same large house in Piccadilly. At about the same time, and in analogous circumstances, Mary Ann Y took up with Edwin S at a house in Pimlico; the only real difference was that the preliminaries lasted slightly longer in the West End. Their respective children were born a fortnight apart, on 14 and 30 November 1851. Another case – same period, same timetable – was that of Esther B, nurserymaid, and George E, footman, in the Hyde Park Gardens household of a Mr Y. The same story every time, give or take a few details; a banal cautionary tale, except that each describes the unique, sad fate of people who really existed. Sometimes these love affairs excited the indignation of contemporary observers who took them for licentious excesses.

There are few women more exposed to temptation of immorality than domestic servants, especially those serving in houses where menservants are also kept . . .[94]

In reality, London was full of maidservants who were not at all threatened by these particular dangers, since their employers –

artisans, shopkeepers and clerks for whom possession of a servant was a sign of status and respectability – lacked the means to keep more than one. But even these maids were often in daily contact with their employers' workers or apprentices, who took their meals on the premises and sometimes lived there too. The possibilities for new idylls were endless:

> *When first acquainted with Father I was working for Mr Q. [a furrier] at Cheapside, where Father also worked. . .*[95]

> *I was living with Mrs T. as servant of all work, I was there six years. . . . Mr T is a builder and the Father is a carpenter in his employ.*[96]

> *I was living with Mr V. at Whitechapel, butcher, as servant of all work, I had lived there 18 months when Father came as a journeyman and lived in the house.*[97]

> *I was living with Mr L., linen draper, Chalk Farm Road. Father was there when I went and was an apprentice.*[98]

Girls who worked in public houses, hotels or furnished lodgings often formed attachments to bar customers or the guests whose rooms they cleaned and whose beds they made. A whole neighbourhood camaraderie, a sort of workers' complicity, flourished in basements and backyards between female staff and the delivery men, handymen and maintenance workers who supplied and repaired the houses of their employers.

The Area Belle, the successful farce mentioned above, gives a comic version of these liaisons whose pathetic results are recorded in the admission files.

> *Let me see – there's Pitcher in the police, and Tosser in the Grenadiers, and there's Dobbs the baker, and Chumps the butcher – They all come by turns. And there's the milkman: he, I believe, is rather sweet upon me, but I have never put the milkman in the dairy yet.*[99]

The Foundling Hospital applications conjure up an endless procession of butchers' boys delivering meat to the kitchen door in a barrage of friendly teasing and light-hearted compliments, milkmen arriving in the quiet of early morning, jovial bakers' roundsmen knocking at the same time every day. The monotony of their daily rounds would have been pleasantly alleviated by the presence of familiar pretty faces on the doorstep, in the kitchen or area.

Out of all the servants in the Square,
She used to shine;
She'd a delicate turn in the ancle,
And a great big crinoline;
When she used to clean the front door steps,
How the chaps they used to stare,
And throw sheep's eyes, and heave big sighs,
Which made me tear my hair – hair.[100]

This song, containing the memoirs of a rejected suitor, sketches with apparent authenticity[101] an atmosphere of some freedom, kept alive by the need for constant practical exchanges between all these young people as they worked at their tasks from morning to night. Visiting carpenters, gas fitters, blacksmiths and painters made their own contributions of improper, knowing repartee.

Workshops and retail premises brought the sexes together too. The man might be a book-keeper or worker sleeping in an adjoining room; or a sales assistant to whom a seamstress would bring the finished product. Sometimes darker, more complex love affairs would arise between an employee and the daughter of the house: relationships, often unsuspected by the rest of the household, which were eloquent on the resentment felt by some employees (as well as the startling naivety of some girls).

I was living with my father at home. He is a bootmaker. Father was errand boy.
. . . Just before going he seduced me in the kitchen and this was repeated once. I was
not aware he was doing wrong.[102]

I was living with my parents at home. My father is a tailor. This was two years ago.
Father came as a foreman to my father. . . he always expressed a regard for me and
proposed marriage whilst I declined. C.C. took place by force on 8th January whilst
I was in the same room as him, employed on some special work which pressed for
completion. . .[103]

Before the disastrous epilogue which brought her before the Foundling Hospital committee, Susan E had been subjected for years to the attentions of a worker, when she was too young, she said, to understand the meaning of his gestures and advances.

In a few cases the family was aware of the relationship: Elizabeth J, for example, was seduced by a jobbing jeweller who worked for the brother-in-law in whose house she lived. While paying court he had promised her marriage in the presence of her sister and brother-in-law.

Many working people tried to compensate for high rents and their small earnings by subletting part of their homes to a person living alone – like the Greenwich shoemaker who, when his two eldest children decided to emigrate to Australia, asked his daughter Jane, who had been working elsewhere for two years, to come back home and replace the migrants at the bench. That is how she met the sub-tenant, a plasterer, who lost no time in paying court. She was already twenty-five and wanting to start a family; but when William Z learned of her pregnancy he vanished immediately, leaving arrears of unpaid rent.

Households practising this system of subletting would have been among the poorest. A labourer with an omnibus company, the father of seven children, in this way introduced under his roof a nineteen-year-old horse-drover. Shortly afterwards his eldest daughter fell for the young man, and the subsequent inevitable, commonplace liaison was pursued over a period of months in the house itself.

Quite often these tenants were friends or relatives of the head of household. A Marylebone blacksmith, for example, rented space to a factory colleague aged twenty-three. When his sister, temporarily out of a job, came to stay at his house, he was quite pleased to see her becoming attached to someone he thought would make a suitable brother-in-law and new recruit to the family. In much the same way, a Knightsbridge shoemaker had as a tenant the jobbing tailor employed by a neighbouring shop. His daughter, whose normal job was sewing uppers in the workshop, was always ready to lend a hand when the tenant had too much to do.

It will doubtless be thought that there was nothing surprising in these gloomy amours between bed and workbench; that embracing a trade can be expected to lead to embraces from the tradesman. But it also happened that people met one another through friends or family in relaxed or festive circumstances. References in the admission files to these very diverse occasions make it possible to re-create an idea of the social life of young working-class people, a life too often caricatured with a handful of moralistic clichés. Workers' love affairs largely arose not from the depravity of the streets, but from the close friendship networks binding young people together. Girls in service, for example, worn down with hard work, often persecuted by demanding butlers, housekeepers and the like, would naturally form an alliance with their room-mates, share knowledge and information with them, walk out with them in a gang on evenings off. If the cook made a new acquaintance – a carpenter, say, or a mason or a gilder – she would naturally introduce him to her friend the chambermaid. People would visit relatives or women friends working in nearby houses. One servant might know a valet:

He lodged at 4 Queen's Gardens and I know Eliza Z. who lodged there also.[104]

Another would have a friend who was a printer, a house-painter, a gardener:

I went with a friend to tea at Mrs. L. and there I met Father he paid me attention. . .[105]

Father was a gardener. . . . I was introduced to Father by Mrs. W. of Hackney Downs, wife of nightwatchman. . . . She is nursing the child now. Father and I were friends.[106]

Off duty, these young workers moved busily from house to house, visiting one another, introducing their friends and their friends' friends. Brothers and sisters came along too. Sometimes there were parties:

Father came to a servants party at Mrs. Y. We were acquainted from that time, merely acquainted. I went from Mrs. Y. to Mrs. C., Porchester Sq. I still kept up my acquaintance with the Father. I went from Mrs. C. to Mrs. Y. at Wimbledon as Upper Housemaid. I found the Father there as butler. Father told me of the place and that way I got it.[107]

The story of Mary Ann M, chambermaid at a house in South Kensington, gives a good idea of the animated spirit in some groups of young domestics.

I met Father the following summer. I was introduced to him by some fellow servants to whom he was known as an acquaintance of their relatives. Father used to call occasionally to see my fellow servants. After 2 or 3 weeks, he began to take particular notice of me and wrote to me asking me to go walking with him. Father was then working for a City firm.[108] I used to walk out with Father once a week and on Sundays – after nearly 6 months in Jan. '61 he seduced me after a servants party – in my own pantry. . . . Our courtship was known to my fellow servants, Hannah E. and Abigail Y.[109]

London underwent rapid demographic expansion throughout the century. It was a young town, where unmarried people met others of their own age all the time, in the street, at home or in the homes of friends. Working girls could expect to meet their future fiancés socially:

I was living at Miss E. in Sloane St as a Needlewoman. . . . I became acquainted with Robert Q. [a coachman] thro' Miss T., who also worked for Miss E. It was about Xmas 1869: he was a friend of hers: we met him when Miss T. and I were out walking together,[110]

recalled Florence Q, who was twenty-four at the time. A friend of Catherine Y, a fellow-seamstress, testified in these touching terms to Catherine's sound morality:

. . . having received your letter respecting my friend Catherine's sad misfortune I have known her for a grate meny years and to be a very respectable girl and she was introduced to the farther of the child through a young man that I keep company with and knowing him to be a steady young man he was introduced to her and my friend he has gon to America and I do not know his address his friend was in a firm in Manchester. My friend that I kept company with I have kowing him a grate meny years he was introduced to me by servents were I lived in Tunbridge Wells that is 15 years ago. . .[111]

Harriet D, a dressmaker, made the acquaintance of William D at Margate, where she was staying with a workmate during her holidays:

I saw the Father on the jetty. . . . A Mr. E., a friend of Mrs. A., introduced the father to us. . .[112]

Fanny J,[113] a garment presser from Clapham, was very friendly with Caroline K. Both aged seventeen, they would go out together on their days off, sometimes accompanied by Caroline's brother. In the course of many such noisy teenagers' outings, a serious attachment grew up between Fanny and the young man. Isabelle, a laundress, was friendly with Annie, a dressmaker,[114] at whose house she made the acquaintance of John T, a cattle-drover at Smithfield Market.

Elder brothers and aunts often played a prominent role in these encounters; it was in their homes that girls whose parents were dead or living in the country would naturally spend Sundays and holidays.

We can see from all this that there were two ways for working-class couples to get together. For a large minority, the first meeting occurred by chance in a public place. But a majority of our sample made the acquaintance of the fathers of their children through relatives or trusted friends, or through work, especially in jobs where people lived on the premises; in other words, the introduction was respectably made in a stable, reassuring environment.

All our seducers, with few exceptions, were in fairly regular paid employment, and their working and home addresses were usually known. Thus they seemed to fulfil the ordinary conditions for working-class respectability: they were in work, they had homes, they were known to a circle of friends. It is noticeable that no mention is made of the suitor's financial situation in accounts of the first meeting, nor at the moment of engagement or the publication of banns. It was only when the break came that the question abruptly intruded. This characteristic of working-class amours gives the wholly unexpected impression, when one reads these hundreds of life stories, of a world of desire and pleasure where, for a time at least, no attempt was made to count the cost.

Parents and employers, for their part, were content to issue warnings about the dubious morality of the young. There is no echo of the rather tortuous and distasteful material calculation which the novelist Anthony Trollope invites us to observe among the young bourgeoisie.[115] Perhaps this impression has something to do with the questions asked by the Hospital committee, which inquired not into the *reasons* for the proposed alliance but into the *circumstances* of the introduction and the sexual relationship. But the fact remains that these women showed a notable lack of interest in the savings or income of possible husbands. Are we to believe, like Engels, that only proletarians are capable of 'pure' love because they possess nothing and have nothing to lose?[116] Could it be that the relative economic independence of these women reduced their interest in matters of this sort? The truth of the matter is that goodwill, and some sort of job, were thought to constitute an acceptable basis for a proposed future together, especially under the rosy influence of amorous emotion. The precariousness and fragility of working-class careers made more elaborate plans unrealistic.

Courtship

He never spoke of marriage or of keeping company. . . . he used to visit me and walk out with me,[117]

said Ruth O, a nineteen-year-old indigent. Those Victorian observers who envisaged encounters between the two sexes as vicious indecency lubricated with beer and gin, or as episodes of bestial abandon provoked by overcrowding in the slums, would have been surprised – had they cared to listen to it – by the careful precision with which Ruth O described the nature of her amorous relations.

Actually the statements of Foundling Hospital petitioners display a sharp sense of the conventions regulating sentimental relationships. Although most were no longer under surveillance in a closed rural society, or supervised by their parents, they still used a traditional frame of reference which prescribed ritual stages for a love relationship.

Social upheavals seem to have had only a slight effect on this aspect of working-class sexual mores. In pre-industrial Hertfordshire, we are told, relations between the young of opposite sexes were subject to an immutable order of gradations: first people were 'speaking', then they were 'walking out together', then later, when mutual attraction was confirmed, they would 'keep company'.[118] In more remote rural societies the ritual was even more complex: meetings on certain days; bundling[119] – a sort of licensed, private physical lovemaking stopping short of intercourse, conducted in the family home; the public exchange of presents; sometimes pitchering,[120] which gave public recognition to pre-nuptial concubinage. None of this survived, of course, in the urban society of the second half of the nineteenth century; yet the terms used by Ruth O to describe different levels of courtship clearly refer back to this tradition.

Only 8·2 per cent of the statements have nothing at all to say about the nature and duration of courtship – not a very significant proportion, especially as the information may have been omitted by accident. Another 11·5 per cent admit that customary procedure has been neglected – a reference implying that the convention was recognized, even if it was not respected. But the great majority of statements describe the modalities of a graduated courtship leading up to the sexual act.

Parents and family

In more than half the cases the existence of courtship was well known to other people; partly, no doubt, because it is natural to want to share the joy and pleasure of such an event, but also in conformity with the popular tradition of a public, formal engagement, whose main function was to establish the young man's commitment in the eyes of the community.

Courtship was no longer made public in the ritual manner still to be found at troth-plighting ceremonies in the remote provinces, but had not yet acquired the solemnity which surrounded engagements from the Edwardian period until the early 1960s. Our statements make almost no mention of exchanges of rings, and none at all of taking an announcement in a newspaper, or parties in the young couple's honour. Judging by the tone used, and making due allowance for the Hospital's discreet approach, what usually seems to have happened was that the intended was introduced without much ceremony to the girl's parents and peer group (usually, in any case, the first to know what was going on).

Sometimes a more detailed account gives us a glimpse of a formal introduction:

> It was about three years ago that he began to pay me attention and having obtained my Parents consent he promised me marriage.[121]

In the case of Nancy E, whose father and fiancé were both carpenters,

> I met Father for the first time at Mr. Q, where Father lodged, whilst on a visit in the evening. Father came afterwards to my father's. A courtship ensued and he promised me marriage (this was known to my father and mother).[122]

87

More light is thrown on the conventional order of events by statements like the one from Emma J, a hosiery worker. She met her suitor while walking one Sunday afternoon with her stepmother, a daily paid laundress. The young man, a butcher's assistant – and evidently a persuasive talker – accompanied them to their door, entertaining them with jokes, and managed to arrange a further meeting with Emma while her stepmother was present:

> We walked together on this occasion and these walks were repeated. About Xmas he visited me in the presence of my parents and proposed marriage, saying he should like to settle and go to America.[123]

Dorcas Q, a chambermaid, was approached by a young stable-hand one day in August 1852:

> I was out walking with my master's under gardener when he spoke to me and proposed seeing me again and he accordingly called. He told me he was living at Wandsworth. . . . He repeated his visit ten days after and he proposed keeping company with me. My sister who has been living 5 years with Mr. Z. knew of this. The keeping company continued for 6 or 7 months. . .[124]

Margaret D was a twenty-year-old seamstress who shared lodgings in the St Luke's district with one of her sisters. On the way to church she met Frederick G, a butcher's assistant:

> He followed me home to my sisters and asked me to keep company with him. I replied that I could not then decide. He saw my sister and spoke to her on the subject. She asked me about him. Father from this time visited me frequently for about 12 months.[125]

> He began to pay me attention and promised me marriage which was known and approved by my parents,[126]

declares a leather-worker. A dressmaker, living at home with her mother,

> . . . met him by accident at my aunt's Mrs. E, No. 2 — street, Bethnal Green. We made an appointment and met accordingly. He courted and came home with me to my mother as my suitor. . . . This went on for months. . .[127]

while another, who worked for a firm of dressmakers in Montagu Place, took up with a gas company worker:

After about 3 or 4 months in acquaintance he began to pay me attention. . . he courted me and promised me marriage. The banns were published at St. James' Church Piccadilly. This known to his and my family.[128]

It should not be assumed that this relatively formal behaviour was only found in girls living at home, who could hardly conceal what was going on from their parents. Harriet E, a maid-of-all-work in Edgware Road, obtained her mother's agreement when she began courting with a carpenter from Paddington Green, although she had been in service for six years. She met him by chance in the street, took him home and introduced him as her suitor. As he seemed respectable her mother made no objection to the engagement, which lasted several months and ended with the publication of banns at St Mary's, Paddington.[129]

Many present this stage of their adventure in a much more laconic way. But it is difficult to be sure whether this is because the event itself was perfunctory, or because the applicant is trying to give a concise account.

He proposed marriage which was known and approved by my parents,[130]

drily notes Priscilla Y, a housemaid engaged to a baker's assistant from Brompton; while Sophia, a Deptford housemaid who had fallen in love with a pattern-maker, describes a more complicated situation:

He is about 23. After 12 months he paid me attention, courted and promised me marriage. The banns were published. . . . His parents did not know this. My parents merely knew I was to be married but not to whom.[131]

Rosina M, a chambermaid near Hyde Park, says only:

He courted me and promised marriage known to his sister and others including my mother.[132]

Introduction to the young man's family, which would have been seen as a further step towards marriage, did not always take place; some girls discovered too late, and to their chagrin, that they did not even know their suitor's address. But Jessica, a seamstress aged twenty-three, even knew the sisters of her lover, a twenty-five-year-old engraver. Their friendship was an old one, dating from a seaside holiday at Gravesend. James had married another, but had been widowed a year later. It was only then that he and Jessica had started 'going out together', meeting at his house or that of one or other of their families. His sisters liked Jessica and considered her his wife-to-be. In fact these working girls from Islington and Dalston played a double certifying role for Jessica and James: they represented the same generation, and thus ensured the couple's acceptance by their peers; and they represented the family, one of whose functions is to protect the material and human interests of its members.

The constraints of working life, the conditions of housing and employment, the relative freedom available to young women to meet members of the opposite sex every day, alone if they wished, help to explain why some girls did not think it worthwhile to inform their families until the amorous relationship reached an advanced stage. Only then, perhaps, did it seem necessary to obtain serious commitment from their fiancés.

Hannah Y was twenty-seven, and had been responsible for running the family household since her mother's death. On the way to the cemetery one day she met a corporal of the Scots Fusilier Guards, and fell in love with him:

> He asked me to meet him again and I consented and used to meet him once or twice a week. About 4 or 5 weeks after we had met I accompanied him one evening to the Sun Music Hall in Knightsbridge (I had never been to one before) and we came away about 11 o'c. he took me into Hyde Park and there seduced me: Father had given me some Brandy and Water. I did not tell anyone. Father then left Chelsea Barracks for 2 months and when he returned he called upon me. I then told my father of our acquaintance. My father did not object. . . .[133]

Besides, even when family opposition was manifest, it did not usually prevent an affair from following its course. Susan T went ahead with hers against the advice of her aunt and uncle, who thought there was too great a difference between her age and that of the building labourer with whom she was courting. Even so they did not withdraw their support, and helped her find another job after her confinement.[134] In another case, the proposed bridegroom was thought too 'unsteady' and to have a 'gay character'.[135] The father of another girl disliked her fiancé because he 'feared that the marriage would not come to anything'.[136] In Rose I's case the problem was that she was a Jew while the man was a Gentile.[137] Emma Q's father thought his daughter's intended was an 'idle, drinking fellow and was always losing his occupation'.[138]

FRIENDS AND WORKMATES

The Foundling Hospital called on colleagues at work, friends, sometimes landladies, to testify to the morality of its postulants. In the minds of the young women themselves, however, even before the unhappy outcome of their adventures, all these people were already cast – symbolically for the time being – in the role of witnesses, substitutes for a family which might be estranged from the girl, might have broken up, or might simply live far away.

> Eleanor Stedman, now in service there states that she has seen Petitioner and the Father speaking together at the door of the house and heard petitioner declare that he was her intended husband,[139]

notes Mr Twiddy, the Hospital's inquirer. And literally dozens of domestics echo again and again, exactly but for the different names, the declaration of Mary Ann T of Manchester Square:

> I used to walk out with him. This was known to the cook (Susan J) and to Cooper the footman.[140]

EMPLOYERS

The relations between young working women and their employers were, as we have seen, liberally mined with sexual ambushes. Where other amours were concerned the attitude of the lady of the house, or in large establishments the head cook or housekeeper, could vary a great deal. It was not unusual for maidservants' love affairs to be treated with tolerance or for advice to be offered. This was especially marked in the households of master craftsmen or small shopkeepers, who employed only one or two people and would have known a good deal about their affairs. But there seems to be more to it than that. One often senses signs of real concern for the future of these girls who worked alongside their employers, who had perhaps been taken on when still very young and served them for many years. One example is that of Louisa K, an orphan aged twenty-three employed by an elderly Woolwich spinster:

> Shortly afterwards, Petitioner informed her that the Father was paying her attention and had promised her marriage and requested that he might be allowed to visit her at the house. The Informant called on Mr. Larkman [the young man's employer] and received a satisfactory account of the Father's character, and consequently she gave permission that the Father might visit petitioner. 2 or 3 months afterwards the petitioner was dejected and she questioned her as to the cause and ascertained that the Father had slighted her. She was recommended to think no more of him.[141]

But usually, to show evidence of morality without going into excessive detail, the petitioners briefly note that the existence of a prolonged courtship was known to other people.

> Father accosted me and agreed to visit me which he was in the habit of doing with the knowledge of Mr. and Mrs. M.[142]

There is every reason to believe that for the majority of the London middle classes, the stability of a relationship was sufficient reason to authorize visits, even if these were sometimes restricted to the kitchen doorstep. This was the case with twenty-one-year-old Emma O, who had been in service with Mrs E in Camden Town since the death of her parents when she was still a child. Her lover-to-be, a carpenter, had approached her on the vast expanse of Hampstead Heath and walked her back home.

> Last summer she was visited by the Father at the street door. Visits continued from time to time for many months and he was acknowledged as her suitor. He appeared to be a respectable working man,[143]

stated her mistress. It seems too that employers treated passing fancies and flirtations with greater indulgence, or anyway tolerance, than the literature generally suggests. Certainly the files contain only a few isolated cases of households which categorically refused to have anything to do with the private lives of domestics, and where all visiting was formally prohibited. This rule was applied by Mrs Q who resided in Belgravia. Michael J only once dared to knock on the pantry door 'because no callers were allowed'. Nevertheless, the other domestics confirmed the existence of a regular courtship.[144]

Everything seems to indicate, then, that relations between the sexes were codified among these young citizens. They were constrained by more or less implicit rules, inherited from parents or employers, and reinforced by the attitudes of friends and acquaintances; most submitted with a good grace. Reading the files of the Foundling Hospital one can discern the outlines of a general set of regulations, or rather a collection of recipes which, like home cooking, were passed on in an imprecise manner and which everyone felt entitled to modify, to season according to circumstances and their personal taste. People *did* keep an eye on girls – we should not be misled about this – but in an approximate, unsystematic way. Manifestations of parental authority were rare and rather perfunctory; as for employers, they showed an indulgence, or perhaps indifference, for which they were roundly criticized in some quarters.

A VERY DISCREET COURTSHIP

In fact, the rules of comportment were so flexible that a number of postulants accepted prolonged courtship without bothering to tell anyone. Sometimes, especially among orphans or those recently arrived in London, this was the result of isolation. Such was the case with Harriet C, barely a month in the capital after leaving her family more than a hundred miles away in Bristol. So when a young man started sweet-talking into her ear, walked her to her door, asked for another meeting, came to see her again, and eventually led her to his room, she found the whole business so extraordinary that she did not breathe a word to anyone, even her room-mate, a laundress like herself. Caroline Z, another newcomer to the big city, declared:

> *I was born at Stratford Bow, both my Parents are dead. . . . He requested to keep company with me. When he had courted me 4 or 5 months, seduction took place. . . . I can refer to nobody who knows or has seen the Father. . .*[145]

While pregnant she had been reduced to seeking refuge in Holloway Prison, then known as the London Female Preventive and Reformatory Institution.

Yes, solitude was an important factor. Thousands of lives were brutally disrupted by death, or by the lure of the capital, where work was always to be had. But we learn that there were also women who sought no outside approval for their actions. Some perhaps were simply secretive; Marian T, who lived with her parents, was wooed for two years by the harness-maker next door, then conducted an idyll for another year, without her parents' knowledge. Others were disobedient, or indifferent and frivolous:

> Father courted me and promised marriage. This was unknown to my father and friends,[146]

says one girl, whose many brothers and sisters gave her substantial help when she was pregnant. In other cases fear of dismissal may have been a factor:

> The Father came as footman in December 1866 after 3 months he courted me and promised me marriage not known to the family.[147]

Whatever its causes – mistrust, duplicity, imprudence – this attitude to courting was always severely criticized once the mistake had become known. 'Total ineptitude . . . disastrous thoughtlessness,' commented Mrs J, a Bond Street milliner, on learning that one of her young workers had been courting without the knowledge of her parents or friends.[148]

And from time to time the Hospital committee was asked to consider declarations of commitment which are so sketchy, so far removed from the prescribed model, that one wonders how the postulants can have believed for a single moment that they would count as proper engagements. These claims seem to be pitiful attempts by women with few resources to convince the judges of their respectability.

'THERE WAS NO COURTSHIP OR PROMISE OF MARRIAGE'[149]

A few, hardier or perhaps more candid than the rest, declared openly and without hesitation that they had dispensed with these formalities.

Here at last is a group of genuine moral reprobates of the sort tirelessly castigated by nineteenth-century reformers. Perhaps owing to the Foundling Hospital's strict regulations, or more likely because, contrary to the alarmist perceptions of the time, such women were never very numerous, they are certainly – judging by the petitioners' confessions, at least – a very small band.

A closer look at the group reveals, first, that these rebels are not distinguishable from the other applicants by origin, profession or age. Nor do their numbers increase with time; their proportion is about the same in each decade studied.

But in the detail of their statements one perceives a different tone, a particular attitude, in which the sexual act seems to be emancipated from prolonged courtship and marriage. There is something of the permissiveness, the frivolity, found in contemporary popular songs and novels; something, too, which is familiar to us today, which anticipates the liberated sexual morality of Western youth in the last decades of the present century.

People would meet, take a fancy to each other, and casually visit one another's rooms, without any real commitment for the future. Hannah J, for example, a nineteen-year-old maid, went home one day with a regular customer of the pub where she worked. Throughout their relationship, he never once offered to marry her. When she became pregnant he said that he would give her money to support the child. The Foundling Hospital inquirer discovered that the man, an employee blacksmith called William C, indulged habitually in adventures of this sort and had fathered two other bastards in the same neighbourhood.[150]

Another domestic, twenty-year-old Mary Ann P, obtained her job through an aunt who worked for the family as a cook. She took a fancy to a footman who also worked there. When her increasingly visible pregnancy caused her to leave the job, they had still never discussed the possibility of marriage. All she had was a promise that the father would send her some money when the child was born, a promise he naturally failed to remember when the time came. Her former employers testified:

We thought her rather forward and did not approve the deportment of either of them, Gill or Mary Ann P., but we did not suspect that the familiarity had proceeded to the length it turned out.[151]

Father did not pay me particular attention. There was no promise of marriage,[152] admitted Jane P whose relationship with a fellow-servant nevertheless lasted some time. Eighteen-year-old Elizabeth T's adventure, a single night in the pantry, was ephemeral by comparison. Almost as casual was that of Susan W, twenty-six, who worked as a chambermaid for Mr and Mrs G of Highbury Place. The coachman 'made advances' to her on several occasions, without getting very far. She moved to another job; and one day paid a visit to her former colleagues below stairs:

> When I left that day, the cook told me to go to the stables as the Father wished to see me there. I saw him there and stayed there about an hour it was then that the seduction took place. There was no promise of marriage and it was with my consent, I knew that at that time he was courting another young woman. I called on him 2 or 3 times and Crim Con was repeated in the stables.[153]

It so happens that in Susan's file there is a letter of intercession, written by the superintendent of a school where her sister was employed, which gives a respectable, edifying version of her story by echoing the language and reasoning of reformist literature:

> She entered service as a lady's maid [George M writes] but mixing with other servants far beneath her in morality and demeanour. She was looked upon by them as too much the lady for her situation, this gave offence: the snare was laid for her fall, she fell head long into it. The coachman of the family became seducer. . .

This account of the facts, which corresponds only in a tenuous way with Susan W's own statement, was nevertheless submitted to the charitable institution's committee.

The postulants in this category are by no means all domestics. Elizabeth D, eighteen, helped her mother run furnished lodgings and worked occasionally as a seamstress. Three weeks after first meeting Edward O, a house-painter of Chelsea, she accompanied him to a house in Sloane Square, close to where he lived. A friend's house? A small hotel that did not ask questions? We are not told. We know for certain that she went there with him on a number of occasions and became pregnant. But, she declared, she never 'kept company with him' and he made her no promise of marriage.[154]

Dorothy Ann A, aged twenty-five, met George R in the music hall. They met on five more occasions, sleeping together each time.

Marriage was never mentioned.[155] As one last example, Nancy S, one of the youngest applicants, was only sixteen when she met her lover, a worker from Rotherhithe, at a music hall near the docks to which she had gone unaccompanied. After a few glasses of spirits they enjoyed a brief physical union standing against a wall in an alley. This was the start of a liaison which lasted several weeks, until the man vanished as suddenly as he had appeared. She never asked him for anything, not even his address.[156]

It would be unrealistic to doubt the veracity of so many statements scattered through a thirty-year period. We have good reason to believe that in the main, young workers did try to conform, albeit in approximate fashion, to a model of relations between the sexes which would tend to discourage fleeting or furtive liaisons. And some individuals, much as one would expect, managed to circumvent the rules. But on the basis of our sample of applications, these appear to have been a minority.

> **'Where they went to I never heard say. . .**
> **But when she returned, Mrs. Gray**
> **Said she'd very much rumpl'd her muslin. . .'[157]**

SEX BEFORE MARRIAGE

Carnal relations between young people have always been tolerated by the working classes in Western Europe, on the express condition that they are followed soon afterwards by marriage.

In some regions, these pre-marital unions seem to have been used to test the couple's fertility.

> *In the Roman Church after 1564 such an action between an affianced couple was a grave sin. In the English church it was a much less serious matter.[158]*

Lawrence Stone has demonstrated the prevalence of pre-nuptial sexuality in eighteenth-century Britain, even after the passage of the Marriage Act of 1753 which formally prohibited all sexual relations until after the ceremony.[159] The practice was so widespread that in some areas, during the second half of the century, more than 40 per cent of children were conceived before the marriage ceremony.

From the figures one can conclude that among the English and American plebs in the last half of the eighteenth century, almost all brides below the social elite had experienced sexual intercourse with their future husband before marriage.[160]

During the first half of the nineteenth century the custom was gradually dropped by respectable artisans, small shopkeepers and the working elite,[161] but remained very much alive among the rest of the working classes and, judging by the Foundling Hospital's admission files, seems to have kept much of its importance for large numbers of domestics and other working women.

The mothers of children admitted to the Foundling Hospital had had, *ipso facto*, one or more sexual relationships outside the institution of marriage. All, or nearly all, had believed at the time that they would later marry their lovers. All, or nearly all, had consented to carnal relations only after a relatively prolonged public courtship. More than three-quarters of the relationships lasted longer than six months.[162]

Duration of amorous liaisons

Two years and longer	29·5 per cent
12 months – two years	24 per cent
6 – 12 months	24 per cent
1 – 6 months	19 per cent
Less than a month	3·5 per cent

Many relationships continued after the couple became aware of the pregnancy, and a few continued even after the confinement.

PROMISES OF MARRIAGE: 'HE PROMISED ME MARRIAGE, THEY ALL DO'[163]

This freedom of behaviour, specific to the working classes, was determined by one element: the 'promise of marriage'. Only this promise, which in traditional practice bound the man by his word of honour, could authorize pre-marital sexual relations. It thus traced the real dividing line between permissible and delinquent conduct.

Ideally, an engagement was made official by introducing the fiancé to the girl's family or to a parent substitute, for example an employer. Only then could a regular relationship begin. In this respect many of these life stories, so disastrous in their outcome, had started out in full conformity with custom.

Sarah M, a housemaid aged twenty-two, took a shine to a butcher's boy of her own age who delivered meat every day at the pantry door. The friendship suited everyone:

> *He courted and promised marriage known and approved of by my Mother. He used to visit me as my suitor. This was known to my mistress. In 1872 he seduced me at the House.[164]*

Nancy, engaged to a journeyman carpenter, said that the promise had been repeated many times:

> *We used to walk out together and he promised me marriage – this was known to my mistress. He seduced me 6 months after I entered the service. Crim Con was repeated. He promised me marriage several times. When pregnant I told him and he still promised marriage.[165]*

And the statement of Caroline Y draws repeated attention to this given word:

> *He courted and promised marriage but not known to anyone in the house. My mother and sisters knew it. . . . He seduced me on the 25th of July last at Brighton. . . . He seduced me under a promise of marriage.[166]*

So does Angelina T:

> *He seduced me in the first week and promised marriage before and after,[167]*

and Emma T:

> *Last February he seduced me at our lodging having previously and afterwards promised me marriage.[168]*

The public character of an engagement could count in the young woman's favour later, when adoption was being sought for her child:

> *In answer to your note which I have received about my sister I can safely say that on last witemonday twelve month me and my sister was at Crystal Palace for a days holiday and there we met with that man Thomas M he was with us all that day, he*

saw my sister home to her situation in the evening he meet her up to November with my sister and in the month of December I wanted to know the reason they did not come to see me and my sister she had told him she was in trouble and he left her and I herd him say he was going to make her his wife and that I was to be bridesmaid and my sister bought things I know to be married in but I was never to his house and his trade was as well as I can remember glass stainer and my poor sister went in the workhouse to be confined because he was not able to pay her expenses. Sir, I cannot remember any more as I can take my oath she was promised marriage. I remain your obedient servant Harriet P.[169]

Many of the statements make the explicit claim that the promise of marriage was decisive:

Courtship continued until 14 May 1870, after he had promised marriage. . . . CC was repeated with my consent, as I expected to be married. When pregnant I told him and he promised to marry me in September.[170]

Father seduced me in September 1869, it was in consequence of his repeated promises to marry me that I consented.[171]

He seduced me in February 1862 at a house – it was repeated in full expectation of the promise of marriage.[172]

All this time he promised me marriage and under this promise I yielded to him.[173]

And conversely, other applicants said they had suspended sexual relations on discovering that the promise was false:

She avows that. . . after she discovered that he would not marry her she steadily refused his solicitations to renew that intercourse.[174]

The given word was still invested with such symbolic importance that it was enough merely to pronounce it in private, orally or by letter, for our young women to regard it as a solemn oath. Of course we have no exact transcripts of these declarations, made at the moment of engagement or during the sexual act. But it seems reasonable to suppose that young women would have expected something formal, probably no more than 'I promise to marry you'. Whatever the actual phrase, it appears to have retained its contractual significance even when uttered during the blaze of sexual passion, or not even pronounced until after the act.

If, on the other hand, the promise had not been made clearly or with real conviction, the applicants spelt the fact out in their statements, with a sense of nuance which would be surprising to someone who did not know that breach of promise was an offence:

> *We used to walk out together in the Parks. This continued for 2 years. He once promised me marriage. . .*[175]

admitted young Nancy E.

> *He promised me marriage but nobody knew this when CC first occurred. His promise of marriage was not repeated after the 2nd occasion;*[176]

> *He continuously said that he would never leave me. I believed he meant marriage;*[177]

> *Soon after he came, he paid me attention but never promised me marriage I, however, expected Father to marry me. After 2 years he seduced me. . .*[178]

confessed, rather pathetically, Fanny T of Mile End, Margaret D of Brixton and Dorcas E of Whitechapel. And Amelia J, a domestic working in a well-heeled neighbourhood overlooking Hyde Park:

> *In Oct. 1861, he seduced me – saying that if anything happened he would marry me.*[179]

Let us pause for a moment on this last remark, for it is a good illustration of working girls' attitude to their virginity. It seems to show that the promise was required not so much to protect an honour sullied by overintimate relations as to provide insurance against the material consequences of any pregnancy. This is underlined by the fact that some women did not hesitate to take the initiative in breaking off relations, after being deflowered, but before becoming aware that they were pregnant.

Others, after arranging to have their child adopted, rebuilt their lives with another man who was aware of the situation.

There is a very marked contrast between this reality and the value placed on the virginity of their heroines by the great Victorian novelists (whom we often believe to have been privileged observers of their time, when in reality they were only projecting their own class values on to the rest of society). By way of examples, 'Little Emily' withdraws from society after being seduced and abandoned by Steerforth, and finds final salvation only by disappearing to the other side of the world; Esther, in *Mary Barton*, is reduced to prostitution after her short affair with an officer, while Ruth, in love with Bellingham, expiates her sin through her death.

This attitude to virginity also contrasts with that of young twentieth-century workers as described by the American historian John Gillis: the men, he asserts, are repelled by the idea of marrying a 'second-hand' woman, while the girls strive at all costs to remain intact for their wedding night.[180]

LOVE NESTS, LOVE TRAPS

The promise of marriage may have legitimized sexual intercourse, but the admission files tend to show that, in general, couples did not engage in it very often. Could it be to avoid shocking the Foundling Hospital committee that so few sexual acts are reported? It seems unlikely that respect for these sensibilities would have been so unanimous. A more convincing reason would be the difficulty young Londoners experienced at that time in finding a private place for a rendezvous.

The fact is that in about half the cases for which the files are explicit on this matter,[181] the woman had sexual relations fewer than five times in the course of the whole liaison. Unfortunately, however, the information is unverifiable[182] and subject to so many different interpretations that no conclusions can be drawn as to the fertility, or the sensuality, of these couples.

Let us note, in any case, that some couples enjoyed much better facilities for lovemaking than others. Living under the same roof, either with the same employer or in the same lodgings, and therefore living, for however short a time, in something like concubinage, necessarily provided many opportunities.

We have already discussed the role of the promise of marriage. Despite the superficial similarity, this promise was very different from the traditional 'plighting of troth' which could mark the beginning of more or less full-time sexual relations. Rather, it created a trusting relationship which might sooner or later release libidinal impulses.

What was the setting for these sexual frolics? For the most part, they seem to have occurred in everyday surroundings, in the workplace or at home. Romantic *billets-doux*, the exaltation of grand passion, are not much in evidence here. Quite often the act was performed in the workplace, in the lodger's room or in the home of the girl's parents. The house would perhaps have been empty, with some people on holiday or on a visit, others at work, the children asleep. People would make love in places where they spent a lot of time: domestics, for example, in the kitchen, others in their rooms. This was especially true where the couple both worked for the same employer or lived in the same lodgings: the normal setting was the girl's room, or the boy's room, or the kitchen; sometimes an 'upstairs' room or the servants' hall.

There were only rare exceptions. The – very young – daughter of a Peckham grocer was seduced by the clerk in a storeroom; another succumbed in the stables. Perhaps the most surprising case is that of Mary D, a chambermaid of Dalston, who gave herself to the household's coachman in the garden on a cold night in January. Even she admits that

CC was repeated once in the house.[183]

It was not unusual, however, for some of these young women to visit their lovers at home. Perhaps because this would have been seen as daring behaviour, not entirely to their credit, they often sought to minimize its importance:

After a year he seduced me in his own house. I was acquainted with his housekeeper and used to visit her. Her name is Mrs. Perry.[184]

So the setting for these seductions is usually described as being homely and discreetly normal – not always, though, as a large minority of postulants paint their adventures in more agreeable colours. We can hardly do better than quote once again from a contemporary song, which might have come in its entirety from one of the Foundling Hospital's statements:

And on next Sunday so fine,
That being a day of their leisure,
He asked her to meet him at nine,

She did, and they went for some pleasure.
To Gravesend they went by the boat
When the fine bottled stout they kept guzzling;
He smoked and she wetted her throat,
And then rolled about in her muslin . . .
At Gravesend they stopp'd very late;
Til every boat had started:
The tailor appeared in a state,
And she was very faint hearted. . .[185]

or these ambiguous phrases from a comic song by Herbert Cole:

If you say 'Have a drink' Well, it's understood,
That you seldom hear a girl say, No; . . .
Or down a country lane with you to go?
And if you were to kiss her on the sly,
Did you ever hear a girl say, No? . . .
If you ask a young girl if she'll go to the play,
Did you ever hear a girl say, No?
If to Brighton you ask her to go for the day,
You never heard a girl say: No![186]

In fact, a day of open-air relaxation and good cheer at the seaside or in the green Essex lanes often led to the first sexual caresses. Circumstances of this kind are mentioned regularly from the 1870s onward, as cheap transport became more widely available and the fashion for excursions spread to the working classes. People did not travel very far. Wimbledon Common, Battersea Park, Epping Forest and especially Richmond are frequently mentioned:

C.C. *took place last summer in May in Richmond Park. I thought he would have married me.*[187]

On the coast, Gravesend and Brighton were the favoured destinations of the London labouring classes:

In March '73 *went with him for a days holiday to Gravesend and we went to the Gardens until it was to late to catch a train or boat and then he persuaded me to stay all night with him at a coffee house, there seduction took place. . . . My mother was very angry at my staying out all night and I denied that anything wrong had happened,*[188] recalled Mary T. It was in Brighton that Hannah Y, a cook, and Thomas A, a painter in the building trade, spent their first night together:

> He seduced me on the 5th of July last at Brighton where I went with him for a day's holiday. He took me to a House which he said was his aunts. He seduced me under promise of marriage. It was repeated on the next occasion in London whilst we were out walking. It was repeated for some time afterwards.[189]

Skilled workers, shop assistants, commercial travellers, policemen and other categories close to the petty bourgeoisie were the first to acquire a taste for Sunday outings in the country. Among domestics, sexual advances were more often inspired by the change of scene during their employers' holidays. The Isle of Wight, the South Downs or the verdure of the Weald could produce sexual impulses even among people who were working as usual:

> It took place at Marine Parade, Dover where we had gone with the family. . . . Crim. Con. was repeated 3 times.[190]

If there was no shelter to be found, the districts of Victorian London contained any number of open spaces, patches of wasteland, dark alleys, where a love affair might be consummated at a pinch. In Camberwell, Lewisham, Battersea, Greenwich, Stoke Newington, even in the royal parks, there was no shortage of secret corners:

> He seduced me one evening in the Park last summer (July or August). It was once repeated in the same way.[191]

> After one year and 9 months he seduced me outdoors. . . . He promised marriage all along, alleging that he was single,[192]

said Ellen T. Naturally, summer was the best season:

> On 27th Aug. Father seduced me out of doors and C.C. was repeated in the same way more than once.[193]

The Hansom cab, that enclosed public place whose steady progress reminded the couple of their imminent separation, was the scene of many seductions:

He took me home in a cab and effected his purpose by violence as we were returning.[194]

We occasionally walked out and in December he took me in a cab where Crim. Con took place.[195]

He seduced me in Aug 1866 in a cab we were going from Uxbridge to Gerrards X . . .[196]

Father seduced me in a cab as we were out. C.C. was repeated in the same manner and he also took me to a coffee house.[197]

Very few girls seem to have been offended by this cavalier treatment. Yet the cab was manifestly a man's invention, a man's convenience whose heavy rumbling could drown the girls' murmured objections, and support – for as long as necessary – the illusion of their consent.

Even less respectable, although often used, were the hotels, refreshment rooms, coffee houses and all sorts of taverns and public houses where beds could be hired by the hour; and of course the sordid, disreputable lodging-houses in the centre of town.

In these cases, to remove any suspicion of the prostitution which obsessed the Foundling Hospital committee, some women offered an explanation which was highly fashionable in Victorian melodrama and trashy novels: they had been induced to surrender by a mysterious potion which robbed them of all willpower and made them easy prey for vice. The same artifice was later used by the journalist William Thomas Stead to prove the existence of the White Slave Trade.

One is not entirely convinced by the notion that carpenters and footmen – men possessing few of the wiles attributed to experienced libertines and cunning pimps – would have used anything more diabolical than strongish drink to dissipate the girls' scruples. Nevertheless, the idea of more sinister techniques did have its devotees. It tended to dilute the applicants' personal responsibility, transporting them at a stroke to the dramatic world of the popular novel:

Yes! Chloroform is the new help[198] *by which lordly men will conquer women. . . . How many women have succumbed rather to chloroform than to the seducer. . . it was as she felt the fresh air on her face that, for a moment or so, she resisted the stupifying effects of the chloroform, and gathered sufficient energy to utter a faint scream.*[199]

The 'poor man's best-seller' *The Mysteries of London* describes two premeditated rapes whose victims have trustingly consumed 'a drugged wine-glass'.[200] This, according to Jane Y, is how her fiancé, a young printer, set about seducing her:

> *C.C. took place last January in a house which he said belonged to a friend of his near Strand. Father had given me a drink but I resisted and cried out in vain.*[201]

> *C.C. took place last June. He had given me a drink which stupefied me and whilst in this state he took me by surprise, by coming to my bed.*[202]

writes another, echoed by a third:

> *He. . . gave me something to drink which stupefied me. When I was in a helpless situation he took advantage of me in the open air, this was repeated 2 or 3 times afterwards.*[203]

Another excuse sometimes offered was that the girl had been misled: she had gone to meet her suitor's friends, or better still his family, only to find herself alone with him in a house of ill repute.

> *Father took me to a house in Sloane St which he said was a friends. CC took place. . . CC was twice repeated,*[204]

complained Annie D, who had been seduced by a house-painter.

> *In November following Father seduced me at an improper house at Knightsbridge. I had a holiday. Father said the house was a friends. Father locked me in. I tried to get out but in vain. C.C. was repeated 3 or 4 times in the lanes, six weeks afterwards.*[205]

> *Last night he seduced me at a house he said belonged to a friend,*[206]

declared Elizabeth Y. Frances chose to emphasize her own trusting nature:

> *The acquaintance continued till April 1850 when he took me to a house in Bloomsbury where C.C. took place. I did not know the purpose for which he took me. C.C. was only once repeated.*[207]

Naivety or immorality? The circumstance is so often recalled that one cannot help thinking of the stock soap-opera invitation: 'Let's go up to my place for a nightcap'.

Nor can one help noticing the sour, plaintive tone of most of these accounts of seductions. A few nevertheless manage to describe the fateful night in more cheerful fashion: marriage had been promised; one Saturday night, after a date at the theatre, the couple had spent a few hours together in a bedroom. Thus, Isabella T's account of her first night with Thomas D:

> *He seduced me 22 August 1860: I had a Holiday – he took me to a House in the City Road after I had been with him to the Strand theatre. I Passed the night with him.*[208]

It was much the same for Sophia C, who had been engaged to a stonemason for six months:

> *He seduced me at the 'Sun' coffee house, Whitechapel, where we slept together all night. This was in Sept. 1855 and continued for about 2 months.*[209]

Sarah Ann G gave a similar account:

> *He promised me marriage after 3 months, he took me to a public house in Notting Hill, having a holiday that day. C.C. took place and was repeated 12 times or more, in the house of my master.*[210]

as did Hannah:

> *We met accordingly and we met frequently afterwards, for six weeks, at the end of this time he took me to Greenwich for a holiday and then at a Coffee House.*[211]

and Jane:

> *Crim. Con. took place at a Coffee House where he took me it was with my consent we slept together there.*[212]

However prudent or foolish they seem, we should not forget that the majority of these first sexual encounters had been legitimized by the promise of marriage. They posed no threat to the love relationship but on the contrary (most couples would have thought at the time) were likely to prolong and strengthen it.

THE QUESTION OF CONSENT

Quite a number of the petitions go into some detail on the responses made by these young women to their fiancés' sexual advances. It is difficult to say what use the Foundling Hospital's committee made of these answers. They do not seem to have influenced the admission of children either way.

The women were probably asked whether they had consented to intercourse, and whether force had been used by their partner. Curiously, although allegations of rape are extremely rare, there are quite a few affirmative answers to the second question. This raises the possibility that we might have overestimated the role of the promise of marriage. A popular song composed and sung by the famous music-hall artiste Arthur Lloyd suggests that a girl could change her mind at any moment, and that the culprit would then be punished for his persistence:

> I followed her home and to speak to her tried,
> She said 'Why d'ye follow me?' and I replied,
> 'I love you dear girl and would make you my bride,'
> You Know! . . .
> Then she said, 'Well, I like you, but silence beware!
> You know!
> I've a very stern parent his bedroom's up there! You know!'
> I struggled to kiss her, she gave a loud cry,
> I heard a door open and ere I could fly,
> A very hard fist struck me twice in the eye! You know! . . .
> A policeman appeared and exclaimed 'What's all this?' You know!
> Oh, said I, a young girl I was trying to kiss! You know!
> To the station he marched me at a very quick pace . . .
> His Worship exclaimed, when the case he had tried,
> 'Forty shillings or one month' – with horror I cried
> 'Forty shillings or one month, for what?' – he replied:
> 'You know!'[213]

What is really at issue here? The most convincing hypothesis is that despite the promise of marriage, many girls retained secret doubts as to their suitors' real intentions. In a society lacking reliable contraceptive methods, a society which seemed to have become incapable of holding people to their promises, the more prudent, less credulous young women would have been reluctant to abandon themselves to passion. This state of mind is well illustrated by the declaration of Harriet P, a cook aged thirty-one:

> It was not with my consent, tho' he did not use violence. C.C. was continued for a month.[214]

Isabella O's ambivalent feelings are also apparent:

> Father... effected his purpose partly by persuasion and partly by force.[215]

Even more significant is the case of Emma Y, a young cook who had been engaged to a footman for more than five months. The young couple were well matched, fond of one another, and the man was sincere – so much so that when she discovered her pregnancy, he did not abandon her: they both left their jobs, took furnished lodgings and tried to find new work. Nevertheless, one day he vanished. Emma took her case before Clerkenwell magistrates, who found in her favour and ordered the father – if and when he could be found – to pay weekly maintenance.

Against this background, a climate of mingled love and mistrust, it is not difficult to grasp the attitude of the young woman who declared:

> He seduced me in the house – we were alone – I resisted him but he over persuaded me.

An equivocal attitude on the part of women is also, of course, a feature of the traditional game of amorous conquest. To agree, then change their minds, resist and at last surrender, would have been just as much part of our petitioners' seduction techniques as they were in the more patrician example of Byron's Julia:

> A little while she strove, and much repented,
> And whispering, 'I will ne'er consent' – consented.[216]

The man's role in the game is to overcome these hesitations by insisting, by offering convincing proof of his love and desire.

> I says my dear girl, with you I shall dine,
> For at Finchbank's, I hear, they sell very good wine;

> *And more than all that, there is a wax-work to be shown,*
> *No matter, says she, can't you let me alone?*
> *I followed this damsel through field after field,*
> *With a deal of persuasion I brought her to yield;*
> *Next day we were married, and she altered her tone,*
> *And she teazes me now, if I let her alone.*[217]

A number of the contradictory or ambivalent statements preserved in the secrecy of these files must owe their existence to these conventions:

> *It was not with my consent – that is – only partly so. Crim. Con. was repeated 3 times.*[218]

> *C.C. took place six weeks afterwards in the house. He used violence. It was at the top of the house in the day time – he was putting up bed furniture – I did not complain to anyone as he begged me not to do so – C.C. was repeated for some time.*[219]

> *At the end of May C.C. took place after many attempts. I did not consent – C.C. continued till the end of June when he left suddenly . . .*[220]

> *He came into my room and forced me. Crim. Con. was repeated.*[221]

> *Father seduced me about 15 months ago at my mistress' house. It was not exactly with my consent. It occurred in the kitchen and was never repeated.*[222]

One might conclude that some of our applicants either were lacking in will-power, or were coquettes expert in the arts of seduction. Let us not jump to conclusions, however. It is patently obvious that some young women were really offended by the way they had been treated at the moment of the sexual act. It is not difficult to see that some of these accusations of violence concern not so much the act itself as the generally boorish comportment of the lover. Asked by the committee to recall this episode of their lives in detail, many women felt resentment, even disgust, at the memory of sexual relations made all the more painful by the desertion which had brought them to an end. Sometimes the Foundling Hospital's questions elicited unconsciously comic replies. Sarah Ann E declared:

> *CC took place at his lodgings. This was June '54 with no great deal of violence and was repeated 3 or 4 times.*[223]

Others certainly retained vivid memories of an experience which had been psychologically as well as physically painful:

Father threw me down. I cried out . . .[224]

stated Susan G, only fourteen years old at the time of the occurrence.

A courtship ensued and he promised me marriage. . . . It was not with my consent. He was violent. I cried out. . . . Father continued to promise me marriage. C.C. was repeated,[225]

says Emma. Matilda R recalls:

C . . . paid me attention, courted and promised me marriage. After 6 months C. took place at my masters. Father lived on the premises. I did not consent – he was very violent. . . . I did not tell my master or mistress as Father said he would marry me.[226]

One last hypothesis: the public admission of indecisiveness, of humming and hawing at the moment of the sexual act, may be the first sign of a new, more modest attitude, or perhaps of greater susceptibility to guilt about pre-nuptial sex. The exhortations of evangelists, moral pressures of all sorts, might have made these girls feel they were doing wrong even though they were sure that they would marry their lovers.

This would have been thought very satisfactory by moral reformers or by anyone else who hoped to graft bourgeois morality on to the working class. But there is nothing in the available sources which really supports this explanation, although there is a faint possibility that the files for the last two decades of the century (which were not accessible for this study) might do so. Comparing the statements for the 1850s with the latest ones available – twenty years later – there is no quantitatively significant change: the proportions of non-voluntary, voluntary and 'mixed' sexual acts remain constant in relation to one another, although there is an increase in the number of statements which leave the information out.[227]

The absence of significant statistical change does not mean, of course, that all the postulants remained deaf to the thunderings of moralists. But we cannot say more than that with any degree of certainty.

These are the interpretations which may explain the resistance of some applicants at the moment of the sexual act. Naturally the different factors would have been present in many different combinations. But in any case, they throw serious doubt on the idea that housing and working conditions at that time gave the popular classes a broad familiarity with sexual matters.

We can hardly forget, however, that most of the postulants admitted more or less openly that they had consented willingly to sexual relations which they believed at the time were pre-nuptial. It seems that the sexual act itself, by ratifying the promise of marriage, was expected to strengthen the engaged couple's relationship and – following traditional custom – make an early marriage more likely. The very tolerant treatment of pregnant girls by most families and friends suggests that the act was seen not as evidence of weakness or immorality, but as one of the preliminaries of marriage.

> He seduced me, not against my consent.[228]

> He seduced me in my bedroom and I then went to his room where Crim. Con took place with my consent.[229]

> Seduction took place in the house – with my consent. . . ,[230]

say these women. Where they had not been read beforehand, the women believed, banns would follow soon afterwards.

Nor should we forget that immediate surrender must often have been the product of amorous passion. Here and there in the byways of these statements – so carefully composed, so ruthlessly stripped of sentimental detail, that it is easy to forget that they are love stories – we come across a variant of the *cri du cœur*:

> I gave way to him because I was fond of him.[231]

Words of love

No direct trace survives of the love talk of these young working women. Our only access to their feelings is through the unreliable channel of extrapolation.

But those daughters of the people who applied to the Foundling Hospital did possess notes and love letters, which they attached carefully to their admission forms by way of evidence. Snippets of sentimental conversation, fragments of vanished exchanges, faint echoing half-phrases in overlapping male and female voices, are thus retrieved from the depths of time.

The most striking feature of this rare and precious material is its variety of tone, content and cultural level.[232] It is most unusual, at least when the young man is still paying court, for one of these letters to be devoted entirely to the expression of amorous sentiments. Suitors who lived or worked in distant parts of a metropolis not yet equipped with long-distance communications wrote mainly to arrange a rendezvous or to apologize for missing one. A large proportion of the letters were written simply to alter an appointment:

> I remembered that I was engaged on Thursday but if you can make it convenient to see me on Wednesday at the same time and place you will favour,[233]

writes a journeyman engraver. Another young man writes hastily:

> Come up to the Race Course neer the Strand this afternoon at ½ past 3 o'clock.[234]

Behind the dry phrases, careful scrutiny reveals the organization of leisure time, the comings and goings of daughters of the people who, outside working hours, were free to go anywhere they wished. So that a young grocer's clerk could write to his friend:

> I will be in Lambeth Road on Sunday evening about past 6 and after that time, I will be at the 'Bird in Hand', so that you will know where to find me, if you should happen to be out.[235]

And a twenty-four-year-old commercial traveller to his intended, a seamstress of twenty-two:

> Where and at what time shall we meet on Thursday. Of course, I leave all that to you. Would you rather go to the Theatre or somewhere else. I shall not suggest where: for you always seem to consider my wishes so that you might be prejudiced – It pleases me beyond everything to think you do consider my wishes but Darling Nancy, you have spoilt me with kindness. . .[236]

The demands of a couple's different jobs could make arrangements difficult, and determination was often needed to organize regular meetings. This helps to explain why these letters are sometimes peppered with expressions of amorous impatience and longing for a more stable, respectable life. If, like John J, you were a coachman, you had to go where your master went and explain yourself to others as best you could:

> *You will think it very unkind of me for not writing to you before but you will not when I tell you the reason I have been to Hastings with my master for a week and I enjoyed it very much indeed I should very much like for you to have been there with me indeed as Hastings is a very nice place. . . . I wish that you were living there with me. . . . Your ever affectionate lover,*
>   *John J.*
>   *XXXXXXXXX*

Communications were slow and working hours endless, as Charles Y, a locksmith aged thirty, writes to Eliza, twenty-three, a chambermaid:

> *My dear Eliza,*
>   *I now drop you a line i am sorry to say that i was not able to come a Round to you this evening as i have been out at Brixton at work all day i have only just come home now at 9 o'clock. . .*[237]

> *My dearest Eliza,*
>   *I just received your welcome letter and was verry pleased to Receive it i was rather Disapinted as i hurried home for you but i know it cant be helped at all times and . . . especially in your stage of life but i hope you will be able to be your own misses before longe. Dear Eliza you mention about comeing to see me on saturday evening i shall be pleased to see you at 7 o'clock or that to ½ past without fail. . .*[238]

James D, twenty-two, gardener, writes to Isabella E, twenty-two, chambermaid:

> *My dearest Isabella,*
>   *I receive your kind letter last night and am very sorry to hear that Miss S is thinking of shuting up the house as you say she is no Lady I should call her an old wich or something worse but never mind Old Gal Brighter days will come again as the darkest cloud as a silver lining cheer up your pecker up Dear. . . dont fret old Gal I am coming to Long Acre on Thursday evening so I shall give you a call at 7 at*

the corner so please be on the look out I hope I shall see the Old Clock out when I come. . .[239]

Illness and injury are frequently mentioned:

I am sorry to say that I shall not be able to see you this evening on account of my knee being so swollen.[240]

I should have come over to see You but I have been very ill.[241]

I have been very ill since I left Southampton Yesterday morning but I hope I shall be better when we get out to sea.[242]

You must excuse me not writing to you yesterday I did not feel very well I have got a bad cold.[243]

I am very sorry to say that I could not come this evening to see you darling on account of my boil breaking which gave me great pain and was obliged to stop in and poltice my hand and go to bed ½ past 8 and you thinking every knock was me at that time.[244]

Dear Emmy,

I have only just received your letter as you seam not to like it because I have not written and so I thought that I would sit down know and just write to you a few lines hoping it will find you better than you was when you last wrote and also Lizzie's cough. . .[245]

The letters swarm with hints and anecdotes about daily life, with adolescent jokes, lovers' private codes, promises of gifts. A pocket-knife or book has not been returned; the friend who knows where to get gloves cheap has not been seen; the weather, of course, is cold, or hot, or damp: 'I'll wait for you in front of the church whatever the weather'; the brother of the beloved has been passed in the street without showing any sign of recognition; 'I have got a pair of gloves and a bottle of Aude Cologne for you'. Sometimes incomprehensible practical jokes are planned:

I shall drop in of course I shall say how are you stranger I shall have to get my sermon of by Heart This week but never mind as you say I think I can play my part mind you don't laugh when I come in and spoil the Game I made a bet with Mrs Minns the other day and I lost so we shall have it on our sunday never mind you don't let the cat out of the bag. . .[246]

or absurd events described, as by this draper's clerk aged twenty to the young servant he is hoping to seduce:

I went to Church a fortnight since and we laughing nearly all the time myself and two young men went and one of them drew a donkey in one of the Mission hymn books and passed it on to James and he burst out laughing and passed it to me and I could not help laughing as well and all the people in the galleries were looking at us and I was quite ashamed of myself I did not know which way to look. . .[247]

Even the most trivial of these exchanges have the merit that they show the young couples in a completely different light from that of the administrative inquiry, and give some idea of what their lives were like before they were brought through misfortune to seek charity: lives made of small joys and great hopes, of wild laughter, impertinent pranks, silly deceptions.

More broadly, though, they bring nuance to the dramatic or grim picture of the life of the labouring classes built up by novelists and Victorian moral reformers, a version which is still more or less accepted by historians of the period. Without going to the opposite extreme, we would do well to keep these amusing vignettes in mind, alongside the established images of physical suffering and moral degradation.

We have already noted how precarious people's lives were made by sporadic unemployment, illness, high levels of infant mortality, the absence of old age pensions, and alcohol. We have shown how arduous the working conditions were, and how humiliating it was to seek charitable aid. The Foundling Hospital postulants and their lovers were all victims of these things in varying degrees.

But their life histories, of which we have access only to brief episodes, show something of the other side of the coin: small oases of joy and relaxation which – however limited they may have been – modify the unrelieved miserablism of our received image of the Victorian proletariat.

The shadowy areas of the picture, which Podsnap[248] would have striven to see in mezzotint, or better still in pastel pinks and blues, have been heavily blackened – largely on principle – by a whole tradition of dedicated social observers, from Engels to Jack London. Reintroducing a sense of the paradoxes of human destiny can only serve to enrich this representation.

The expressions of amorous tenderness and sexual desire which comprise the other main aspect of this correspondence are very helpful

here. Kisses, spelt out or represented by symbols, fly back and forth
with the letters:

> *I long to see you to have one kiss from you.*
>   *kiss kiss kiss,*[249]

writes Alfred Y to Ellen I. An apprentice mechanic says lovingly:

> *. . .hoping you are happy and well. . .*
>   *kisses xxxxx*

while others end on an anticipatory note:

> *I hope dearest that you have got plenty of kisses for me to night,*[250]
>
> *Dear*
>   *I must now conclude with love to my own dear Lottie. P.S. I will be at your
> gate at 5 o'clock to have a kiss of the only girl I like in this world. . .*[251]

The letters give a compressed version of the events which punctuate
these humble amours, their moments of solicitude and remorse:

> *I am sorry that I was obliged to leave you as I did on Sunday your poor heart seemed
> quite full and I felt much grieved after I have left. . .*[252]

and the loneliness of waiting:

> *I shall be very sorry to miss your company on Sunday but I do hope my darling that
> you will write to me soon. You know, dearest how I love you and I am sure that you
> hav some affection for me. I won't darling, abuse your trust in me it would be my
> greatyst wish to marry you I often wonder if I shall, I should like it very much, but I
> suppose I must wait a while yet. . . . You told me darling, that you did not wish to
> go out with anyone else, be assured dearest I don't want to. . .*[253]

Other letters contain declarations and heartfelt effusions some of
which, like this one from a gardener, give away nothing to the novelist
Madame de Scudéry:

> *Dearest Harriet,*
>   *I spend one Sunday with Pleasure and the other with the Blues but hop some*

day to spend them all with Pleasure when I have got the one I love Fast well good night Dearest. . .[254]

I begin to think you are right in saying absence makes the heart grow fonder and not as I thought stronger. Indeed I find my heart gets every day fonder and more feeble on your account,[255]

sighs another, while a third declares with tremulous sincerity:

All my love to you my own dearest Judy, I remain your true and devoted lover and soon husband. . .[256]

All these letters express feeling in a much less light-hearted, offhand way than contemporary popular songs lead one to expect. We can quote by way of example a verse of 'Sally in our Alley', supposedly sung by an apprentice who is courting a young street-trader:

> *Of all the days that's in the week*
> *I dearly love but one day,*
> *And that's the day that comes betwixt*
> *A Saturday and Monday;*
> *For then I'm dressed all in my best*
> *To walk abroad with Sally;*
> *She is the darling of my heart*
> *And she lives in our alley.[257]*

It seems, on the contrary, that young men and women of the people sought a language in keeping with their ideas of distinction, or at any rate charged with strong emotion; while the authors of popular ballads used a pastiche of popular speech to express *their* ideas of the simple satisfactions of the masses.

We also find lovers' quarrels in these letters, and the anguished pleas of the rejected:

I do trust Margaret that you will give way to your better feelings and meet me, it makes me very sad when I think how happy we were together only a week ago, it is an awful contrast. I really believe that if I had not sent that letter this would not have occurred. I have often told you Margaret, how well and truly I love you and I sincerely trust that I shall always do so, even if I never see you after to night. . . if I were able to call you dearest and to once again kiss your sweet pure lips, would make me very different to what I am at present. . .[258]

> . . . You told me that you thought because i done what i did i did not want to see you again,

explains Gabriel B, a groom (and later a farm-worker) to his friend Mary Ann G, a nurserymaid of Leicester Square. He goes on:

> . . . No one could have more love for you than i have for you i think i have not do you think that if i had not loving feeling towards you i should never of sent these letters to you in such a little time no my dear Mary Ann i shall think more of you now than before so forgive and forget and i only wish you wos by my side now i could tell you something that would make you happy and i should be live me dearest Mary Ann you can see that i feel it very much. . .[259]

Some lovers make desperate attempts at moral blackmail.

> If you don't come I shall never forgive you so if you want to be good friends not like last Christmas I beg you on my knees for you to come to dinner as I love you so dearly that I don't wish for rows. Dear Liddy I shall be waiting anxiously to see you at one but not after so I must conclude with my best love to you. I am your accepted husband,[260]

concludes a Stepney house-painter. Others hint at jealous feelings and erotic longings:

> I did not receive a note from you this morning as I expected and very much disappointed I was. . . how many sweethearts you have got already not mentioning how many you will get But enough of that foolery I should very much like to be with you to sit beside you with my arm round your pritty little waste how happy I should be. . .[261]

> I accept the kisses you sent in your note with pleasure and will return with interests on friday night althou I would rather had them from your lips than your hands.[262]

Apart from two or three very gross references, allusions to sexual desire and sexual acts are very oblique – often, one feels, because the writer did not want to say anything which might later be used as evidence in a paternity suit.

The usual tone of these references is apologetic, embarrassed and concerned. It conveys the element of risk in pre-nuptial carnal relations, and the sort of pressures exerted by some women to prevent their partners from taking things too lightly.

In any case, the letters contain no hint of the Rabelaisian enjoyment, indifferent promiscuity or sexual licence commonly associated with love among the people.

I see you trusting dearest Annie that you are in good health and feel no ill effect from being with me.[263]

I was not at all well although I would not say anything about it but I think that I hurt myself on Sunday night with you but I am in hopes not much I know it was all my own fault but I cannot think that you love me Judy as I do you but I hope you will in time, do not let anyone get hold of this or else they will be thinking something of you and me. . .[264]

Sarah Ann's application gives no detail on the exact circumstances of her seduction, but the above extract from her lover's letter suggests that she put up quite a fierce struggle.

William G by contrast writes in apology rather than reproach. An engraver by trade, he forced Matilda W to yield to his advances during a visit to his room in Islington one afternoon in January 1860. A few days later he writes to ask her to forgive him and to promise that he will not do it again:

Dear Tilly,
    I am very sorry that I should be the cause of so much trouble to you. I would have seen you before but I have to much feeling for you. I am extreemely sorry for what I have done I have made up my mind not do so any more for I have thought of the great trouble it gives you and what might happen by doing so I am so pleased that you are all right. If you will only wait for a little time before I see you I shall be all right and quite to promise I have made you. . .[265]

In her statement to the committee, Matilda confirms that he kept his promise. A dressmaker who lived in Dalston with her mother and sister, she expresses an unusually deep fear of the social consequences of a bastard in the family. But William's promise not to touch her again had come too late: she was already pregnant. On learning this he left London immediately, and a few months later married someone else.

Let us end our exploration of these fragments of love talk with another sample of the impassioned if somewhat scrambled, prose of the farm-worker Gabriel B, manifestly very upset by his fiancée's reactions:

March 23 1863

My dear Mary Ann,

I returned tonight and i am very sorry to hear that you are no better but i hop, please God, that you will soon get better again. forth i do assure you that it makes me worries me that i fell a grat deal for you but i hop please God these few lines will find you better you say in this letter that you hop that i shall enjoy myself better next time my dear Mary Ann i should never wish to enjoy myself better than i did this time i could not enjoy myself i could not do it my dear Mary Ann i turn to som thing else and i feel it very much i do assure you don't you think that i feel sorry for all you think i could not rest till i rot to you a bout it now you my [illegible] by this letter this time and i hop you will forget all for i am very sorry for all and i hop when we meet again things will be all right again for you will always be a good friend in me and you will find my words true and you say that is the only thing you have against me so i hop my dear Mary Ann you will forget all this time and when we see each other we can put all things rite again i dont think that i can say any more about but i am very sory for all past i shall rite again on Sunday but i wanted to send you answer to your last letter as you wished me, so I think that will be all this time but i trust again i hope these few lines will find you better so ishall be only too happy to see or hear from you if you can get out so i must conclud with my kindst and most affectionately and best love to you so ihop to remain yours ever and kindst so good by and God bless you from yours ever,
    G.B.[266]

Gabriel's fear that he might have lost her for ever seems not to have been simulated or exaggerated in any way, for this letter was followed a day later by another written in the same breathless and frantic style.

'NOW LOST TO ALL, HER FRIENDS, HER VIRTUE FLED. . .'[267]

In principle, according to the dominant code of sexual morality, if it became known that a girl had been deflowered before marriage both she and her family would be excluded from society. The family might well expel the miscreant from its own circle, or at the very least make her pay dearly for her offence. This is the treatment meted out in literature to characters who have allowed themselves to be seduced: women like Esther Dombey and Alice Marwood in *Dombey and Son,* Emily and Martha Endell in *David Copperfield,* Martha in *Mary Barton,* Ruth or Hetty Sorel in *Adam Bede.*[268]

In real life, however, even when pre-marital relations were not legitimized (and perhaps concealed) by a hasty marriage, the social consequences were usually a good deal less dramatic. Of course the lovers, the families, above all the young mothers themselves, were faced with heavy psychological, physical and economic costs. But except in a very few cases the arrival of an illegitimate child did not entail systematic rejection by a social circle whose main concern continued to be its own survival.

Just as – however strong their mutual affection and desire – the couples half-feared, a moment eventually came when pregnancy was established beyond doubt. Sometimes they had already separated: a new job, a simple loss of amorous interest, had sent the young man and woman in different directions.

> *He courted me and promised marriage for about 3 years. . . . CC was once repeated within a week which was the last time I saw him.*[269]

> *I did not tell anyone but left the place a month after and the Father a fortnight after that.*[270]

But this was quite rare. What usually happened was that one day the lover suddenly learned that he was to become a father. According to custom, the news should have been followed more or less immediately by a marriage ceremony. In these cases, as we know, no such ceremony took place.

**'He promised to marry her soon,
But soon he forgot all about her. . .'[271]**

Thus cornered, with what ingenuity, with what agonies of conscience, how brutally sometimes, the young men acted to disentangle themselves by cutting through bonds of affection cemented over time! There is something very cruel about the suddenness with which these stories turn from idyll to misery.

POSTING BANNS

Some couples – about twenty in our sample – continued to follow traditional practice for a time. When pregnancy was confirmed, banns would be posted, generally at the woman's request as marriages were celebrated in the woman's parish. The posting of banns was still imbued with a certain solemnity, although people who failed to follow it up by getting married were no longer excommunicated for 'mocking the Church'. In theory, it committed the young man absolutely.

In nineteenth-century London, however, it was not too difficult to evade the vengeance of the Church or to escape the consequences of dishonourable behaviour. The Bible Women, among others, complained from time to time about the feckless attitude of some couples living in sin, who allowed the period of banns to elapse and thus obliged the missionaries to start the process all over again.

Where Foundling Hospital applicants were concerned, this move often had the opposite effect to the one intended: instead of bringing the marriage date forward, the posting of banns accelerated the break-up of the relationship as the father-to-be, completely cornered, vanished before the appointed day.

In the roll of honour of those who sought salvation in flight we find James E, a carpenter of Spitalfields, who had been courting Louisa G for several months. Learning that she was pregnant, her uncle tried to help her by posting the banns at St Mary's.

This however had not the desired effect as the Father, immediately afterwards decamped,[272]

reported the Foundling Hospital's inquirer. Panic, or some other reason, could make the husband-to-be vanish on the very day fixed for the marriage:

The Banns were published in Thornhill Sq. Church. . . in August and a day was fixed for the marriage and I went to the house of his sister Mrs P to meet him but he failed to come. He borrowed me £8 which he required to [illegible]. I met him by chance in january last and I asked for the £8 which he refused to pay unless forced.[273]

Eleanor M was twenty-seven and a cook; Thomas was a mason. The banns were published. He left her on the morning of the appointed wedding day.[274]

LIVING IN SIN: 'BEFORE EVERYTHING WENT WRONG'[275]

Unwilling or unable to marry as planned, some couples chose second-best and made arrangements to set up house. This was the very decision most feared by so many Victorian philanthropists.

The more virtuous women at first resisted the idea, like this kitchenmaid, engaged to a plasterer who had been courting her for three years and promising marriage:

> *When pregnant I told him and he said he would marry me in March* [i.e. two months after conception]. *He wanted C.C. to be repeated but I refused. He excused himself as to marriage because he was out of work. I left my situation in August and went to Mrs. D. a friend, Blackfriars Rd. Where I was confined attended by a midwife. Father wished me to go with him to America but I refused because he would not marry me first.*[276]

Others lacked these scruples, but their cases – only about twenty out of our whole sample – are exceptional.

Fanny P's story is a remarkable illustration of the way a young woman's initial matrimonial ambitions could gradually be narrowed down, under pressure from the fiancé's personality and aspirations, the circumstances of their relationship and the couple's economic situation. Fanny was an orphan. Four years before she knocked at the Foundling Hospital's door her aunt had found her a place as under-chambermaid with Lord A. in Belgravia. Before that, everyone agreed, her behaviour had always shown perfect modesty and reserve.

After courting her assiduously and officially for two years, Frederick W, a house-painter of Bloomsbury, promised to marry her. One autumn afternoon, during a walk among the red and gold foliage of Wimbledon Common, she allowed herself to be seduced. At the time, no doubt, her future appeared not only secure but positively luminous. Soon she was expecting a child and left her job on her fiancé's advice. 'We thought she was going to get married,' Susan Thane, the head chambermaid, declared later. But they did not get married yet. They took a room in Manchester Square, where on 29 May 1875 their daughter was born.

Everything had not gone according to the original plan; but Fanny was not destitute, and Frederick was still promising 'from time to time' that he would marry her. Then the future came apart. A week after the child's birth, Frederick, a model worker who had always behaved in a 'decent and worthy' manner, disappeared literally into thin air. Perhaps, his foreman suggested, he had emigrated to the colonies with another painter named Hardy. Nobody knew for sure.

Fanny tried to live alone with her baby. She managed to survive for nine months on subsidies from friends and by taking in needlework; but eventually starvation threatened, and she had to try to get the child accepted by the Foundling Hospital so that she might find another job as a domestic.[277]

The point here is that, contrary to the usual reasoning of Victorian moralists, living with the father of her child for three months had been enormously helpful to Fanny. It had enabled her to avoid what so many others had to suffer: the mortification of workhouse or hospice, the anguish of a dishonoured pauper's daily existence following close behind the pains of childbirth. Cruel though the father's abrupt defection may appear, the fact that he supported his fiancée until the birth of their child does argue a certain sense of responsibility. And it is here that one discerns the harm philanthropists could do by striving blindly to separate those couples whose union was not blessed by the Church. The moralists had great difficulty in understanding that a valid relationship could exist in the absence of official conjugal ties.

Henry P, thirty-four, was a tailor specializing in cloaks. He had lived with a woman for eight years and they had a child. Two years before the events described in the Foundling Hospital files, he became enamoured of Eliza J, one of his seamstresses, ten years his junior, and started a love affair with her. When he learned that she was pregnant they took lodgings in Kilburn, and he gave her a ring so that people would think they were married. But he died of a heart attack before the child was born. It was registered in his name, and his brother agreed to take in the mother and baby for a time.[278]

Sometimes the prospect of marriage seemed so intolerable that – as the reports of philanthropic associations constantly point out – it led directly to final breakdown of the relationship and the material desertion of women and children. This pattern can be seen in the story of Hannah E, a domestic aged twenty, and Francis Y, a carpenter by trade.[279]

More than a year of keeping company, followed by an official introduction to the girl's family – which was delighted with his serious mind and other qualities – had authorized Francis Y to love his fiancée physically. A few months later Hannah discovered that she was with child. Francis suggested that they take lodgings in Paddington, and they began their life together. Nothing in the young woman's statement indicates that this arrangement aroused her scruples in any way. She had nevertheless received a religious upbringing: her mother had taken her to church, she had been a regular Sunday-school pupil, and all her employers praised her moral qualities.

But her mother did not like her attitude. A widow who had never remarried, still supporting three children and strongly influenced by her local vicar, she worked on Hannah until she persuaded her to leave her lover who, for his part, was nagged incessantly to post banns. The result was that before the period of the banns was over he left London, deserting his three-months-pregnant lover.

The choice between marriage and concubinage seems not to have been an ethical matter but more a question of personal convenience, although decisions must have been strongly influenced by the importance attached to legitimate union by the philanthropic organizations.

ABORTION ATTEMPTS

Not much is known about any precautions the couples might have taken during the sexual act to prevent conception. The incredulity and astonishment shown by some men on learning that their lovers were pregnant suggests that they had tried to use the most widespread contraceptive method of the nineteenth century: *coitus interruptus*. Throughout the century, in fact, Malthusians and neo-Malthusians, eugenicists, socialists and feminists had done everything they could to spread information on the control of fertility.[280]

Often some attempt would have been made to choose a time when the woman was considered not to be fertile.[281] Even under cover of the promise of marriage, efforts would most probably have been made to make conception less likely, if not to prevent it altogether. This may be a specious argument, but the written statements do describe a variety of male reactions to news of a pregnancy. Some simply record a brutal denial and rejection ('He slighted me and denied paternity'); others the hope that there might be a false alarm ('He said he hoped not'); and still others the man's fear of being dishonestly saddled with someone else's offspring:

> When 3 months gone with child, I told him, but he did not believe it. Subsequently he said it was not his and told my Father so.[282]

Some fiancés, while expressing great surprise, did not reject the young woman and even offered to help:

> I told him of my pregnancy but he would not believe it 'til I consulted Dr Johnson who told him it was so.[283]

> . . .he would not at first believe it was so; he at length became concerned and promised to assist me through my difficulty.[284]

Two letters from a valet, Edward O, express these feelings:

> . . . I cannot think how or by who you came in the family way being quite sure it was not by me. . .[285]

> Ruth, I hope you are not as you think if so it is a very bad job but I am in hopes it is only fancy but of course if you persist in my being the father of it why I must do my best for it after it is born. . .

The certainty that he *could not* be the child's father was spelt out by a constable, who said in so many words what others hinted at, but left unsaid:

> But I cannot believe that you have been burdened by me for I was never allowed to enjoy you sufficiently for that.[286]

Whatever contraceptive methods were used, it is clear that in the cases we are considering they had not worked. This unwelcome realization brought some men to try to persuade their lovers to terminate the pregnancy.

All human societies have practised abortion in one form or another, and nineteenth-century working-class women were no exception. The use of abortifacient potions seems to have been more widespread than surgical intervention to remove the foetus. A study published in 1825 lists among other methods bleeding and taking emetics, cantharides (Spanish fly), mercury, powdered savin and juniper essence. In the mid nineteenth century colocynth, quinine and a concoction of gin and gunpowder were added to the list. Pills containing lead enjoyed a brief vogue around the turn of the century.[287]

Daily and weekly newspapers contained numerous advertisements offering, in veiled but far from impenetrable terms, to rid women discreetly of any 'temporary inconvenience'.

From reading the Foundling Hospital files, it is apparent that recourse to abortion was by no means exclusively a matter for women. While it is only to be expected that none of the postulants would have admitted trying illegal abortion methods (even though one declared 'I did everything I could to produce abortion'), quite a number of men seem to have regarded it as an obvious, almost a normal, expedient.

We can ignore the possibility that some applicants might have been trying to blame any illegal acts on their partners, since the letters quoted here were written before application to the hospital. A social breakdown of the men favouring abortion tells us very little; those who proposed this solution to their partners came from every category of the working people: farm-workers, skilled industrial workers, artisans, domestics, salesmen, soldiers. Only one was a pharmaceutical dispenser.

One example is William O, sales assistant in a Hammersmith shop. When his lover, a housemaid, realized that she was a month pregnant, he sent her a letter containing a strange mixture of threats, apologies and advice:

26.12.51

Dear Ann,

We whent to Westminster as I said it was my intention but I cannot tell you the result of it until you are a little more composed. I whent to the arcade at about 25 minutes after. I then came to the conclusion that Mrs H. was taken ill and that you did not visit the arcade during that time. I wish you never to mention my letters or anything else that I have given you unless you wish me to commit an act which may be far from meeting with your approbation. Your character you recolect is as I consider at a discount and I think I should endeavur to show it to all I know were you to commit it yourself in the way you mentioned. I must own you have experienced much pain or unkindness from me within the 2 months past but I say it shall be my study to repay you for all if not in one way I'll make sure the other. I cannot come down to see you until I receive an anwert to this but I would advise you to take a good dose of salts and senna directly if it belongs to me if not let it go where it belongs. . . [288]

In the same callous vein the domestic servant James D insists, between chatty asides and requests for news, that nothing could be easier, more natural or more effective than 'getting something' from the chemist. He scolds his lover, a chambermaid aged twenty-four, as if she were a child refusing to take her medicine:

> *My dear Fanny,*
>   *I wish you would do what I tell you and not be so stupid but go to the chemist and get something but that you must please yourself about it can be prevented if you like you did not tell me how you mother was nor how the new footman are getting on and wether he was likely to stop I am getting on all right as yet hopping you are the same why do you not ask Barbera she would get you something so I must conclude with love. . .* [289]

Gabriel B also believed that these potions, which were supposed to work by causing vomiting and intestinal spasms, were effective if used in time:

> *My dear Mary Ann,*
>   *I received your last with the greatest surprise if that the case i hop things will be all right with you i only wish that i had of heard of it before but that of no use now. . .* [290]

A bootmaker who urged his lover to ask her mother what to do confirms the idea that remedies of this sort were supposed to be part of women's traditional know-how. At the same time he supports the rest of our sources in indicating that it was men, desperate to evade their responsibilities and go back on their promises, who generally proposed abortion.

Women, on the other hand, usually had to be persuaded, almost compelled. Doubtless they still hoped that their concession of pre-nuptial sexual relations, and the resulting pregnancy, would tie their lovers down and make marriage a certainty. But we should also remember that abortion in the nineteenth century was an alarming and dangerous experience.

In any case, the insistent attitude of these men, and their apparent indifference to the consequences of some of the methods used, are very striking. The reasons are most probably a mixture of ignorance, callousness and a certain resignation to sickness and death. We know already, of course, that during and immediately after childbirth the lives of Victorian women were under very serious threat. Perhaps the risks posed by this radical chemotherapy did not seem much greater.

For all these reasons, some men brought strong pressure to bear on their former lovers, as we can see from this letter 'of a very disgraceful character'[291] from a soldier based in Winchester to a girl he had seduced:

> *Dear Sarah,*
>
> *I regret to hear that you are in the state you describe and also that you have taken the medicine without result. But surely you cannot have taken enough to gain a result. I wish you to take it to procure abortion: you can get a medical adviser under the 'Rarra' – that old doctor's shop there. You must take the medecine or else I shall not speak to you any more – it may not induce your courses but it will prevent anything serious. Mind what I say. . .[292]*

'I TOLD HIM AT WHICH HE SEEMED FRIGHTENED'

That is how George T, a draper's assistant of Oxford Street, reacted to the news that he was to become a father. Then he took to his heels and vanished without a moment's hesitation. Later his fiancée learned from a friend that he had gone abroad. Although it may seem surprising in the light of all the oaths and promises we have seen on record, such behaviour was far from unusual.

We mention this case because no other petitioner thought fit to describe her partner's emotions at what amounted to a turning point in both their lives.

On receiving the news, doubtless, the fathers-to-be suddenly became less certain of their feelings – if, that is, they had ever been certain of them in the first place. We should bear in mind that Victorian law was quite severe with seducers, who could be prosecuted for breach of promise and, naturally, pursued with paternity orders. This explains why so many chose the radical, if not very admirable, solution of flight.

'I told him when he deserted me immediately,'[293] recalls Mary Ann

C. One imagines that before the lover's final departure there would often have been a stormy interview, or an exchange of polemical letters, as his duplicity or cynicism was at last revealed.

Emily J and John Z had worked in the same workshop since their apprenticeship, which means in effect that they had been childhood friends and known one another all their adult lives. He promised to marry her 'as soon as he got on his feet'; they became each other's first lovers. Life and work separated them for two years: then there was an emotional reunion with new promises, new embraces. He did not inform her that he had married someone else in the meantime. On discovering that she was pregnant, Emily hurried to see him at work, but he would not listen to her. It was only on going to his home accompanied by her sisters that she realized the extent of her misfortune:

> *He banged the door in our faces and told me to sue him. We found he was married. His wife was at the door, Miss Alexander* [his superior at work] *told me he had sold off his things and gone to America.*[294]

Some men just shrugged the news off:

> *When pregnant I told him and he said he could do nothing for me,*[295]

reported Letitia D in 1853, words echoed exactly by Susan P seventeen years later. Sometimes the rejection was outrageously brutal and unpleasant:

> *He admitted the paternity but laughed at me and would do nothing. . . .,*[296]

said Caroline P.

> *When pregnant I told him and he told me to drown myself,*[297]

said Emma D. Isabella B got a similar response from Alfred D, a soldier:

> *I told him and he slighted me and told me to drown myself and that he would help to do so. He did not deny paternity.*[298]

> *When I told him my condition he laughed and desired to repeat the intercourse but I refused,*[299]

complained another girl. Some of the men's letters are notable for cruelty and heartless impudence:

I am going to be married shortly to a very nice young woman.[300]

If I had any intention of marrying it has been dispelled since coming home.[301]

The announcement of a pregnancy could bring to light extreme forms of deceit. The rough behaviour of some lovers may have exposed their ambiguous intentions, but did not always destroy all affection between the couple. It was quite different when a woman learned that a man she had considered her husband-to-be and introduced to her family, a man with whom she had planned a joint future, had been married all along and was himself the father of a family.

I witnessed her horror and grief when her mother called and told her she had had a letter to say he was a married man,[302]

recounted Mary Ann E's woman employer, who had been present when the young servant discovered her betrayal. Things were not always so clear, however, especially when – as a number of files confirm – there was a genuine attachment between the couple. In some cases only the last-minute discovery of an earlier marriage prevented bigamy or concubinage. The reports of charitable societies, incidentally, bulge with references to happy bigamists and contented common-law husbands!

Among our files is the case of Dorcas A, courted at length by a carpenter from Holloway. He made a good impression on her parents, but one day in June 1857,

Petitioner's mother was accosted in the street by a working man of decent appearance who said he had been watching an opportunity to see her in order to inform her that. . . he was married.[303]

When questioned the culprit confessed, then departed without another word. Richard H, a tailor, got as far as marrying Sophia J, a flower-seller, although he was already married. She laid a complaint and he was jailed for eighteen months for bigamy.

Alfred A, a commercial traveller, seemed very taken with Ann E – so much so that he went on courting her long after the beginning of her pregnancy. The idyll ended when the girl's mother received an anonymous letter alleging that he was already married and had three children. Hurrying to his wife's address, the mother found the family 'in a starving condition'.[304]

One of the most romantic cases must be that of James W, a porter with the South Eastern Railway who fell madly in love with a young laundress. He was already married in his native Cornwall to a woman 'moving in a much higher state of life than the young man's family', but was denied the right to live with her and their child. While he was preparing for this new, more suitable marriage, his sister arrived on a visit and gave his secret away. After this second matrimonial setback he threw everything over and went off to try his luck on the other side of the Atlantic.

But it seems that most of these men were just trying to keep the adultery going for as long as possible. Having never revealed their addresses, they were in a good position to disappear as soon as it became absolutely necessary.

The threat of fatherhood also precipitated the departure of those scoundrels and ne'er-do-wells who had been playing on their fiancées' tender sentiments, and were using marriage preparations as a pretext for relieving the girls of their meagre savings. One of these, a grocer's assistant, managed to borrow £7 from his fiancée and another £50 from her aunt (both domestics), ostensibly to set himself up in business.[305]

Vincent T seduced Annie G, a housemaid past her first youth – she was thirty-two – who had managed to save a few pounds during long years of service in the home of the Reverend D at Notting Hill. They kept company for a long period, until pregnancy intervened.

> Father deluded me from time to time, borrowing money 'til 8th of this month, when he deserted me. . . . The Banns were published in St. James Church,[306]

explained Annie sadly. These situations are heart-rending: the poor swindled women saw their dreams of a better life dashed, and were reduced to penury after years of saving. Isabella P, a housemaid aged twenty-five, believed that she was on the point of marrying her intended, a milkman two years older. The banns were published in Thornhill Square Church and the wedding day was fixed. The inquirer notes:

> *Then he entirely deserted petitioner who had placed all the money she possessed into his hands, at his instigation, with a view to providing a home after their marriage.*[307]

Eight pounds! Hardly a fortune even in those days, it would at least have helped her to avoid a depressing nine-week stay at St Mary's workhouse, Islington.[308]

There is nothing surprising about the high incidence of liars and conmen in the Foundling Hospital's files; after all, the institution was geared specifically to rescuing the victims of such people. But these cases do give an idea of the minefield created for young working women in the Victorian metropolis by the rules of sexual morality, the thirst for amusement and pleasure, the quicksands of love, the fear of being 'left on the shelf' and, last but not least, the longing for a happier, less exhausting life.

The presence of so many contradictory elements made these young women vulnerable to opportunist manoeuvres by unsavoury characters who saw London's working girls as an inexhaustible reservoir of prey. The capital's vast anonymity did the rest.

A code of sexual morality which under certain conditions tolerated pre-marital sexual relations placed young women in an obvious position of weakness in dealing with these specimens. We are not in a position to comment on the scars left by such adventures when the sexual relations did not result in pregnancy; but when they did it was the women, alone and unaided, who had to bear the physical, psychological and social consequences.

'HE SAID HE WOULD SEE ME THROUGH MY TROUBLE'[309]

Do not imagine that all these stories are about shameless blackguards and their victims. Indeed, a majority of the men showed a less than callous attitude when the time came to separate.

Some reacted to news of the pregnancy by starting to drag their feet. They told the girl that they had changed their mind and no longer intended to marry; but at the same time, they promised to support the coming baby. This attitude seems hardly to have surprised the women. The use of wet nurses and babyminders was common practice among people who had to carry on working; the Foundling Hospital was itself based on this principle. But knowing, as we do, how these stories ended, we can see at once that the offer of help was usually just an expedient to soften the shock of desertion.

When Mary Ann's mother, for example, tried to get the money promised by the father of her daughter's child,

> *He treated her with insolent defiance, and refused to contribute anything towards the maintenance of the child. . .*[310]

John P, a coachman of Chelsea, was already married; when Ellen C announced her pregnancy, he confessed that he could not marry her, but swore in the same breath that he would take care of the child. He even gave her £7 to find a place to live. But he soon realized that it would be impossible to support two households, and stopped sending money.[311] Walter C, for his part, was manifestly too unstable and selfish to contribute to the support of his offspring for long. His letters indicate that when his fiancée had left her job, he installed her in the home of a couple he knew, promising to pay a weekly sum for her food and lodging. References to time-honoured male social pastimes also show how strong the temptations of bachelor life could be for these young men:

> *I sit down to write you all particulars of my not coming down on Sunday I went out in the morning and got drinking consequently I was not in a fit state to come to you. . . . Now Susan, you did not make yourself unhappy as I shall see you on Sunday and not before and let me tell you that it will be no use sending anyone to see me as it would do no good I think you now me well enough to be able to judge better that to send anyone to see me. I will send plenty money before Sunday so that you shall not be without. Now Susan, be of good cheer and all will be all right before the time.*
> *Hoping you will forgive my unkindness to you.*[312]

We should note in passing that some of these relationships ended in a more tragic way: that sometimes it was death that deprived the child of a legitimate name.

James T, a gas worker, was carried off by typhus on the last Sunday before the banns were due to be read.[313] Betsey Y assured the committee that George E would have married her if he too had not died of illness.[314] Henry J, an office worker aged twenty, had had a stroke.[315] Virginia P, who worked in an arms factory at Lambeth, had known Charles Y, an engineering apprentice, for seven years. The banns were published, then withdrawn because Virginia had contracted a serious illness. Their bad luck seemed to have arrived in an avalanche: Charles was drowned before the child was born, and the sick Virginia was forced to seek refuge in the Lambeth workhouse.[316]

William P died of a heart attack at the age of thirty-four, when Sarah J was four months pregnant.[317] Alfred Hartwell, twenty-four, a turner, died in an accident while working on a railway line. Walter E, an engraver aged twenty-four, succumbed to a fever on the same day as his stepmother.[318] Illness and death were always present, and sometimes struck at the worst possible moment.

When Fanny P was eighteen, she fell in love with a young butcher's assistant who promised to marry her. They went out for walks and to music halls, and she was soon pregnant. Preparations began for a hasty marriage to take place before the child was born. But at three in the afternoon of 23 November 1862, Edward D injured himself mortally with one of the knives he used for cutting up carcases. He was rushed to St Bartholomew's Hospital. A Sister of Charity who was present testified that the petitioner had been at his bedside when he died and behaved in every way as a lover and 'wife-to-be'.[319]

Drowning, burns, fever, tuberculosis – all had a place in the long list of unforeseen obstacles that could sabotage these young people's matrimonial plans.

This insecurity helps us to understand young women's anxieties about the sexual act. Their own amorous yearnings, and their reluctance to rebuff their suitor's advances, were always counterbalanced by a vague fear of unknown dangers. Remember that all these young people were raised from childhood to an understanding of sexual matters which is partly veiled, here, by the Foundling Hospital's outlook and investigative method. Girls as well as boys had been raised in overcrowded dwellings and heard the jokes and chatter of courtyard, music hall and workshop. Young women knew that once they were courting openly and the promise of marriage had been given, pre-nuptial sexual relations could strengthen the relationship and perhaps speed the transition to the conjugal life which was their dearest wish.[320]

But people were also aware of the liberties which could be taken with courtship customs: they knew how easy it was to disappear in the swarming, constantly changing city, and how widespread, nowadays, was the dream of starting a new life overseas. Nevertheless, a pregnancy did not usually entail the immediate scrapping of marriage plans. What usually happened was that the father-to-be suddenly discovered, or claimed to discover, that there were pressing reasons for postponing the wedding.

In practice this situation seems to divide humanity into two main groups. Libertines – men who live from day to day – tend to marry at this point and later desert or deceive their wives, seduce other women, get into debt, do moonlight flits, waste time and money on ephemeral adventures.

Men of this type were products of the capital's working classes: people marginalized by the decline of traditional industries and their related skills, enslaved in bourgeois households or business establishments, crushed by the economic machine, hardened by the permanent insecurity of lives which religious belief could no longer explain or make endurable, which categorical social rules no longer helped to control. They were men stupefied by work, suffering and ignorance, men fearful of the future. In these disorderly amorous relations, in this callous and dishonest behaviour, we can observe a whole population adrift, guzzling and carousing, despicably ready to fleece its own poorest and most vulnerable members, pleasure-seeking, egotistical, a population which arouses what Flora Tristan calls 'horror of the people – so venal, so cold, so selfish and disagreeable';[321] a group of which Engels wrote:

> A class about whose education no one troubles himself, which is a playball to a thousand chances, knows no security of life – what incentives has such a class to providence, to 'respectability', to sacrifice the pleasures of the moment to a remoter enjoyment, most uncertain precisely by reason of the perpetually varying, shifting conditions under which the proletariat lives?[322]

Alongside this group existed radically different individuals, who had on the contrary an acute concern for the future. These clumsy heirs of utilitarianism and evangelism were pulled in two directions by contradictory inclinations: although convinced that marriage would be a disaster, they were very loth to betray a woman they loved.

Traditionally, among the artisans and tradesmen of London as among rural folk, marriage was linked to the acquisition of a skill or trade giving economic independence. This was not the case among the unskilled proletariat for whom early marriage meant, among other things, combining two sources of income.

Our male sample consists essentially of daily paid workers, clerks and book-keepers with little hope of one day becoming masters themselves, and domestics whose promotion chances were equally slow and poor, especially if they stayed with the same employer. Nevertheless, the reasons they gave for breaking off relations suggest that these young people were not completely deaf to the arguments being developed by workers' organizations and institutions for moral and religious education. Inspired largely by evangelism and the theories of Malthus, these bodies mounted tireless campaigns against early marriage which they held responsible for poverty and overcrowding in the slums. The working classes were ceaselessly exhorted to delay conjugal union and organize their lives around prudence, foresight and thrift.

One example is the work of the Society for the Diffusion of Useful Knowledge, whose criticism of marriages undertaken without forethought is a leitmotiv of the first half of the century:

> The great improvidence of the able-bodied labourers was that of improvident marriages – of marriages contracted while the parties were mere children, and with the direct intention that the offsprings of such marriages should be paupers. . .[323]

Although the political principles are different, the ideas are similar to those put forward by Robert Tressell's creation, the evangelized workman Slyme, in a novel published over sixty years later:

> 'Early marriages is another thing,' said Slyme, 'no man oughtn't to be allowed to get married unless he's in a position to keep a family.'
> 'How can marriage be a cause of poverty?' said Owen, contemptuously. . .
> 'Wot I mean,' said Slyme, 'is that no man oughtn't to marry till he's saved up enough so as to 'ave some money in the bank; an' another thing, I reckon a man oughtn't to get married till 'e's got a 'ouse of 'is own. It's easy enough to buy one in a building society if you're in a reg'lar work.'
> At this there was a general laugh.[324]

The fathers-to-be named in the Foundling Hospital petitions not only had no savings; they followed trades subject to every fluctuation of the market, and lived under permanent threat of unemployment. It was no easy thing to escape this condition. For example Henry A, who worked for a butcher when he first met Alice M, later tried to set up as a dairyman. A long illness prevented him from getting the project off the ground. On leaving hospital he managed to find work in a City restaurant, but was still eager to have his own business. After some time he tried to get started by going into partnership with a friend. Three months later they were bankrupt and had to close down.[325]

When all else failed there was always the army, which at least offered secure employment; or the colonies, where everything seemed possible. 'The colonial empire of England. . . is one of the safety-valves of English society,' Charles Knight had written in 1840.[326]

What were they to do when they had met a girl, fallen in love with her, promised to marry her, and finally neglected one of the fundamental dogmas of lay and religious morality: control of the passions and the senses? They were not all liars, by any means. Many sincerely believed that they were deserting their woman and child only for a limited time. The precariousness of existence for the mass of the people made it difficult to imagine the sort of linear career conceived by the well-off. It meant that people often had to choose the lesser of two evils.

It could easily seem less cruel to leave mistress and child behind, in the hope that the situation would improve, than to risk dragging all three into a spiral of destitution. This was the reasoning used by James O, a policeman, in a letter to his fiancée's mother:

> I venture for a first time to address you on circumstances that are painful to me and no dout to you. it is this that I being present unemployed and no chance of employment in this town I will be compelled to leave here and you are aware that in your daughters present state I cannot or I might say it is not prudent for me to take her about with me as I have no particular place to go to, so under the circumstances she has made up her mind to go to Camden Town to morrow I therefore trust you will act a kind mothers part to her for the present, until I am able to assist her or till I get settled some place I trust you will keep her in best possible cheer and not form a bad opinion of me for I will act as honourable as I can. I do not feel that with my present feelings I can say anymore but believe me yours truly,
> James O.[327]

James did come back, a month before the confinement. But in this couple's case there was another complication standing in the way of marriage: he was a Catholic and refused to convert. The child's acceptance by the Foundling Hospital would enable the mother – or so she said – to leave the capital and emigrate.

The same sort of reasoning was probably at work in the case of Charles P, a butcher's worker who, in their courting days, had dreamed with his fiancée Mary Ann of emigrating to America and starting a new life there. When she became pregnant in March 1848 he left straight away, promising to send her a boat ticket as soon as possible so that she could come to join him. She waited a long time for news – as long as possible, it seems, for she did not decide to start adoption proceedings until the very last moment allowed by the Foundling Hospital. Did they ever meet again? We do not know. But the circumstances of separation are very different from those described earlier.

Here and there, a child's file contains specific information on the subsequent course of one of these life stories. Like that of George H, a jobbing carpenter of Spitalfields, and Amelia G, who had so many brothers and sisters that she was sent at the age of nine to live with distant relatives. They met in 1858 and began officially keeping company, going out together on their days off. One day when her uncle and aunt were out they made love in her room, but she was so terrified of pregnancy that after only two more occasions she refused to continue the sexual relationship. It was too late. When she knew she was pregnant, Amelia took lodgings. George H continued to help, sending her £4 a week, but could not make up his mind to marry her: he thought she should get the child a nurse and find a new job.

Perhaps George's behaviour was influenced by the suicide of his father, his only surviving parent. The result in any case was that on 18 October 1860 Amelia gave birth alone in her lodgings. A few days earlier the girl's uncle had had the banns published, hoping to encourage a last-minute marriage. Irritated by this move, which did not fit in with his immediate plans, George H disappeared the day after his son was born. And the mother duly presented herself a month later at the Foundling Hospital, which accepted her child.

However painful it may have been, this separation had undeniable advantages under all the circumstances. A reliable third party had undertaken to raise the child; the young mother could go back to work; and the father was free to seek elsewhere the means to support his family. The documents in the file do not say much about what became of him, or whether he eventually married Amelia. But about five years later, on 4 May 1865, he wrote to the hospital asking for his child to be returned to him:

> Sir,
>
> Not being able to attend myself I have writen to you – to acknowledge my being the Farther of the child named John T. entered in your Establishment on the 27 of November 1860 and with your kind permission Should like to Clame my child.
> Please accept my sincere thanks for your kindness
> George H.[328]

Letters from the fathers of these children sometimes display the sort of cruel fatalism forced upon people who despair of reconciling work with family life.

One mason from Islington waited until his daughter was five months old before deciding to desert her and look for work in the provinces. Perhaps without realizing it, he was following the advice of social observers, who tried to encourage professional mobility among the poor, and criticized them for cluttering up the London workhouses when there was employment to be had elsewhere. But he was demolishing the immediate plans he had made with Ellen E. Ellen was already thirty years old and had some small savings which she had been spending to set up home. After leaving her, Thomas O sent a letter whose defensive, bitter tone is ironically highlighted by the repeated allusions to happiness:

> Nov 11 1851
>
> Dear Ellen,
>
> I write to you these few lines to let you know that I am now on the road for Gloster I shall stay there all winter. if all is well. Do not make yourself unhappy. There is plenty of nice young men in holloway it is not in my power to make you happy if I was ever so willing. I never made you any promas that would case you to leve your place.
>
> So I wish you all the happyness that this world can aford and everlasting happyness in the next, farwell
> Thomas O.
> I shall write to you when I get to my jurney is end[329]

Finally, this correspondence illustrates the ideas people had about their lives and identifies the roles they assigned to love, sexuality, father-hood and marriage.

From the standpoint of the dominant ideology, extra-marital sexual relations and the birth of a bastard were seen as such serious moral errors that they justified specific measures, like the application of the Poor Law system and the deployment of a whole range of activities by the charitable societies. These efforts were not fruitless; our documents show clearly how transgressions were assimilated, sometimes painfully but without excessive guilt, into the happy or unhappy course of individual lives. So long as the father was showing a proper interest and struggling to improve his own material situation, many mothers waited without impatience. Their complaints, echoed in their lovers' letters, are about material worries and difficulties, rather than any feeling of shame or the fear that they may be marked with an indelible moral stain.

All the evidence suggests that these couples simply grouped the birth of their child, and their separation, with other unfortunate episodes in their lives; even if they retained a tenacious hope that one day another turn of fate might enable them to make up for – and at last forget – their mistakes. Here lies the vast ethical gulf which separated the social classes in the nineteenth century: because from the middle-class point of view, serious moral transgressions should cast a perma-nent blight on the future.

The characteristic attitude of the working classes can be seen in two sequences of letters. The first sequence is from a milkman, Thomas J, to Frances P, a housemaid aged twenty.[330] As none of the letters is dated we do not know the exact duration of this correspondence, but it certainly lasted less than a year. The first letter is devoted almost entirely to the young woman's state of health, and the urgent necessity for its author to go elsewhere in search of work. Written just after the birth of the child, it ends – like the second letter – with good wishes to the mother and baby. The second letter is full of depression and impotence mingled with hope:

Dear Fanny
I again just write a line to you to say that I am going all wrong for I have not got a place yet but I think I shall soon have one and then we shall be all write so you see I can not give you an adress yet for I have not got one Now jest rest contented

with your lot and hope for me for I will write to you again as soon as ever I can –
Then I hope to tell you some better news so until then believe me to remain ever the
same with love and kisses to you and baby.

The third letter is the last Frances received before she decided to
separate from her child. It suggests that things are beginning to look
up slightly. Subsequently, however, unforeseen events were to delay
the couple's reintegration and perhaps prevent it altogether.

My dear Fanny,
  I am very much surprised that you have not answered my letter that I wrote to
you on last Thursday week but I am now thinking that perhaps it was lost but
however now I will tell you now again that I have got on and am at South
Kensington station my number is No 15. Fanny I hope you are getting on all right
still as it leaves me at present but of course you know that we don't take any money
the first week so I can't send you any yet but I will as soon as I can and I hope soon to
have you up here along with me but that will take you a week or two as I borrowed a
£1 of a friend and then get what fund I can from home. Fanny I am rather unsettled
just now and am very busy so cannot say any more this time but will write to you
again as soon as I can. Please excuse awfully dirty paper.
  Yours ever
  the same Tom

The most abundant correspondence consists of a series of letters
from Gabriel B, a groom aged twenty-seven born in Gloucestershire,
to Mary Ann G, aged twenty. We have already seen some extracts.

The ten long letters were written between 23 March 1863, just after
the seduction, and 10 March 1864, when the baby was two months
old.

Mary Ann left London for a time, accompanying her mistress to
Scotland. She remained in this employer's house throughout most of
her pregnancy; when the father eventually disappeared, the same
mistress agreed to take her back into service. But her wages of six
shillings a week were too meagre to enable her to pay a nurse, and she
thus found herself before the Foundling Hospital committee.

It is a great pity that only half the correspondence between this
couple has been preserved. The passage of well over a century entitles
us to cast an intrusive, indiscreet eye over this very precious material.
When the first letter was written the child, a boy, was a week old. He

was soon to be put to nurse as the young mother was already eager to resume work. At this stage the father was in full agreement:

> *December 24th 1863*
>
> *My dear Mary Ann,*
>
>   *With the greatest of please and i am glad to hear that you and the child is all right and i quite agree with you about the child it will be cheapest and i will do all i can and if you get another place for a time and then we will have a home of our own please God i cant send you any money now but i understand it will be 5/- a week for the child you are coming home to London on Wednesday next but i did or else sent to you be fore. . .*

It was a happy time for Mary Ann; she was recovering her strength and beginning to grow fond of her child. All she lacked was a little money. Soon she even began to have ideas about living in indolent domestic happiness. It would be good not to have to look for jobs any more, to keep her child by her all the time, to look after him, to have a home. These were dreams without substance, as neither she nor Gabriel had a penny. No doubt they would have money before long, but they still had to wait a while. Gabriel began to worry that his poverty might look to her family like desertion, that she might become an object of scorn.

> *January 14, 1864*
>
> *My dear Mary Ann,*
>
>   *I am pleased to hear that you are both back quit safe and i am glad to hear that you got so well and when i hear from you again you will be right and strong you tell me you feel better now than you were twelve months ago you told me it was nice to have a child it is all for the best for you i will do all i can for it but i cant just at present i have been getting me some more clothes but if i had of been aware that would have been the case with you would not of had them for a time. . . send me word how the child is getting how you are also i shall have quit as much love towards you as before an i hop you will love me i should like you to come down here for a day or two. . . i am in the same lodgings and if you will come we have a sparebed so that you will be made all right. . . please to give my kind regards to your brothers and sisters and i hop they are well tell me if they dispise you i may waz will you do all you can and we will have a home as soon as we can and then it don't matter to anyone so that will be all this time. . .*

Eight days later, about a month after the birth of their son, Gabriel had still sent no money. But the young woman loved him as much as ever, and even seemed quite satisfied with life. She was getting slightly irritated, though, with the contrast between his ready promises and his stinginess in practice. Gabriel for his part had changed his mind about the baby: he had decided they could not afford a nurse, it would be more economical to take lodgings and look after him themselves. In the next letter he returns to the question of their social standing and proposes a discreet marriage whose date can be kept secret:

January 21 1864

My dear Mary Ann
    I received your kind and affectionate letter and i was glad to hear that you are as well as you are. . .
    i was very sorry that you where disapointed about the monney and i feel it as much as you i think about things and intend to do all for the best for you and the child i think it will be a great expence for us booth and what i tell you this time it will be for the best and i think you will think the same i think i can have furnished apartments and it would cost no more that it do for the child it wont cost so much for booth so i dont see why we should pay all that so i think it will be best for you and me to do so wee can get married down here on the quiet so that no one wont know at least I shall say we have been married over twelve months and you say the same and then it will take all disgrace from you now I think you will agree with me please send me answer next time the child name is alright i know you want the child with you and it is quite right for you to have it. . .

Mary Ann was thrilled. Not to have to separate from her child was, for the moment, all she desired. Of course she agreed to the new plan immediately. His letter dated 4 February is serene, even optimistic in tone. He was ready to join her as soon as she wished it. The only slight problem was her family, which seemed worried about the sincerity of this father who, incidentally, had still not sent a single penny. Gabriel seeks gently to prise Mary Ann away from her family – he may have feared a court action – and at the same time tries to get back into their good graces:

February 4 1864

My dear Mary Ann
    . . . we can take apartments for a time and then we will have a home of our own i have no fixed time so i shall leave that to you do all you can in return to Mrs Stone [her mistress] *for all kindness to you. . . as soon as you can leave to then we*

will arrange things but i have no fixed time So dont you leave to offend me in any
way will see you if all will before you go out if i have not sent you any money yet i
will make things all right with you when i come the child will be best to stay there till
you leave it will solve all trouble.

i will let you know before i come and i thank you and your brother for your kind
offer and invitation i shall be only to happy to be in your company. . .

After this reassuring letter, Gabriel gave no sign of life for over a
fortnight. He had moved jobs and a problem had arisen, about which
he remained vague. Mary Ann complained bitterly. Her family
seemed to have been tormenting her with nasty remarks about the
phantom father. In an eighth letter he tries once again to reassure and
encourage her.

. . . Let me beg of you not to be so down hearted i will do all i can to make you
happy i think so much about you if i have been to see you so dont think any other
way. . . for i think more about things as you for i can see how you are treated and
when you are away from all of them you will be much happier than you are now so i
shall have it to you about comming to me i shall have to try hour luck and i am not
the least afraid that we shall soon be all right dear Mary Ann. . . it of no use to frett
now we must put up with things now it is as much trouble to me as you for i want to
do the best for you and myself to the child is allright. . .

By 26 February the child had finally been placed with a nurse, whom
the father was promising to pay. He urged Mary Ann to come and join
him; her family, which had initially been fairly reserved, was becoming openly hostile.

. . . any time that you think well You shall have a home as I have told you before all
that i want is for you to come to be with me. So i hop you will do so please send me
the address where the child is at and i will writ to them so that the money shall be
paid all right. . .

send me word how much money there is to pay up so i hop you will soon come
to be with me and i hop my dear Mary Ann you will be happy you shall never want
for a home so the sooner you are away from them the better. . .

Mary Ann's sister now went to see Gabriel. In a letter written soon
after her departure he heaps praises on the sister's goodness and on the
wisdom of her suggestions. Sincerely or not, he mentions the good
impression left by the visitor five times in the space of a short letter.

Otherwise this last missive is pretty vague. Gabriel is still unable to get away from work:

March 10 1864

> *My dear Mary Ann,*
>   *. . . dont you think it unkind of me that i have not been up to see you before now i have the same love for you now that i had twelve months ago so i hop you will make yourself happy and i hop your dear sister got home alright my dear Mary Ann You have one kind sister and the way that she wants to arrange things it will be all for the best so let me beg of you to make yourself happy. . . excuse my short letter this time i can't any more this time i am at work all the time i can now please give my kind regards to your sister and my kindest love to you so that will be all this time you ever true and affectionate*
>   *G.B. . . .*

When Mary Ann arrived to join him, Gabriel had disappeared.

Seduced and abandoned

The young women whose statements we have been examining – and whom we know to have been sufficiently determined to get through the Foundling Hospital's admission procedures without major *faux pas* – were people who proved in adversity to have great strength of will and a certain physical robustness.

All – or nearly all – continued working as long as possible, usually for as long as their employers would keep them on the payroll. Quite a few managed to keep their condition secret until they went into labour. This phenomenon, widespread at the time, always surprises twentieth-century readers. It is forgotten nowadays just how completely petticoats and aprons disguised the outlines of the body, and to what extent plump figures were taken for granted, whether as a sign of prosperity[331] or of some medical condition.[332]

Mary Ann G, whose love life we have just considered at some length, revealed her pregnancy to her mistress – with whom she had lived in close proximity for several years – only three weeks before confinement.

In Lambeth, where Ruth Y lived with her father, no friend or neighbour noticed anything amiss:

None of my relatives knew I was pregnant until I was actually confined.[333]

any more than Emma Y's workmates in the lace workshop of a big fashion house:

> *This situation Petitioner relinquished the day before her confinement, her condition being quite unsuspected by other employees with the exception of the forewoman who pitied her and treated her kindly.[334]*

Twenty years earlier another Emma, this one a chambermaid, had described a similar experience. Judging by the way her mistress and the manservant who had seduced her reacted to the news, she had excellent reasons for concealing her pregnancy from everybody:

> *I was taken ill and confined suddenly in the house no one knowing previously of my condition. . . . Father decamped suddenly on hearing of my confinement,[335]*

she told the committee. The Foundling Hospital's inquirer describes her employer's attitude with slightly malicious irony:

> *Mrs. Y. keeps a boarding school for young ladies, she is an elderly maiden lady, and views the subject of Petitioner's disgrace with much repugnance. She is extremely anxious that the birth of Petitioner's child, which occurred immediately after the pupils had left the house for the midsummer vacation should be kept a secret.*

Sometimes the secret was kept so well that a maidservant managed to give birth in her employer's house and nurse the baby for days before its cries drew attention. Not everyone had the good fortune of Isabella T, a chambermaid whose employer, a retired military surgeon, was able to help with her delivery (which lasted thirty hours!)[336] Another wrote:

> *My situation was not discovered 'til the day of my confinement. . . I was removed from Eccleston Sq.* [where she had been employed as a chambermaid] *a fortnight after my confinement.[337]*

While these hard-working, pain-resistant mothers-to-be were still carrying their babies, their lives retained a semblance of order and tranquillity. But at the moment of confinement, and during the early postnatal period, they were suddenly exposed to the full cruelty of their situation, and might get a first taste of extreme destitution.

Even then, those who had savings, or were still getting support from fiancé or family, were bothered only by fears for the future. During this short respite they were sheltered by friends or took furnished lodgings. We should note that in every decade studied, this group was by far the largest. But what of the others? When labour pains began they were, so to speak, in the street with nowhere to go. The choice was between hospital and workhouse.

The bulk of Foundling Hospital petitioners had been confined either at Queen Charlotte's Hospital in Bayswater or at the General Lying-In Hospital in Westminster Bridge Road.

Both were founded for the care of 'the wives of poor industrious tradesmen, or distressed housekeepers'. From 1810 onward the General Lying-In Hospital, to discourage suicide and infanticide, accepted unmarried mothers on condition that the child was their first. They were segregated from other patients in a special department.

At Queen Charlotte's Hospital, too, only 'deserving unmarried women with their first child' were accepted. They were allowed to stay for fourteen days; at the end of this fortnight, the hospital would recommend suitable candidates to ladies who wanted to employ a wet nurse for their own babies.

Both hospitals required women to submit their marriage certificates. If they could not do so, they were expected to display an appropriate attitude of humility and repentance. Any subsequent help from the Foundling Hospital, or one of the temporary shelters which existed for the purpose, depended partly on whether this posture was deemed satisfactory.

St Mary Magdalene's Home in Paddington, which required the young mothers to stay for at least a year, had been founded

> . . . to endeavour to rescue those who have once fallen, to aid them in obtaining situation, and to assist them in placing their children out to nurse.

In Kilburn, Queen Charlotte's Convalescent Home had been founded in 1822

> . . . to provide a temporary refuge for single women with their first child, who on leaving Queen Charlotte's Hospital are too weak to return to service, and who have no friends who will receive them.

Others included the Temporary Home for Friendless Women in Crawford Street; the Home for Single Women who have Fallen for the First Time, in Carlton Road; the Home for Deserted Mothers and their Children, Great Coram Street, founded '. . . to provide a temporary home for women after their first fall and to help in boarding children out when mothers are placed in service'; St Cyprian's Beth Esda in Dorset Square, founded for 'the reformation of Girls of the Servant Class, under 18 years of age'; St George's Home, Mount Row, 'to receive girls under 20 years of age, after a first fall'; and The Anchorage in St John's Wood.

The girls' conduct while they were staying in these places, the visitors who came to see them, the plans and ideas they innocently revealed, were all noted and used in evidence for or against them when the time came to find a job or go through a Foundling Hospital inquiry. Of Louisa K, who had been confined at Queen Charlotte's Hospital, the Head Sister declared approvingly that she had been visited by

> . . . several highly respectable ladies who appeared to take much interest in petitioner – and spoke much in her favour respecting her former general conduct.[338]

The Sister Superior of St Saviour's Hospital wrote of a woman who had been confined there:

> . . . I found Martha Q. a hard working, industrious woman during her stay here (of 2 months) which character also her late mistress gave her and considered her greatly ruined against by her seducer.
> Wishing others similarly situated now here could partake of the bounty. . .[339]

But although Sarah Z's conduct had been satisfactory during a three-month stay at a Holloway shelter, 'the probability of her having been previously upon the street was hinted at'.[340]

The supervisor of the Newington workhouse gives by implication a very precise idea of the sort of attitude he judged appropriate in fallen women:

> . . . She was some time an inmate of this workhouse and during her stay here her conduct was uniformly good. . . . She was willing to do the work allotted to her and was civil and obliging. She always expressed a great desire of bettering her condition

but from the unfortunate circumstances that has occurred she was prevented doing so. . .[341]

Everything was noted: excessively loud cries during delivery, signs of irritation or impatience, coarse language – all were liable to go down on the record. Those who were confined at home escaped this close surveillance. Only one landlady in our sample shows an intolerant attitude, declaring to the Foundling Hospital inquirer:

> *Petitioner was confined of a male child. Petitioner's conduct was not correct, she refused to suckle her child until the Dr. insisted on her placing it to the breast as there was a good supply of natural food.[342]*

Many applicants came to the Foundling Hospital from nearby workhouses: St Pancras, Marylebone, Strand Union, St Giles's, St Luke's, Clerkenwell, Islington, and even as far afield as Kensington, Lambeth or Greenwich. Several had been rushed to the workhouse already in labour, like Alice T:

> *On Xmas day, being taken in labour in the street, while on a errand, I got into a cab and went to my sister, who, having no accomodation, I was obliged to go to Clerkenwell workhouse where I was confined and remained 10 days. . .[343]*

Others stayed for weeks or even months. Where else could a penniless eighteen-year-old orphan seamstress like Susan P find shelter? Where could she stay alive and feed a baby, except somewhere like the Lewisham workhouse where she lived for six months?

Pauperism, the social observers called it. Indigence. Idleness. The passive indifference of half-beasts. Culpable depression: they put on their institutional stockings and wait dully for their pittance.

If we consult our sources, however, we discover that on the contrary, doctors and friends could not help noticing how acutely the women feared the future. The files of the General Lying-In Hospital contain tragic references to the intense anxiety which afflicted many unmarried mothers. In the hospital's Case Books can be found, for example, an account of the case of Louisa N, aged twenty, who gave birth to a stillborn child. She was

> *. . . a large made woman who states that about a fornight before admission after*

walking to the hospital and back home again (some considerable distance) she felt a pain in and about the rectum perineus. . . her situation being single has caused her to fret a great deal and being poor to live badly.[344]

Mary P

. . . suffered from excessive mental sufferings also had an absece in Breast. after labour was seized with puerperal mania (alias delirium from exhaustion) calomel and antimony were administered by Dr. Hutton. Brandy, opium and porter by Dr. Cape and myself but she sank and died after 10 days.[345]

Sophie T's father reported in a letter to the Foundling Hospital:

. . . For it appears from what the matron told her mother that she did nothing but fret during the time she was in the hospital although she had such good treatment.[346]

Amelia Z's baby was born prematurely as a result of its mother's 'mental anxiety'.[347]

In addition to the pain of desertion and their fears for the future, these women had to contend with physical exhaustion, difficult to avoid even if their health was good, as they were usually obliged to go straight back to work. They thus tended to appear at the Foundling Hospital in a weakened state, having tried to resume work without taking a proper rest after childbirth. Mary Ann A, an eighteen-year-old housemaid, did not last long at the refuge where she was placed after leaving hospital. The inquirer reported:

The poor girls strength was quite unable to do the hard scrubbing and other work required to the inmates directly after a confinement and the Manager will not keep the infant without the Mother.[348]

One more ordeal remained: to endure the pain of separation from their child. Elizabeth D was in the same position as many other petitioners. At the end of her statement, which spells out faithfully and soberly, in words which bring tears to the reader's eyes, the litany of her misfortunes, she appends this appeal:

Gentlemen: This is all true, indeed it is. I have left my situation 7 weeks, when they never knew or suspected my misfortune; and now I'm nearly starving, quite destitute, and shall soon have nowhere to hide the little child. Please take it and give me an other opportunity of beginning life afresh. Your servant.[349]

It was almost impossible to feed a child, let alone pay for boarding or a nurse, on a salary barely sufficient for the ordinary costs of a single person. Ann D, to take a clear example, could call on nobody in London for help, having arrived there alone leaving a widowed mother in Ireland. Some time before confinement she left her job and took furnished lodgings in Greek Street. When the time came, she went to St Anne's workhouse to have the child; after staying there for ten days, she decided to go back to her lodgings. Arriving at the house half dead from cold and fatigue, late in the winter of 1853, she found there were no rooms free and

> *. . . passed the night with her baby on the common stair leading to the street.*[350]

She managed to keep alive until her child was admitted to the Foundling Hospital by pawning a few old clothes. Not all these life stories are as terrible as Ann's, but many women lived in what the committee's inquirer called 'great poverty', 'ulcerated', emaciated and weakened.

All in all, it was a most wretched procession of helpless shadows, bowed down with suffering, which filed past the committee's desk. One would expect that such miserable creatures would have become submissive, that some at least would admit feelings of shame or repentance. None did, however, not one – surprisingly, given that any show of breast-beating and hair-tearing would have impressed their reformers. Sometimes, especially if her family lived in the provinces, a woman would ask that her father or mother should not be informed of 'the present circumstances'. This was ostensibly to avoid worrying them, but would also have left undisturbed any illusions they might have had about a daughter getting on well in the capital. It was rare, too, for a woman to try to convince her landlady that she was legally married.

Another astonishing thing about the girls was their pugnacity. These young workers had not subsided into indigence, or agreed to place their children with a public charity, without a fierce struggle. Whenever they could, with the support of family or friends, they took legal action against their seducers – usually in the form of a paternity suit, sometimes of an action for breach of promise.

Until the Poor Law reform of 1834 it had been fairly easy to compel a man to honour a promise of marriage, or at least support his child born out of wedlock. Popular culture and tradition retained traces of these customs, and comic representations of reluctant seducers being forced to support their bastards were common. In 'I Never Take no Notice' (a song satirizing busybodies and neighbourhood gossip) a baker's boy called Carroty Bill

> . . . done a thing I heard 'em say
> No odds to me it may be,
> He's got a half-a-crown a week to pay
> For Mary Wilson's baby.[351]

and in 'The Muslin':

> She brought forth a son – so they say,
> But quickly the tailor was missing,
> She vow'd that she would make him pay,
> For nobody else she'd been kissing;
> She took him before the old beak,
> Who told him, instead of his guzzling,
> He must fork out a half-crown a week,
> If he would run after the muslin.
>
> So young gents I'd have you take care,
> Never run after the ladies,
> Or a half-crown I declare,
> You'll have to pay each of your pay-days. . .[352]

To relieve parish funds of the burden, the law had formerly supported the right of deserted women to some sort of subsistence allowance. Under laws passed in 1662 and 1733, and modified under George II and George III, women had the right and the duty to prosecute a man they deemed to be the father of their child; if convicted he was compelled to marry the mother or pay an allowance, in lieu of which his goods could be seized or he could be imprisoned. The allowance paid by the father, or by the parish administration should he default, went to the unmarried mother.

The new Poor Law passed in 1834 altered these arrangements fundamentally. Members of the commissions of inquiry which prepared the 1834 law violently attacked the moral depravity which was supposed to have been encouraged, especially among women, by the old regulations. Strongly influenced by Malthusian theories, the commissions asserted that hitherto the law had implicitly 'legalized' pre-marital sexual relations and encouraged the celebration of improvised marriages. It was claimed that this made socially undesirable births more likely.

Much was also made of the great cost to the community of supporting increasing numbers of mothers and illegitimate children, since parishes were now finding it difficult to make the fathers pay up. Finally, it was said that some women and some parish officials had exploited the old arrangements in a corrupt manner; that women of doubtful morals had thus been able to marry men with comfortable incomes; that this means of husband-hunting had been encouraged in some families; and that parish authorities had sometimes colluded in these manoeuvres by compelling 'innocent' men to marry.

After interminable debates the 'bastardy clauses' were added to the Poor Law, withdrawing from unmarried mothers all legal aid and all material aid other than that dispensed by workhouses. For it was important to conform to natural law by making a bastard 'what providence seems to have decided it should be: a burden to its mother or, failing that, to her parents'.

At a stroke, paternity suits and actions for perjury or breach of promise were reduced to symbolic status. Some petitioners still tried, despite everything, to ensure that their rights were respected. Very few succeeded. Annie V, for example, had insufficient evidence of her lover's guilt. Sarah I failed to make her seducer appear in court:

> The case was brought before the Magistrate at Marylebone Police Court. Two summons were issued and served at the Father's without effect. The Father's friends appeared and produced a letter for the Father which satisfied the Magistrate that the Father was not forthcoming. The Father being at sea on his way to New Zealand. . . . Petitioner made her statement to the court in a straightforward manner, and her case was considered a hard one, by the Magistrate, who gave her five shillings through compassion.[353]

The case brought by Dorcas Y, an apprentice dressmaker aged twenty, turned against her: she herself, the police court decided, had set a matrimonial trap for Henry J, a quartermaster some twenty-five years her senior. Her local vicar confirmed this in his evidence to the committee:

> *I am sorry I cannot speak favourably of the general conduct of Petitioner and her family and as far as I can make out the present case is marked by much misconduct that does not make the unhappy mother of this illegitimate child the object for pity that one sometimes feels. She has attempted to father it on a man I believe to be innocent. . .*[354]

When the courts did find in the mother's favour, the father usually wasted no time in putting himself out of reach. In 1866 Eleanor O, for example, obtained an order for £100 compensation for breach of promise from a clerk aged thirty. She never received the money. Sophie D was supposed to receive a weekly allowance of 2s 6d. The father started the payments, then suddenly stopped them.[355] Dinah Y was ordered to be paid the same amount by Clerkenwell magistrates on 3 January 1857, but the father could not be traced and never paid.[356]

Georgina T obtained a judgement for repayment of sums she had lent her lover, John A. When she applied for admission to the Foundling Hospital he was being sought by the police for bigamy, for John A had agreed publicly to marry her, and banns had been posted.[357]

Seducers knew perfectly well that these actions had little chance of success. Numerous letters and statements make it clear that they no longer had much to fear from the rigours of the law. When Vincent Y, a jobbing tailor, was asked for compensation, he replied that 'he'd do no more than the law compelled him'.[358] Walter A, a harness-maker, told his fiancée's father that

> *He would not pay a farthing unless compelled, intimating that he would soon be out of the way,*[359]

and Augustus T, a baker's assistant, reacted in the same way to pressure from his fiancée's employers:

> *Mr. Burns threatened him, when born the child would be sworn to him when he replied that he would not give her the chance to do that for he should go over the water.*[360]

And of course, when a man signed on in the army, all hope of prosecuting him was lost for ever. Otherwise, though, even if the action failed get any help for the mother, it was likely to force the father to leave his job, and sometimes to leave town, as well as making trouble for him with his family. Vengeful feelings may well have played a part in bringing these cases.

John C's letters illustrate this clearly, for he suggests that two can play at that game. A butler aged twenty-nine, who had been engaged to a workmate (a cook), he was also an addicted gambler who first learned of his friend's pregnancy just after losing all his savings.

> *27 November 1865*
>
> *. . . It is of no use for you to throw out any threats to me as it will only make me more obstinate you said you had a great mind to go to my Mother for her to take you in do you think for one moment that she would for I know her too well. . . for then I swear I will never give you a farthing until I was made to . . .*
>
> *. . . But if you cause anything unpleasant with my Mother and me I myself will write to your mother and send one or 2 of your letters and they will see. . .*

By March 1866 the baby was a month old and Annie Q, ignoring its father's threats, had informed both families. John's tone is still threatening, but it is clear that he feels beleaguered:

> *It is of no use for me to say that I can come to any terms for I cannot get a place and my Father has told me that I had better soon get away. . . it has made a great change since your mother or you I do not know which wrote to my mother. . . . You say you will get the law to protect you but you will not so expose yourself and me so much as that for if it comes to that I will pawn the last thing that I have to defend me and then perhaps it will not be all your way. . .[361]*

In a farewell letter to Ruth C, Jonathan J lists the options open to a man on the run from his fiancée, and accuses her of making things unnecessarily difficult for both of them:

> *I have left my situation as I could not think of stopping after you saying you had wrote to Mr. J. more over I cannot send for a character to him what if that I got another place but I must try to get in some Hotel. I mean to go to Manchester or Liverpool I dont know which yet and if I can't get something soon I shall try to get in the police or if I miss at that I must go for a soldier as I am no trade and I wont do any work if you had not written to my master – as you said you had I should have been able to have done something. . .[362]*

But the mothers did not all engage in vengeful behaviour, and some, doubtless wishing to put their mistake behind them as soon as possible, refrained from going to the law – like Mary Q, a chamber-maid who refused to have anything more to do with the father of her child, a coachman, even though he had promised her marriage:

> I wish to break off all communication with the Father. He is a man of bad habits and character. He never denied paternity;[363]

or Martha Y, aged eighteen, who thought her lover, an apprentice printer, too immature for fatherhood:

> Father is not aware of my having a child nor do I wish it.[364]

Frances J refrained because the man who had promised to marry her was in the final stages of tuberculosis.[365] Parents, employers and supervisors often give full support to these decisions.

Even after all hope of marriage, or at least regular material aid, had been lost, many of these women held out for as long as they could before resigning themselves to separation from their child. Best placed were women who had an ample supply of milk, and made a good enough impression on the hospital or workhouse to be recommended as wet nurses. For this they were paid 19s a week, a considerable salary for the time, and were fed well to ensure that the foster child would not go hungry. This enabled them to pay a nurse for their own child. But when the foster child was weaned – after about a year – this largesse came to an end. Even if their employers liked them and wanted to keep them on, they could no longer afford to board their own child on an ordinary domestic's salary. Hence the letter in support of Maria Z's application to the Foundling Hospital from Mrs Y, who had employed her as a wet nurse for her own child:

> She has been paying 7/- a week for the maintenance of her child which charge she can no longer sustain, as her duties as a wet nurse have ceased. The hour of separation from her present home is much dreaded by her as she has no place to go other than the workhouse of which she has a great horror from her past experience there.

Maria had spent four months in the St Pancras shelter before her confinement.[366]

Sometimes the girl's family was able to help. The son of Nancy Y, who worked as a folder, was suckled for some time by his own grandmother, whose baby had died. But the household was so poor – eight people crammed into two small rooms in an overcrowded Blackfriars alley – that eventually the child had to be sent for adoption.[367]

These family arrangements could also be upset by disagreements, as Rose P explained in a letter to the Foundling Hospital:

> *I have received a letter from my mother this afternoon to say she cannot have the child any longer as her husband has a great objection to her keeping I beg to state it is not my father at caused my mother great uneasiness having a large family of her own to support by her own exertion as her husband will not support her entirely. . .* [368]

Despite everything, these mothers still hoped that by suffering great privations if necessary they might contrive to work for a living and raise the child themselves. Margaret D, whose child was born in July 1862, managed to pay its boarding costs until Christmas. Then the woman who had been looking after it for an exceptionally low fee moved away, and Margaret could find no substitute for less than four shillings a week – her exact salary as a chambermaid. She left her job and tried to live with her baby in the workhouse; but after a while made up her mind to separate from it.[369]

The inquirer wrote of Emma E, aged twenty, that she had

> *used every exertion to place herself in a position which would enable her to retain her child. . . her last effort was to apply to Marylebone workhouse for a little pecuniary assistance; but the cruel repulse she met with there determined her to accept the proferred aid of Your Institute.* [370]

Skilled workers fared little better: Ann M, a dressmaker, fetched up at the Foundling Hospital after ten months of struggle, owing considerable arrears to her child's nurse.[371] Even with the help of a brother or sister, these efforts usually ended in failure. Isabella Y's whole family contributed to the seven shillings a week charged by the nurse. Isabella had given birth secretly in a corner of St Thomas' Hospital, where one of her sisters was a night attendant.[372]

After devoting herself to a child's survival for months on end, spending all her earnings and most of her strength to keep it alive, it must have taken an immense effort of will for one of these mothers to turn round and implore the hospital to take the baby away.

People were not always brought to the Foundling Hospital by lack of money alone. For a few mothers it represented an honourable way of hiding a mistake, but these were only a small minority. In most cases the long delay before a reluctant application, the expressions of sorrow, the compulsive explanations for applying at all, the many reservations included in the statements, project sadness, not shame. Mary P's first letter to the hospital is an illustration. She was twenty years old and had been working as a housemaid when a baker's assistant made her pregnant.

> *I have made up my mind to part with my baby as I find my mother is very changeable so I think it is much better to study my child's welfare before my own feeling as I am unable to support myself in a proper manner it would be much better to have her taken care of but I hope you will pardon the liberty I have taken to ask you if I can hear of my child by inquiry on Monday and if she should die would they please let me know of it as I feel it a great trial to part from her and I beg to state it is not the disgrace that persuades me to part with her, pure necessity compells me to do so hoping sire you will forgive me the trouble I have given you when am I to bring her sir if you would be kind enough to let me know. . .[373]*

Few of the statements are as moving as this one. But everywhere in the archive one discerns the conflict between necessity and mother-love, between a woman's wish to have her child properly fed and clothed, and the grim prospect of never seeing it again, or even knowing whether it was alive or dead.

The inquirer, Mr Twiddy, explains why Louisia O, a tapestry-maker aged thirty-one, has finally decided to let her child go:

> *Petitioner is deeply distressed at the thought of parting with her child and declares she has put off, from month to month, her application to the Institution in the hope of being able to support her child but her declining health renders her incapable.[374]*

Annie I had been trying to raise her baby alone for nine months when she applied. Her (woman) employer wrote:

> *However hard she tries the difficulty to keep herself respectable and pay 5/- per week*

for the child besides clothes is next to impossible and the trial seems to depress her at times so much that I must beg most urgently your kind sympathy in taking her child; it will I am sure be hard for her to part with it but still I can see nothing else that can be done. . .[375]

Another story of misery, distress, fierce struggle and powerlessness is that of Margaret A, forced to separate from her child very much against her will. Her mother, a home-based washerwoman, was utterly infuriated by what had happened to her. On learning that Margaret was pregnant she threw her out into the street, hoping perhaps to compel the child's father to meet his obligations. The couple did in fact then live together for several weeks. But the girl's troubles were not at an end; her intended, an assistant butcher, was dismissed from his job for theft. When her time came Margaret took shelter in the St Pancras workhouse, emerging a few weeks later to find that the father had married someone else. But she still wanted to keep the child. It was only after several months that she was brought to the point of writing:

Sir having taken it into consideration about parting with my child i shall feel most thankful if you will receive it as my friends so very much wish it and any time that you wish i will attend. . .[376]

There is a mass of evidence for these mothers' attachment to their children, their continuing solicitude for their welfare:

I was then confined at Queen Charlotte's Hospital with a beautiful little boy I was very ill and kept the bed for several months. . . . I am still in a very weak state I am quite unable to keep my poor little boy. . .[377]

declared Eleanor O in her application. At the workhouse where Sophie O was living, the authorities noted that

Her devotion to her baby has been motherly and it is purely in the childs interest that she applys for a place. . .[378]

After her child was born, Georgina Z found a new job as a housemaid in Camden Town. According to her employer, she then became worried about the way her baby was being looked after:

She therefore, requested to leave her (informant's) service so as to nurse the child herself, at her grandfather's house, until she could get it better provided for when she would gladly return to her (informant) service.[379]

Some mothers, having put off separation for as long as possible, began writing to the hospital authorities soon afterwards. Sarah E, a domestic aged twenty-six whose son was admitted on 5 September, wrote less than a week later to ask for news of him:

Dear Sir,
I hope you will excuse me troubling you so soon but I feel very anxious about my Baby if you will be kind enough to let me know you will oblige your humble servant. . .[380]

And a few, like Emma T, who worked as a domestic in Belgravia, found the separation so unbearable that they retrieved the child. A month and a half after Emma's child had been admitted, the Foundling Hospital's inquirer brought these facts to the committee's notice:

. . . She declares that the separation from her child acts upon her mind in such a manner as to injure her health and unfit her for her duties as a servant. She has agreed with her uncle and aunt, Mr. and Mrs. T., to receive and maintain her child. Your enquirer has visited Mr. and Mrs. T. at their residence, and ascertained that Mr. T. is a coach wheeler in the employ of Messr. M. His wages average 30/- a week. They have only one child – a daughter who is married – they state that they had no knowledge whatever of the existence of petitioner's child nor of the circumstances connected with its birth till three weeks ago. . . . Mr. and Mrs. T. appear to be respectable persons and seem anxious to have charge of the child, the responsibility of which they appear fully to comprehend.[381]

Mary Y managed in similar fashion to find a way of continuing to see her child, if only occasionally. She too wrote six weeks after the child's admission, as the arrangements had obviously taken time to finalize. She had already waited eleven months before deciding to place the baby. Then, after many attempts, she managed to persuade the mother of her lover (a Knightsbridge restaurant waiter who had emigrated to America) to look after her grandson:

March 26th 1864

Sir,

    Pardon the liberty i take in writing these few lines to you but i have wrote to ask weather you would be so kind has to lett me have my little boy out as the father's mother of my child wishes verry much to take him and bring him up as there own i am truly sorry to think that i have given you so much trouble hoping you will not refuse me this favour. . .[382]

Some time later, the committee having apparently given a favourable answer, she wrote again as follows:

I beg to inform you that if possible i will be sure and attend the Committee on Saturday morning next and if you could make it convenient for me so that i should only have to come up once as i shall not be able to come up again being in service and so expensive and if you thought that if all was satisfactory anyone else could fetch the child or should i require to bring any clothes with me i am very sorry to give you so much trouble but i have got a very nice place and i should like to keep it. . .[383]

Even where this providential family aid was lacking, mothers were comforted by the hope that they might one day be able to take their child back and care for it. A month after her child was born, Eliza T, installed in a new job, was already dreaming that by 'saving her wages . . . she might somehow repair the wrong she has done to her child'.[384]

These hopes were not always illusory: sometimes the longed-for reunion did take place. Amelia D, who at the age of eighteen left her newborn baby at the Foundling Hospital, wrote four years later asking for permission to take the child with her to Australia.[385] When she married, five years after leaving her daughter, Elizabeth O wrote to ask whether a woman friend and protector would be allowed to collect the child from the hospital.[386] Frances I, a kitchenmaid aged twenty-five, eventually married her child's father five years after the event. The couple returned to the Foundling Hospital together and left with their little daughter.[387]

What, then, characterized the reaction of these mothers to their misfortune, to the unforeseen and crushing responsibility with which they were faced?

First, they were in no way ashamed of their love for their children. Their attitude is in sharp contrast with this sad lullaby, in which a child's tears represent

A mother's fault, a father's shame,
A hapless state, a bastard's name –
Balow, my babe, weep not for me. . .[388]

Nor is there anything rebellious in their attitude; nor any attempt to repudiate the immoral relations of which the child is the fruit, except in a single case at odds with all the others. It concerns a tailor's family in Aldgate, where Jessica I, a Jewish girl of eighteen, fell in love with a Gentile. She concealed her pregnancy until confinement and never saw her child, who was removed while she was unconscious and put immediately to nurse. From the time of its birth in May to its adoption in August, she made no attempt to see it.

Thus there is no sign of the indifference and callousness – supposedly engendered by the presence of too many children, too often carried off at an early age by disease – which were perpetually denounced by philanthropic associations, doctors and health visitors. Well into the twentieth century, public health institutions were still criticizing mothers of the labouring classes for 'ignorance and fecklessness'.[389] Worse still, it was claimed, the poor neglected their children more or less deliberately in the knowledge that if they died there would be one less mouth to feed. 'Babies abounded,' recalls Margaret Nevinson, a former Whitechapel rent collector, 'meeting with scanty welcome at their birth, and chiefly conventional regret at their death. . .'[390]

The admission files in no way support this view. On the contrary, even though the mothers, their parents and families were often much too poor to be able to feed another mouth, they made extraordinary, heroic efforts to ensure the survival and well-being of these bastard children.

Family and friends

One hundred and sixty-four of the admission files in our sample make no allusion to the family's attitude, while several dozen others indicate that the petitioner's family knew nothing of her pregnancy. Of course many applicants were orphans or had only tenuous contact with their families in the remote provinces.

The majority of cases give the consistent impression that where their views were expressed, the family – parents, sometimes grand-parents, but especially aunts, brothers and sisters – reacted to the misfortunes of the Foundling Hospital's young postulants in a tolerant and reassuring manner. Often the family had been more or less attentive bystanders during the girl's affairs of the heart. When misfortune struck, they moved into the role of sympathetic confidants.

The first and most natural reaction was to try to force the perjurer to honour his promise: he would be hunted down at home or at work, and new assurances would be extracted:

> *I last saw Father at my brothers who pressed him to marry me. My brother, since my confinement has sought for Father, in vain.*[391]

> *. . . In February my mother discovered my condition and accused the Father and talked to him very severely and he kept on saying he would marry me but after Nov. he never came near me and my mother went to his lodgings but he'd gone away.*[392]

The mother of Sophie M, who had been abused by her employer with his wife's complicity, went to see the wife and

> *. . . threatened to knife her. My mother went to the magistrate but nothing could be done until the child was born.*[393]

On learning that his daughter was pregnant, Martha T's father, a former steward with seven other children, fell into a violent fury. He went to see the young carpenter responsible and

> *in his first bursts of anger at this disclosure. . . threatened Father with personal chastisement. Father immediately decamped.*[394]

The anger was sometimes reciprocated, and fierce quarrels broke out between families, especially when the couple were very young. All for nothing, as the lover usually took to the hills before he could be found:

> *My mother enquired at Mr. E.'s and learnt that Father was discharged.*[395]

> *After the birth of the child* [the mother] *sought for him at 10 Dean St., Holborn, but without effect.*[396]

*My mother immediately sought the Father at his home found that he had gone. . .
no one knew whither. I never heard of him since.[397]*

*My mother went to the butler of Father's previous employer's house, for Father's
address and he gave it but I did not go to address after him as butler said Father was
married with one child.[398]*

Events of this sort, almost identical except for names and places, are
described in statement after statement, decade after decade.

Very occasionally, we come across a family which refused to help
the girl when she announced her pregnancy. The father of Matilda O,
a sick man who had seen better days, declared to the Hospital
committee:

*I have no means to support the child and feel that in my state I could ill bear the noise
and worry of a baby and to be daily reminded of my child's shame and disgrace.[399]*

According to Mary Ann D's file her mother, an elderly domestic
working in Ireland, 'has entirely discarded her'.[400] The case of Sophia
P, a lacquer worker, suggests that some very poor parents, who had
been greatly relieved to see their daughter earning her living at last,
could become so exasperated on seeing her instantly 'caught' through
a thoughtless adventure that they would not have her back in the
house, especially burdened with a child. Sophia had been seduced by
her employer, Augustus E, but after they had lived together for three
months he had married someone else. Then her parents would have
nothing to do with her; she was taken in by a sister whose house-
painter husband was out of work. Attached to Sophia's file is a letter
written by her mother to two of her sisters, a document which is
especially interesting in that it is wholly private, not written for any
official purpose:

*. . . i now take up my pen to write after waiting so long and not hearing from you
you must not be offended at my not writing before as i have had such a very heavy
trial about your sister Sophia she was confined on last saturday with a little boy by
Mr E. and he got her to take the shop and E. has botted off to America and left his
wife and family behind him. . . now you know the reason I have not wrote because I
had nothing but bad news to tell you. . . we never found it out till after he was gone
because she denied it since I wrote last to you you must know that her father is very
indignant against her and has forbid me going to see her and you must know that I*

have a nice life on it I have started to write several times but could not have courage to send you word before and i hope you will excuse me sending you so much of my trouble your sister Susan is still at the old place and they enquire about you. . .[401]

Sometimes a pregnancy could cause real family dramas. Such was the case with Ruth P of Camberwell, whose invalid mother ran a family boarding-house. Her father had worked for the same firm, Meeds, for years, and had sent Ruth to Sunday school. The family had lived in the same neighbourhood for sixteen years. When the lover had been tracked down, and refused to contribute to the child's maintenance, the Foundling Hospital's inquirer notes,

> . . . *The dread of exposure, which an application to a police court would bring upon Petitioner's parents constrains them to keep the case a secret, which they have hitherto done at the cost of the destruction of their peace of mind.[402]*

In the end they decided it would be better to abandon everything – house, business and neighbourhood – than to risk anyone finding out about their daughter's disgrace:

> *Parents and girl removed to their present house when the child was born, and where they live alone, estranged from their friends and under the hope that the child may be received into the Foundling Hospital and so relieve petitioner and her parents from the cause which now oppresses them heavily.[403]*

A less agonizing case, but one also dealt with in total secrecy, was that of Ellen P, a machinist. Her family had lived for twenty years at the same address in Highgate until Ellen's 'fall' forced them to move. In general, however, such displays of shame and despair were as rare among these families as the angry, brutal expulsion of the sinner.

Efforts were generally made, however, to keep the news from spreading, which suggests that the status of unmarried mother was not regarded with the sort of calm indifference observers believed to be normal among the working classes. The reason most often given was that the parents feared the effects of such a bad example on their younger daughters. Mr J, for example, refused to allow his daughter in the house

> . . . *while she has the child on account of the moral example to the other three, younger children.[404]*

Elizabeth B, daughter of a window-blind maker, confided in her parents, but the birth of her child was kept from her brothers and sisters.[405] In other cases the pattern was different: Lily E, aged seventeen when her child was born, got support from her mother and sister, who helped her fake a holiday visit to the country to avoid arousing her father's suspicion.[406]

Most of all, people feared neighbourhood gossip and rumour. Caroline K looked after the children of her sister and brother-in-law, a bootmaker of Gray's Inn Lane; there she met her lover, who deserted her when she was pregnant. Her parents lived nearby; her father was a carpenter – she noticed her pregnancy after returning home to live with them. It was immediately decided that she should stay with her sister for the confinement 'to prevent the discovery of Petitioner's circumstances to the neighbours'. Her mother paid the midwife and the baby was removed and put to nurse.[407]

It is generally believed that this attitude is most often found in specific class subcategories, and it will therefore be assumed that secretive behaviour would have been more frequent in the families of master craftsmen, small shopkeepers and others supposed to have strong aspirations to respectability. This view is not supported by the facts. The reasons for secrecy seem to have been much more complex, and subject to numerous variables: regional background, religious beliefs, ages of parents and children, relations between family members, circumstances of the seduction, and so on (suggesting, incidentally, that historians would do well to reconsider certain schematic classifications). This observation converges with Alastair Reed's criticism of the over-rigid division of the labouring classes into different strata, elaborated during the nineteenth century and often accepted more or less uncritically by later writers.[408] In any case, our sample includes skilled workers and master craftsmen who helped their daughters without trying to hide the situation from the neighbours; and unskilled and casual labourers who behaved differently. We may take as an example the case of Dorcas B, who lived with her mother in Hackney. The mother, a widow with nine other children, worked as a laundress, an extremely low-status occupation. Nevertheless she acted vigorously to prevent the birth of an illegitimate child from disgracing her among her neighbours.

Dorcas's child was the fruit of illicit relations with a recently widowed brother-in-law. Her mother's social anxiety may have been rooted in the girl's age (she was only seventeen), in the whiff of incest, or in the nature of the sexual act itself (a single, furtive coupling which occurred while Dorcas was delivering laundry). Whatever the reason, the matter was kept secret. The girl slipped away for confinement at Queen Charlotte's Hospital; then the neighbours were told that a baby had been taken on for nursing, and the newcomer took its place among the six other children still living in the maternal home.[409]

The family is the natural source of support in difficult times. People got their parents to help persuade the recalcitrant lover to make amends, and turned to them again for financial and material aid.

Of course the father and mother, who might be old and sick or already supporting a large family, were seldom in a position to look after the baby themselves; although there are a few examples of parents doing so, among them Nancy's father, a docker who already had seven children including one still in infancy; or Emma B's, a Bethnal Green shoemaker who also had seven children.[410] The situation recalls the fisherman in Victor Hugo's 'Pauvres Gens':

> *Five children we had, that will make seven;*
> *Already, in the hard season, there are days when the*
> *Pot stands cold and empty. What will we do now?*[411]

More often the child would be entrusted to a brother or sister, usually against a small financial contribution. Elizabeth A's sister sheltered her for several months before her confinement, then helped to pay the nurse.[412] Ann A's sister, although herself only just above the poverty threshold, paid for her room and the costs of her confinement.[413] Georgina Y was confined at the home of her brother and his wife.[414] Louisa had three brothers:

> *Alfred P. of the police Station, Hunter Street; Henry P. of the public house in*
> *Oxford St. and Charles P. of Brooks Mews, Grosvenor Square. I had savings to*
> *the amount of £7 and this by the help of my brothers has supported me.*[415]

Jane's brother paid for the care of her child, while she subsisted with the help of her savings.[416]

Despite the financial burden of an illicit pregnancy, despite the worries and complications brought by the child's presence and the young woman's disgrace, the relatives of Foundling Hospital applicants usually made excuses for their conduct. It may be thought that they would hardly have been so foolish as to blacken their relative's character while trying to get her child adopted; but they did have the option of using the language of guilt, like the brother of Lucy Ann M who wrote of the burden 'so improperly broat upon herself and parents' by his 'unfortunate sister'.[417]

Few families took this line. Sarah T's father, a small shopkeeper whose daughter had been seduced by a neighbour, spoke of the matter to the Foundling Hospital in these terms:

> *Such cruelty seldom heard of as he confessed his fault but would make no recompense knowing as he did my large family of 7 daughters and 3 sons it appeared the more cruel. And there is some excuse for her as he was a single man and often professed so much respect for my family, and our premises behind are open together in one yard therefore they could have intercourse together at any time without suspicion. . .*[418]

There is no trace of blame, either, in this statement by the sister-in-law of Matilda J:

> *She is in my opinion entitled to the sympathy of every person. I was in the company of Mr. T. several times and he appeared to me to be all that a member of a family could wish when one branch of it is engaged to be married. . .*[419]

or in the evidence of Elizabeth T's sister, who puts the blame on Elizabeth's employers:

> *She expressed herself warmly on what she considered to be an act of great impropriety on the part of Mr. and Mrs. Z. namely leaving petitioner and the Father alone in charge of their house during a period of 3 weeks, that in her opinion, petitioner's present unfortunate condition is to be attributed to that circumstance entirely.*[420]

or in the long letter from Susan T's father, a Knightsbridge bootmaker (although he does cast doubt on the girl's common sense):

> *She was such a fool as to believe him. I must acknowledge that she was always a very simple and unsuspecting girl and an easy prey for such villain like him. . .*[421]

We can sum up this section with two important conclusions. First, petitioners' families were much less permissive, less indifferent to illegitimacy, than the standard ruling-class view would have us believe. Secondly, it can be said that in the main they fulfilled their proper role by providing material and moral support.

'No Sir, Missus don't permit no followers'[422]

In much the same way, these documents broadly contradict our received ideas on the attitude of bourgeois Victorians to faults committed by their maidservants. These ideas too can be traced back to the nineteenth century. Henry Mayhew had this to say about domestics:

> *They are badly educated and are not well looked after by their mistresses as a rule, although every dereliction from the paths of propriety by them will be visited with the heaviest displeasure, and most frequently be followed by dismissal of the most summary description, without the usual month's warning, to which so much importance is usually attached by both employer and employed.*[423]

William Acton asserts that

> *. . . A woman found pregnant is usually dismissed from her employment without a reference,*[424]

and this theme was also dear to Mrs Gaskell, who often denounces employers, notably in *Ruth*, for their indifference to the welfare of their workers.

These sociological prejudices probably result from the strong impression made on sensitive Victorian observers by a few scandalous, well-publicized cases. Otherwise it is difficult to understand why, according to our sources, so few employers behaved with this sort of cruel rigour, and why so many made great efforts to help domestics who had got into trouble.

It would of course be a gross error to suppose that there was any general tolerance of illicit sexual relations. Most of the petitioners left their jobs spontaneously, as a matter of course, when their pregnancy started to become noticeable; and the blackmail used by some lovers, who threatened to give girls away to their new employers if they did not drop their demands, shows that the bourgeoisie in general frowned on the condition of 'child-mother'. The response could be very harsh indeed: Eliza Z, for example, was sacked on the spot when her mistress discovered that she had had an illegitimate child six months earlier.[425]

There remained, however, a dense and diverse throng of distinguished persons whose dealings with the petitioners were marked by 'common humanity'.[426] Many employers turned a blind eye to a maid's pregnancy, and continued to shelter her during confinement and immediately afterwards. Georgina O gave birth in her mistress's house, where she had been working since the age of twelve. The employer wrote:

> We were unaware of her confinement when of course it would have been inhuman to have sent her away, she having nowhere to go. . . . Her mother and her stepfather are very poor and unable to give her shelter even if her stepfather was disposed to do so which he is not. . .
>
> I need not tell you that it would be quite impossible to keep her in our service with the child.[427]

Georgina was able to resume her place in the household, for the child was accepted by the Foundling Hospital.

Other employers supplied a financial safety-net during the period of confinement, like the master baker Mr J;[428] and like Mrs J who rented lodgings for her maid in Bishopsgate and covered the costs of the midwife and other needs:

> Mrs. J. has been induced to assist Petitioner in her present difficulties in consideration of her former good conduct and her promise of future amendment,[429]

confirms Mr Twiddy. According to their surgeon, Mr and Mrs A of Grosvenor Place House begged him 'to act for them in every way that might be probable to advance her welfare and they assisted her during her confinement'.[430]

Where the liaison was between two of their employees – either when both were servants or when one or other was a worker or apprentice – employers often felt a moral obligation to speak to the young man and try to get him to honour his responsibilities. The intervention was sometimes indirect, like the one described in this letter from the Reverend R. P:

Lord E. asked me as Parish Minister here to speak to that E. about you and your child which I have done. . . he excuses himself concerning his sin with you saying you were as much in fault as he was if not more. . . . He gave me a sovereign for you for which I now enclose a Post Office order. . . . I am sorry to have to tell you that E. is married to Mary R. and they have gone to Australia – he promised me that he would send you money from thence.[431]

All sorts of employers showed concern in this way. At the other end of the social scale from Lord E, we find a couple running a grocery and cheese shop in Islington, who threatened the father of Alice Z's child with dismissal unless he married her. He promised to do so, but dragged his feet and hesitated until they sacked him, without a reference, after six years' service. Mr and Mrs I then shared with Alice's new employers the costs of her lodging and confinement; finally her new mistress, Mrs P, accompanied the girl to her interview at the Foundling Hospital.[432]

Ellen P, maidservant to a Mr Q who owned a coffee house, received decisive moral support when her fiancé, a butcher's boy, changed jobs and vanished. Her master discovered the deserter's new address, went to see him and obtained the promise that he would marry Ellen the next spring.[433]

Employers could be relied upon for this very valuable support. It was rare indeed for a reference to be refused when the time came for an applicant to produce evidence of her morality for the Foundling Hospital, even if she had left the job eighteen months or more earlier. This example was written by a Lady X:

Emma J. was in my service twelve years as lady's maid and during this time always conducted herself in every respect as I could wish. . . . I could have taken Emma J. back into my service in consideration of her serving so long with me and from her previous good characters but could not do so owing to the unpleasantness it would have caused with the other servants. . . . I consider Emma J. quite worthy of the kind consideration of the Committee of the Governors of the hospital. . .[434]

Others went further still, taking the trouble to put in a personal appearance or helping their servant to go through the necessary procedures to gain the committee's attention. One example is that of Mrs Charlotte T, for whom Elizabeth E worked when she was seduced by a young soldier. The pregnancy caused no great fuss in the household; Elizabeth admitted what had happened and was half-forgiven. She stayed in service until confinement was near; then she was taken gently to lodgings rented nearby in Pimlico. If the child could be adopted, Mrs T said, she would take Elizabeth back into her service. She wrote three letters to this effect, of which we quote the second:

> I must earnestly recommend the Bearer Elizabeth E. to your kind consideration soliciting you to take her child into your noble Institution. . . . I never have had a steadier or better conducted young woman in my service and was shocked and astonished to learn what had befallen her. . . . As the Man is out of the country, and in consideration of her natural propriety of conduct, and in hopes of Saving her from further misfortune and ruin, I will take her back to her situation provided she gets the child off her hands into some Institution. . . . I only add that I am daughter and sister of clergymen of the Established Church and will be at the Foundling Hospital at 2 o'clock. . .[435]

No doubt people did disapprove of sexual misconduct by maid-servants, but it certainly did not lead to instant dismissal, or cause the disgusted rejection that the effusions of Victorian moralists lead us to imagine. Many employers had no difficulty in finding convincing excuses for these vicissitudes of the people: it was an aspect of their condition, the inevitable fate of those who allowed themselves to be carried away by their senses.

Indeed, bourgeois families were so far from rejecting women merely for transgressing the rules of marriage that mothers unable to feed a newborn infant would send out to a hospital or workhouse for an unmarried mother able to stand in for them. If they were satisfied with her services, these mistresses might later support the nurse's application to the Foundling Hospital in the hope of keeping her:

> She is an industrious and deserving girl. . . My husband took her as a wet nurse from the Greenwich Union on the 10th of July last (a fortnight after her confinement) and her story appeared such a sad one. . . . Should her child be received into the Hospital, I intend keeping her as a nurse after her engagement as wet nurse expires. . .[436]

Some employers were prompted by wholly unselfish reasons, like a Mrs Knapp who, Mr Twiddy reported,

. . . states she has been induced to take Petitioner into her service purely from a compassionate motive, hoping to reclaim her from her present lost position.[437]

But most of these employers kept their maids on when they were pregnant, and took them back into service after confinement, simply because they liked and valued them. The hospital's inquirer quotes the reasons given by Mr D, a draper:

Petitioner's former good conduct, her sincere penitence for her present error, together with the kindness she had always shown her widowed mother by allowing her 2/- a week out of her wages, are circumstances which have induced informant to look over her recent fault and retain her in service.

For her part Agnes, the young girl in question, confirmed that her mistress had paid the costs of her confinement.[438] 'I returned to Mrs O after my confinement,' states Harriet M. simply, 'and am there still and shall remain.'[439] In another case the Foundling Hospital inquirer notes with equal simplicity: 'If Petitioner is relieved of her child, she will remain in her present service. . .'[440]

All this is remote from the alleged cold selfishness of the ruling classes, aped in *The Mysteries of London* by the butler of the Markham household:

The young water-cress gal was confined with an unlegitimate child; and so I told her mother never to let her call here again, as we didn't encourage immoral karikters.[441]

RULES OF SEXUAL MORALITY

Not least of the surprises yielded by analysis of the Foundling Hospital's archives is the partisan position often adopted, in real life, by the middle and upper classes, when they assisted working women whose sexual behaviour had strayed outside the social and moral norms.

Conversely, as we have seen, the alleged anarchic sexual behaviour of the labouring classes, denounced so violently and insistently by Victorian and Edwardian observers, is nowhere perceptible in the actual comportment of these young people and their families.

Of course the naivety and thoughtlessness of some girls, and the duplicity and unreliability of some men, are more than apparent. Still more obvious, however, is the general wish to create conditions in which the pre-marital sexual act would fit in with an ideal social, biological and institutional programme. For the most part, these couples were a priori in a situation where both partners were free to marry. For the women, almost any husband offered the possibility of an honourable outcome. From the male point of view, domestics had extra value on the matrimonial market: their household skills and the possibility of savings guaranteed a well-run household and offered the added, glittering possibility that the couple might start a business.

Moreover, the lover usually came from the same professional or family background as the girl or, if he had been met by chance, had been introduced to her family and friends without delay.

In most cases the sexual act occurred only after more or less prolonged courtship, and relations were maintained up to and even beyond confinement. There is every reason to believe that it served partly to *materialize* the amorous relationship and, by reference to established customs, was expected to lead to an earlier marriage. It was accompanied, almost invariably, by a formal promise of marriage.

We have also seen, however, that a whole range of factors might visit failure on the planned partnership – whether or not the programme included formal marriage – and lead to separation. The lover might meet someone else, or his feelings might simply cool; and some men, of course, never really intended to get married in the first place.

The bonds of affection could also be strained by the lovers' trades or professions, which often demanded quite a high level of mobility. Unemployment, underemployment and accumulated debts could drive a man out of a neighbourhood, into the provinces, even abroad; it is not surprising that so many hesitated to take on responsibility for a wife and child.

Finally, some men recognized – too late, but with crude clarity – that there were better opportunities elsewhere, or that they were not yet ready for marriage.

These situations, although typical of the second half of the nineteenth century, were not basically new. The difficulties faced by couples in the pre-industrial period had been just as great, judging by that epoch's late marriages and high level of illegitimate births.

The nineteenth century was notable, however, for the virtual depenalization of male neglect in cases of illegitimacy, following the Poor Law reform of 1834. This placed an intolerable economic burden on women by denying help to those living at home.[442] By the same token, it had a markedly inhibiting effect on the traditional permissive attitude to pre-marital sexuality. Although people still retained traces of the old mentality, and the women or their families would instinctively seek out the father and try to obtain reparation, we have seen that these efforts usually had little or no effect.

Men, on the other hand, had been given a large degree of freedom to evade the material consequences of the sexual act – all in the cause of the struggle against vice and 'immorality' among the labouring classes. Some men do seem to have felt genuine pangs of conscience, while others had to disrupt their lives to escape from pregnant fiancées; but the fact remains that, with no welfare state and no easy access to contraception or abortion, the quest for amorous and sexual pleasure was ultimately far more costly to women.

Women were certainly victims of this new balance of forces which left them hopelessly exposed, barely able to reconcile defence of their material interests with the unpredictable demands of sexual desire. When the worst happened, all they could do was produce the pathetic evidence of their 'respectability' and try to persuade one of a few private institutions to take care of the child. The separation often caused lasting pain, and some mothers wrote letters year after year, asking again and again for news of the child's welfare. A woman might get a baby 'off her hands' only to find that the emotional mortgage was for life.

The admission files of the Foundling Hospital provide a varied picture of the sexual behaviour of the working classes. Here are women who give themselves easily and without fuss when convinced they have found a father for their children; predatory men willing to spend time with a girl, pay court, feed her gin and compliments, the better to seduce and then forget her; families and friends powerless to defend their daughters' honour, unable to hold men to their given word; and poor wronged women sacrificing their lives in a desperate struggle to raise their bastards alone and unaided. Charitable institutions, employers, landladies hover in the background, ready with humiliating demands for a full confession, or at least a convincing display of repentance; and waiting in the shadows beyond them is the sadness of separation, probably for ever, from a child destined to be raised by strangers.

We should not forget, however, that there were other more positive aspects: the fun and pleasure of 'keeping company', the free choice of partners, backstairs flirtations, evenings of entertainment at the music hall, the triumph of stepping out on the arm of one's 'young man', or being treated as a lady by a passing gentleman; and the tender feelings aroused by newborn babies, the support given by families, the sympathy and compassion of some employers.

The rules of the game were generally understood and, up to a point, observed. It is precisely this awareness of a moral code which defined Foundling Hospital petitioners as respectable women, worthy of receiving help. Without it, anything could happen – abortion, prostitution, a prolonged sexual liaison, being 'kept' – in a system which had become far more adaptable and tolerant than ever before.

One day, surely, Britain during the second half of the nineteenth century will lose the reputation carefully manufactured for it by Victorians with an eye on posterity. Just as imperial Rome felt threatened by decadence in the triumphantly prosperous century of Augustus and Hadrian, so Victorian England at the pinnacle of its glory believed that its elites and its people were insufficiently virtuous, inadequately protected against their passions and instincts. The elite were offered as a model the image of a prudish sovereign. The people, on the other hand, were presented with a luridly mutilated, penny-dreadful reflection of their own morals and behaviour, one designed to capture their attention and promote a commitment to reform.

The people were told that they were *dirty*, that their houses were *filthy*, that their souls were *unclean*, that they lived in *scandalous* promiscuity, that their daughters became pregnant *before* they were married, were more or less prostitutes living outside the sacrament of holy matrimony, and that by so living, like *scum*, like *animals*, they had become the *shame* of the world's leading nation.

Yet in the archives we have been examining, the accused remonstrate that they are neither particularly depraved nor especially virtuous. They admit that they were free to associate with anyone they wished, outside the control of their parents or peer group; that they could move from one dwelling to another without surveillance, since their homes were open to the staircase and the street, and this was accepted as normal by families and neighbours. The sexual act, and such matters as abortion, were treated as subjects for open discussion; and the loss of a girl's virginity aroused no real disapproval, or even anxiety for the future, in her immediate circle.

But sexuality outside marriage was accepted on the understanding that the woman would not be deserted if she became pregnant. People were not excluded from the social group merely for living in sin. For the most part, they did not live in the 'militant concubinage' advocated by followers of Tom Paine or Robert Owen, nor in the negligent form practised, for example, by widowed people who simply could not be bothered to go through another ceremony. Extra-marital liaisons were seen more as the obvious arrangement for a certain stage of life: people would live together during a pregnancy and when the woman could not work, while awaiting an upturn in their fortunes or a final decision on the future.

Marriage was seen as the ideal, natural state for adult life, a coalition of forces and affections, an alliance of inestimable value in dealing with a harsh, hazardous, bitter existence and ensuring the care of children.

Even so, the discovery of illicit sexual relations did not usually lead to exclusion from the family or social group; exclusion and blame, when they did appear, were directed against social ineptitude rather than any moral failing. If great efforts were sometimes made to move a girl out of the family home for confinement, it was not to hide her shame from the neighbours but for health reasons: to remove her from a cramped and overcrowded dwelling.

There is no sign in all this of the unstructured and undisciplined state, the confusion of bodies of all ages and both sexes, the bestial, anarchic copulation so insistently alleged and described.

On the contrary, all the evidence points to a set of rules common to everyone – albeit rules whose principles and practice set them apart from the dominant code of sexual morality. The repeated account of a measured progression through stages of intimacy to amorous commitment, of decorous sexual behaviour, with a more or less prescribed ritual preceding carnal union, is ultimately in sharp contrast to the familiar picture of individuals brutalized by poverty and the absence of religious faith, wholly dominated by coarse passions, driven by violent, hurried desires.

All this raises the urgent question: why, against so much evidence, did Victorian observers attribute such a degree of moral depravity to the working classes?

Part of the answer must lie in their natural political and social fears. The residual presence, in working-class sexual morality, of pagan customs in which the sexual act is dissociated from marriage, helps to explain the vehemence with which reform was promoted. For our observers were all Christians, more or less committed to the ardent struggle being waged against the de-Christianization of the masses.

Another reason is the observers' wish to distinguish themselves from other groups. For the most part, the authors of these horrified descriptions of working-class sexuality came from the middle classes and the bourgeoisie, preoccupied at that time with establishing ideological dominance over the rest of society (hitherto a privilege of the landed aristocracy). This necessarily involved the moral disqualification of the other social classes: first the aristocracy, then the poor.

If the image of a depraved populace seems to have been maintained for somewhat longer than might be thought necessary for this purpose, the reason is that it was still needed to justify another immense enterprise: the imposition of marriage and promotion of a standard model of the family, giving the husband complete supremacy over his wife and children. The extent to which this effort succeeded would require another book.

For the time being, though, we should be content to let the archives speak, and thus contribute to a never-ending task which is a precondition for human progress: the effort to keep the past alive so that later generations can learn from it, and measure themselves against it. It is an ordinary paradox of history that, through a new reversal of values in sexual morality, the young Europeans of the late twentieth century have much more in common with these dropouts from Victorian society – these artisans, these domestics who disappeared abruptly in the aftermath of the First World War – than with the contemporary moralists who slandered them with such total conviction.

Epilogue

An excessive and partisan preoccupation with the heroic sufferings of women has led some historians to depict them, much as the working class has been represented, in the martyred posture of victims; or to consign them just as inaccurately to the halls of Valhalla.[1] The compassion and admiration which inspire these hagiographic efforts are laudable emotions, but are of uncertain value in the search for a comprehensive understanding of things.

Anyone who examines a whole social group patiently and systematically – not in the absence of theoretical conceptions, but without trying to protect such theories from the real facts and evidence – discovers an astonishing and contradictory history, a history made up of contrasts: of impudence and morality, cynicism and tenderness, cruelty and generosity; a history, in short, amazingly like real life.

But it is a version which may come as a shock to those, for example, who are persuaded that philanthropy was nothing but a trap – worse, an effective trap – designed solely to crush women and the poor; those who imagine the nineteenth century in primary colours: a bourgeoisie bound by strict sexual morality, a people given over to its fleshy instincts, the tyranny of fierce factory bosses; and women victimized a thousand times over, victims of everyone and everything, in all social classes and all circumstances – mother, prostitute, shop-girl, servant, seamstress – victims of a patriarchal, bourgeois plot to keep them in perpetual subjection.

It is difficult to maintain indefinitely so loud, so strident, a note. Of course these radical classifications do have their role; they are undoubtedly useful for arousing indignation, encouraging action, and so on.

The time and inclination to examine things in detail may be lacking, but useful perceptions can still arise from simplified, simplifying ideas. These ideas may then accede to a measure of validity, in the context of the time which has adopted them. But they remain of limited interest to the historical researcher, for whom the repetition of activist slogans necessarily involves bad faith.

As an example – one among hundreds – we can quote an assertion by Peter T. Cominos:

> *Thus it is clear that an unmarried or married woman's known sexual behaviour classified her either as a respectable member of the social system of the family or one who had fallen below the line of respectability into the subsocial system of prostitution, the negation of the family. . .*[2]

We happen to know that although sexual transgressions are often treated in this way in the novel, the real Victorian society, and the real individuals within it, dealt with them altogether differently. Civil society created and financed, through private philanthropy, refuges and hospitals which were dedicated to moral reform, but also provided aid and relief for mothers and children. Support also came from individuals, for example the employers of these child-mothers whose sexual conduct had slipped into heresy; masters and mistresses who kept the girls in their service and sometimes entreated them to stay on. And the Foundling Hospital did everything in its power to ensure that the 'child of sin' would receive an upbringing, to enable the mother effectively to 'rebuild her life', remarry, and perhaps one day take her bastard child back, raise it with the others and melt into the crowd.

All this suggests that perhaps the persecution of some of its members is not, after all, essential to the logic of an urban industrial society; but rather that time, space and practical necessity at certain moments sharpen the contradictions between the moral aspirations of a particular group and a larger socioeconomic logic. Like a machine which needs oiling but otherwise works well: the wheels may suddenly seize up, then start to move again.

Few would deny that the Western world in the last century developed a civilization which was deeply biased against working-class women. There is nothing to be gained from demonstrating this fact over and over again.

On the other hand, a great deal remains to be done before we can understand how this situation of injustice is constantly reworked and recycled, how from time to time it is affected by sudden flashes and upheavals which modify its effects without changing its nature.

The documents we possess should be analysed as a continuous whole, without denying their inexplicable features, without excluding the parameters of social class and gender. This may help us to grasp the ways in which injustice survives, understand the aims of those who perpetuate and exploit it, and perhaps find weak places where the fetters can be broken. In this way, and in this way only, we may hope to see, apart from any nostalgia, the past as a lesson for the present. We may hope to see the passage of time as ceaselessly enriching these historical records: not only preserving them, but making them more intelligible, and more vital.

Notes

INTRODUCTION

1. See H.L. Beales 'Victorian Ideas of Sex', in *Ideas and Beliefs of the Victorians*, E.P. Dutton & Co, London, 1949; Ronald Pearsall, *The Worm in the Bud: The World of Victorian Sexuality*, Weidenfeld & Nicolson, London 1969.

2. William Logan, *An Exposure from Personal Observations of Female Prostitution in London, Leeds and Rochdale, and Especially in the City of Glasgow*, Glasgow 1843.

3. The best-known are: Dr Elizabeth Blackwell, *The Moral Education of the Young in Relation to Sex*, London 1879; The Rev. Lyttleton, *Training of the Young in the Laws of Sex*, London 1901.

4. John Maynard, *Charlotte Brontë and Sexuality*, Cambridge University Press 1984; Peter Gay, *The Bourgeois Experience, Victoria to Freud*, vol. 1, *Education of the Senses*, Oxford University Press 1984; Alan Macfarlane, *Marriage and Love in England, 1300–1840*, Basil Blackwell, Oxford 1986.

5. C.F.G. Masterman, *From the Abyss*, London 1902.

6. The archive of the Thomas Coram Foundling Hospital. Files more than a hundred years old containing adoption applications, which contained information on the professional and love lives of the applicants, were available for inspection until 1980. The institution then decided that to protect the privacy of their living descendants, the files would be closed for another fifty years. Thus only those prior to 1840 are currently available.

1 LABOURING CLASSES, DEPRAVED CLASSES

1. 900,000 in 1801; 4,500,000 in 1901

2. For example, 1,033 dwellings were demolished to make room for St Katharine's Dock.

3. The rich also moved to residential suburbs across the Lea River, especially on the fringes of Epping Forest.

4. City Press, 'City Dwellings of the Working Classes', 12 September 1857, p.49.

5. The Poor Law was a body of legislation dating back to the early seventeenth century,

which regulated the assistance given to indigents. After 1834 administration of the Poor Law was taken out of the hands of parishes and given to committees which administered larger districts.

6. Jules Vallès, *la Rue à Londres*, Les Editeurs Français Réunis, Paris 1951 (1866), pp. 366–7.

7. *The City Mission Magazine*, 'A District Formerly Occupied by the Mission', vol. XII, 1847, p. 217.

8. Robert Roberts, *The Classic Slum, Salford Life in the First Quarter of the Century*, Penguin Books, Harmondsworth 1977 (1971), p. 33.

9. John Matthias Weylland, *These Fifty Years Being the Jubilee Volume of the London City Mission*, London 1884, p. 59.

10. Jules Vallès, p. 37.

11. S.F. Swift, *In the Slums*, London 1889, p. 1.

12. Anon. (Walter), *My Secret Life*, Grove Press, New York, 1966 (1882–94), p. 279.

13. Françoise Basch, *Relative Creatures, Victorian Women in Society and the Novel*, Schocken, New York 1974, p. 7.

14. 'Link after Link; or, The Bible Women Nurses', in *God's Message in London* (Seven Missing Link Tracts), 1871, pp. 44–5.

15. Michelle Perrot, 'La Femme populaire rebelle', in *L'Histoire sans qualités*, Galilée, Paris 1979, pp. 141–2.

16. The *London City Mission Magazine (LCMM)*, 'The District of St. Giles's', vol. XIII, November 1847, p. 241.

17. *The Book and Its Missions, Past and Present*, 'Dust-Heap Women at Paddington', A/RNY/96, 1860, p. 94.

18. *The Book and Its Missions, Past and Present*, 'Bible Tea-Party in St. Giles's', A/RNY/96, 1860, p. 186.

19. *The Book and Its Missions*, 'The London Heathen and their Missionaries', A/RNY/96, 1860, p. 186.

20. *The Book and Its Missions*, 'The London Heathen and their Missionaries or the Bible Women of St. Giles's', A/RNY/96, 1860, p. 175.

21. R.W. Vanderkiste, *Notes and Narratives of a Six Years' Mission principally among the Dens of London*, London 1852, p. 5.

22. Octavia Hill, *Our Common Land and other short essays*, London 1877, pp. 108–9.

23. People saw behaviour in factories in much the same way that they saw behaviour in the streets: 'A witness in Leicester said that he would rather let his daughter beg than go into a factory; that they are perfect gates of hell; that most of the prostitutes in the town had their employment in the mills to thank for their present situation ...' Engels, *The Condition of the Working Class in England*, Marx and Engels, Collected Works, vol. 4, Lawrence & Wishart, London 1975, p. 441.

24. Andrew Mearns, *The Bitter Cry of Outcast London. An Inquiry into the Condition of the Abject Poor*, London 1883, pp. 13–14.

25. Founded in 1834.

26. The Salvation Army, *Saved in Time*, London 1893, p. 7.

27. If we are to believe the London City Mission, large numbers of celebrated performers and West End actors played in these places. The main difference was that drinks were served and smoking was allowed throughout the performance.

28. *LCMM*, 'Sunday Taverns', vol. V, 1840, p.139.

29. Ibid., p. 140.

30. *LCMM*, 'On the Prevention of Iniquity', vol. VII, 1842, p. 193.

NOTES

31. According to George Sims, these disappeared, along with 'free-and-easies', during the 1880s (*How the Poor Live*, London 1883, p. 47).

32. James Greenwod, *The Seven Curses of London*, London 1869, p. 315. Sims is almost alone in finding nothing wrong with music halls, although he heard 'suggestive songs' in them (p. 51).

33. *LCMM*, 'The Providers of Amusements', vol. XV, 1850, pp. 234–5.

34. Derek Hudson, *Munby, Man of Two Worlds, The Life and Diaries of Arthur J. Munby,* 1828–1910, Abacus, London 1974, p. 103 (Munby took part in one of these games in the bushes near Crystal Palace on 10 July 1861).

35. *LCMM*, 'Westminster', vol. X, 1845, p. 162.

36. Michel Foucault, *The History of Sexuality*, 1, *An Introduction*, transl. Robert Hurley, Penguin Books (Peregrine), Harmondsworth 1984, p. 45.

37. But Medical Officers of Health complained that it was difficult for them to make inspections at night to ensure that the rules of public hygiene were being observed. Cf. J.W. Tripe, 'Suggestions for the Amendment of the Artisans Dwelling Acts', *Transactions of the Society of Medical Officers of Health*, session 83–4, p.30.

38. One example is Henry Mayhew, *London Labour and the London Poor*, Dover Publications, New York 1968 (1861–2), vol. I, pp. 407–23.

39. *Parliamentary Papers*, CVII, 1908, 'Report of an Inquiry by the Board of Trade into Working-Class Rents, Housing and Retail Prices...', appendix B, p. 60.

40. *Parliamentary Papers*, LXXXI, 1887, 'Tabulations of Statements Made by Men Living in Certain Selected Districts of London in March, 1887', p. 34.

41. In his work on sterility, published in 1884, Dr Duncan quotes the figures of the *Royal Statistical Society* on the district of St George's-in-the-East. They show that the average number of children conceived in 31 years of marriage by women married between 15 and 19 years of age was 9·12; while among middle-class women, who tended to marry later (at an average age of 25) the number of children conceived during the period of fertility averaged 6 (J.M. Duncan, *On Sterility in Women, being the Gulstonian Lectures delivered in the Royal College of Physicians in February 1883*, London 1884, pp. 29–31.

42. Philippe Ariès, *L'Enfant et la vie familiale sous l'Ancien Régime*, Plon, Paris 1960, pp. 444–51.

43. Ibid p. 47.

44. Ibid.

45. But the attitude of the working classes was not without its own contradictions. Havelock Ellis was struck by the modesty of young workers who concealed their genitals with their hands while crossing the beach.

46. Walter, p. 73.

47. See, notably, the Criminal Law Amendment Act passed in 1885, and the application of the Common Lodging Acts and the Industrial School Amendment Acts (1880); also clauses on the application of the 1870 Education Act.

48. Later in the century the arrival of psychoanalytic theories gave added scientific support to this tendency and endorsed the attitude of those parents who wished to shield their children from the trauma of the 'primal scene'.

49. Arthur Morrison, *A Child of the Jago*, London 1907 (1896), p. 15.

50. Raphael Samuel, *East End Underworld* (II) *Chapters in the Life of Arthur Harding*, History Workshop Series, Routledge & Kegan Paul, London 1981, p. 63.

51. Thomas Sarvic MD, MOH, *Annual Report of the Medical Officer of Health of Bethnal Green*, 1871, p. 4.

52. Matthew Corner, MD, *Report on the Sanitary Condition and Public Health of Mile End*

Old Town, year ending March 30 1867, p. 13; J.W. Tripe, 'Suggestions for the Amendment of the Artisans Dwelling Acts', p. 32.

53. Archibald Alison, *Principles of Population and their Connection with Human Happiness*, vol. II, London 1840, p. 135.

54. Havelock Ellis, *Studies in the Psychology of Sex*, 3 vols, F.A. Davis Company, Philadelphia 1910 (1887), vol. III, p. 217.

55. John Simon, *Sanitary Conditions of the City of London*, London 1854, pp. 148–9.

56. George Paddock Bate, MD, *Annual Report of the Medical Officer of Health of Bethnal Green for the Year 1878*, p. 50.

57. *The Missing Link Magazine*, 1 June 1880, p. 167.

58. Hector Gavin, MD, FRCSE, *The Habitations of the Industrial Classes, Address delivered at Crosby Hall, Nov. 7, 1850*, London 1851, p. 55.

59. Emile Zola, *Germinal*, transl. by Leonard Tancock, Penguin Books, Harmondsworth 1954 (1885), p. 166.

60. Mrs Ranyard, *The Missing Link*, 'Want of a Bible Mission in Bethnal Green', 1859, p. 126.

61. Ibid., p. 169.

62. *The Book and Its Missions, Past and Present*, 'The London Heathen and Their Missionaries', p. 123.

63. Lawrence Stone, *The Family, Sex and Marriage in England*, 1500–1800, Weidenfeld & Nicolson, London 1977, p. 255.

64. Building and redevelopment had an important role in the spread of lodging-houses. In 1848 a member of the London City Mission, overworked by the number of newcomers to the Mint district, noted: 'The number of lodging houses has increased since I have been on the district from 12 to upward 30, occasioned by an influx of bad characters from several low neighbourhoods which have recently been broken up.' (*LCMM*, 'A District formerly occupied by the Mission', vol. XII, 1847, p. 216.)

65. According to the London City Mission, a night's shelter cost a penny without a mattress, and 3d. with mattress and bed. Sims gives the cost as 4d. to 6d. a night. Gavin says a separate room cost 3s. 6d. a week in rent. Children were charged half price. Tenants were fairly sedentary, often staying for three months or more.

66. Large dormitories where people slept leaning on ropes stretched across the room. These were released in the morning to awaken the guests.

67. George Sims, p. 14.

68. Henry Mayhew, p. 409: 'There is no objection to any boy and girl occupying a bed, even though the keeper knows they were previously strangers to each other.'

69. *LCMM*, vol. X, August 1845, p. 176.

70. Henry Mayhew, vol. I, p. 409.

71. William Acton, *Prostitution Considered in its Moral, Social and Sanitary Aspects in London*, London 1857, p. 28.

72. *LCMM*, 'A District formerly occupied by the Mission', vol. XII, 1847, p. 216.

73. Anthony Wohl (*The Eternal Slum*, Edward Arnold, London 1977, p. 74) notes that in mid century 80,000 people lived in these furnished lodgings. In 1907, Jephson gives the same resident population for a total of about 5,000 lodging-houses.

74. This reasoning has seldom been questioned by historians. Cf. notably Neil Smelser, *Social Change in the Industrial Revolution*, Routledge & Kegan Paul, London 1959; Louise Tilly and Joan Scott, *Women, Work and Family*, Holt, Rinehart and Winston, New York 1978; Michael Anderson, *Family Structure in Nineteenth Century Lancashire*, Cambridge University Press 1971.

75. Vanderkiste, p. 42. Vanderkiste had found that the mother and daughter of a family he was trying to help each had several children by the same man, with whom they both lived.

76. George Sims, p. 24.

77. Arthur St John Adcock, *In the Image of God, a Story of Lower London*, London 1898, pp. 1–2.

78. *The Ninth Annual Report of the London City Mission*, 1844, pp. 15–16. The Mission eventually persuaded him back on to the path of righteousness: he renewed his subscription to a Chartist magazine and bought a Bible for each of his children.

79. LCMM, 'Brompton District', vol. VIII, 1843, p. 191.

80. Mrs Ranyard, pp. 122–3.

81. Engels, p. 173.

82. Painted by Frederick Barnard, it was the frontispiece of George Robert Sims's *How the Poor Live*. Sims refers to the picture on p. 11.

83. John Matthias Weylland, p. 101. The survey examined 1,600 pupils of the 'ragged schools' which tried to give basic instruction to the poorest children before the establishment of municipal schooling in 1870.

84. The Salvation Army, *Saved in Time*, 1892–3, p. 11.

85. George Gissing, *The Nether World*, Dent, London/Dutton, New York 1973 (1889).

86. Ibid., pp. 5–6.

87. LCMM, 'The Providers of Amusements', vol. XV, 1850, p. 234.

88. James Greenwood, p. 19.

89. George Sims, p. 45.

90. Elizabeth Blackwell, p. 105.

91. 'How Wears the Missing Link?',in *God's Message in Low London*, 1871, p. 39.

92. Ibid.

93. R.W. Vanderkiste, p. 53

94. *The Missing Link Magazine*, 1 May 1873, p. 141.

95. William Acton, *Prostitution*, pp. 22–23.

96. LCMM, 'St. George's-in-the-East', vol. XX, 1855, p. 99.

97. *The Book and Its Mission*, 'Wanted a Treasurer for Each District', A/RNY/97, 1862, p. 281.

98. Emile Zola, *l'Assommoir*, Le Seuil, Paris 1970, pp. 384–8. See also in *A Child of the Jago* the scuffle between Sally Green and Hannah Perrott (pp. 44–5).

99. W. Somerset Maugham, *Liza of Lambeth*, Heinemann, London 1976 (1897), pp. 105–6.

100. *The Book and Its Missions*, 1 February 1864, p. 46.

101. Mrs Ranyard, pp. 130–31.

102. Arthur St. John Adcock, *East End Idylls*, London 1897, pp. 188–9.

103. A.J.B. Parent-Duchâtelet, *De la prostitution dans la ville de Paris*, J.B. Baillère, Paris, 1836, vol. I, p. 134.

104. Harry Campbell, *Differences in the Nervous Organisation of Man and Woman*, London 1891. His survey was carried out among fifty married male workers resident in London, who were patients in his department.

105. Havelock Ellis, vol. III, p. 217.

106. Ibid (footnote).

107. LCMM, 'Southwark', vol. XVI, 1851, p. 59.

108. Judith Walkowitz, *Prostitution and Victorian Society, Women, Class and the State*, Cambridge University Press 1980, p. 32.

109. W.R. Greg, 'Prostitution', *Westminster Review,* vol. 53, July 1850; William Acton, *Prostitution,* London 1857.
110. William Acton, p. 20.
111. Jabez Burns, *Retrospect of Forty Years Ministry,* London 1875, p. 239.

2 THE FOUNDLING HOSPITAL

1. Only one child in five was admitted. Cf. John Brownslow, *History and Objects of the Foundling Hospital with a Memoir of the Founder,* edn revised by W.S. Wintle, London 1881, pp. 70–1.
2. Joseph Massie, *Farther Observations Concerning the Foundling Hospital . . . ,* London 1759, pp. 1–2.
3. These sheets are folded in three, with the rest of the file contained inside them. They are stored in bundles of ten, tied together with red cotton ribbon.
4. Michel Foucault, *The History of Sexuality* I, pp. 61–2.
5. The admission files are so numerous and detailed that it was not possible to make an exhaustive analysis of them; nor was it really necessary. After looking through more than a thousand files, we chose a decade in the second half of the century (1860–70) for exhaustive analysis; then added three years from the previous decade (1851–2–3) and three from the following one (1871–2–3). Various aspects, especially the letters between applicants and the fathers of their children, were surveyed in detail for the period 1850–79. Applications from the provinces, and from women whose origin or occupation placed them in too high a social class, were naturally excluded. Thus only applications from women whose social origin and occupation identified them with the popular or working classes were analysed.

3 LOVE AND MARRIAGE

1. Declaration of Elizabeth E, aged seventeen.
2. There are 26 cases of alleged rape: 13 by men of the same social class, 11 by social or professional superiors and two involving unknown persons. The victims' ages varied from 17 to 29.
3. In order to respect privacy and to adhere to the regulations of the Thomas Coram Foundling Hospital, I have not dated any of the extracts from the Hospital's archives, and have altered other dates, and petitioners' first names and surname initials. To distinguish them from other sources, all extracts from the archives will simply be referenced as 'FH' in the notes.
4. FH.
5. FH.
6. FH.
7. 'Buteau slyly tortured her with little familiarities, slapping her on the bottom, pinching her thighs, all kinds of brutal caresses', Emile Zola, *Earth (La Terre),* transl. Ann Lindsay, Elek Books, London 1954, p. 249.
8. FH.
9. Special prayers were said to prepare women in labour for eternal life.

10. FH.

11. FH.

12. In one case, for example, a petitioner, clearly anxious to conceal her frivolous attitude, claimed to have been in a job for seven months; her former employer, when contacted, corrected this to two months (1862).

13. Henry Mayhew, vol. IV, p. 257.

14. 'Milly's Cigar Divan', written and composed by John Cook Jr, arranged by E.J. Symons (undated).

15. Arthur J. Munby, *Red Note-Books, 1860–61*, 4 vols, MSS., 27 March to 22 June 1861, p. 195.

16. Henry Mayhew, p. 217.

17. Arthur J. Munby, 1 October 1860 to 26 March 1861, pp. 125–6.

18. FH.

19. Described by the inquirer as 'an ill-famed district'. We should note here that individuals clung to some parts of the capital. Matilda Z's family home was about half an hour's walk from the place where she worked. She later found new employment in Montague Square, then in Portman Square, even closer to her family.

20. James Greenwood, *The Seven Curses of London, Scenes from the Victorian Underworld*, Basil Blackwell, Oxford 1981 (1869) pp. 180–81.

21. FH.

22. Sarah might easily have been one of the group of dancers seen by Munby one Sunday evening at the Manor Tavern in Walworth; she must have had a similar, respectable appearance in order to be received by the Foundling Hospital: 'The women, workgirls, dressed without any pretence of fashion, and some servants. I noticed among the girls several pleasant ruddy faces, and several red homely hands. The dancing was spirited, the talk cheery and unreserved but modest.' 11 September to 31 December 1861, p. 218.

23. The London Bible Women and Nurses Mission was one of many charitable institutions which existed at the time. It attempted to improve women whose morals were bad.

24. Arthur J. Munby, 1 October to 26 March 1861, p. 99.

25. 'The British Weekly' Commissioners, *Toilers in London, Inquiries Concerning Female Labour in the Metropolis*, Hodder & Stoughton, London 1889, p. 102.

26. W.T. Layton, 'Changes in the Wages of Domestic Servants During Fifty Years', *Journal of the Royal Statistical Society*, vol. LXXXI, 1908, p. 515.

27. 'Modern Domestic Service', *Edinburgh Review*, vol. CXV, April 1862, pp. 426–7, in John Burnett, ed., *Useful Toil, Autobiographies of Working People from the 1820s to the 1920s*, Allen Lane, London 1974, p. 160.

28. Mrs Beeton, in her *Book of Household Management* (London 1861), devotes nearly twenty pages to the different tasks carried out by chambermaids, from lighting the fires in the morning and carrying hot water to the bedrooms, to the ways of laying out clothes for all the members of the family, answering the door to visitors, cleaning marble, copper and silverware, serving at table, washing, ironing, etc.

29. Arthur J. Munby, 1 October to 26 March 1861, pp. 140–41.

30. Arthur J. Munby, p. 99.

31. 'My Mother's Customs', in Thomas Crampton, *A Collection of Broadside Ballads Printed in London*, London 1860.

32. Factory workers worked only ten hours a day and from the 1870s began to get Saturday afternoons off work. Of course they did not work on Sundays.

33. *Toilers in London*, p. 102; Munby, 1 January to 31 March 1862, p. 59.

34. Arthur J. Munby, 27 March to June 1861, p. 193.

35. The heroine of a ballad of the 1870s was only a servant, 'But to marry a Milkman she did not feel inclined'. She describes her ideal husband:

Oh, the man who has me must have silver and gold, A chariot to ride in and be handsome and bold, His hair must be curly as any watch spring And his whiskers as long as a brush for clothing.

('Polly Perkins of Paddington Green', in Thomas Crampton, vol. 8, p. 38).

36. 'The Factory Girl', in Thomas Crampton, p. 140.

37. Mrs Gaskell, *Mary Barton,* Dent, London/Dutton, New York 1967 (1848), p. 75.

38. FH.

39. FH.

40. FH.

41. Munby, 23 June to 26 August 1861, p. 111.

42. 'Rosemary Lane', in James Reeves, *The Idiom of the People,* Heinemann, London 1958, p. 223.

43. Alain Corbin, *Les Filles de noce, Misère sexuelle et prostitution aux XIXe et XXe siècles,* Aubier, Paris 1978, p. 305.

44. Arthur J. Munby, 1 October to 26 March, 1860–61, pp. 113–14.

45. FH.

46. Henry Mayhew, vol. IV, p. 122.

47. FH.

48. FH.

49. FH.

50. FH.

51. Arthur J. Munby, 1 October to 26 March, 1860–61, pp. 127–32.

52. FH.

53. Octavia Hill, pp. 58–9.

54. FH.

55. FH.

56. FH.

57. FH.

58. Arthur R's brother complains in a letter to his mother of the upset caused to holiday plans by the confinement of their young housemaid at the Isle of Wight: 'I suppose it will be impossible to go there for the present, since the story is known to everyone.'

59. FH.

60. FH.

61. FH.

62. FH.

63. FH.

64. Once again, as with the reports of charitable societies which were read by middle-class women, or in William Thomas Stead's press campaign, we note how limited in reality was the alleged taboo on sexual questions.

65. FH.

66. Sarah Stickney, *The Wives of England, Their Relative Duties, Domestic Influence and Social Obligations, dedicated by permission to the Queen,* Fischer & Son, London 1843, p. 304.

67. Elizabeth Blackwell, *The Human Element in Sex, Being a Medical Enquiry into the Relation of Sexual Physiology to Christian Morality,* London 1885, p. 5.

68. Ibid., p. 25.

69. Anon., *The Servant Girl in London Showing the Dangers to which Young Country Girls are Exposed on their Arrival in Town with Advice to Them, to their Parents, to their Masters, and to*

their Mistresses, respectfully dedicated to all Heads of Families & Benevolent Societies, London 1840, p. 8.

70. Ibid.

71. FH.

72. Anon, *The Servant Girl in London* . . . , p. 8.

73. Martha Vicinus, *Independent Women, Work and Community for Single Women, 1850–1920, Virago Press,* London 1985, p. 17.

74. Anon., *The Servant Girl in London* . . . , pp. 55 and 49. This ideal age was 24.

75. As described by François Bédarida, 'Londres au milieu du XIXe siècle: une analyse de structure sociale', *Annales,* vol. XXII, No. 2, March–April 1968.

76. 'Going to Chelsea to Buy a Bun', in Thomas Crampton, p. 55.

77. Arthur J. Munby, 1 January to 31 March 1862, pp. 57–8.

78. FH.

79. FH.

80. FH.

81. FH.

82. FH.

83. FH.

84. FH.

85. FH.

86. In J.S. Bratton, *The Victorian Popular Ballad,* Macmillan, London 1975, p. 167.

87. William Brough and Andrew Halliday, *The Area Belle,* 1865, in M.R. Booth, *English Plays of the Nineteenth Century,* 5 vols, Clarendon Press, Oxford 1969, vol. III, p. 244.

88. 'The Special Bobby', Disley Printer, 57 High Street, St Giles's, in Thomas Crampton, p. 54.

89. FH

90. FH.

91. Anon., *The Servant Girl in London,* . . . p. 37.

92. FH

93. Anon., *The Servant Girl in London,* . . . p. 37.

94. William Acton, *The Functions and Disorders of the Reproductive Organs in Youth, in Adult Age, and in Advanced Life* . . . , London 1857, p. 207.

95. FH.

96. FH.

97. FH.

98. FH.

99. *The Area Belle,* vol. 2, p. 239.

100. 'Organ Grinder', in Thomas Crampton, p. 153.

101. Except for one detail: the crinoline was not well adapted to household labour. Maidservants wore cotton dresses, which they usually protected with aprons of sackcloth when kneeling.

102. FH.

103. FH.

104. FH.

105. FH.

106. FH.

107. FH.

108. He worked as a gilder.

109. FH.

110. FH.

111. FH.

112. FH.

113. FH.

114. FH.

115. For example John Eames or Adolphus Crosbie in *Small House at Allingham*, London 1864.

116. Engels, *Origin of the Family, Private Property and the State*, in Marx and Engels, *Selected Works*, Lawrence & Wishart, London and New York 1976: 'The ruling class continues to be dominated by the familiar economic influences and, therefore, only in exceptional cases can it show really voluntary marriages; whereas, as we have seen, these are the rule among the dominated class.'

117. FH.

118. John Gillis, *For Better, For Worse, British Marriages 1600 to the Present*, Oxford University Press 1985, p. 29.

119. Peter Laslett, *The World We Have Lost*, Methuen, London 1965; Lawrence Stone; Jean-Louis Flandrin, *Les Amours paysannes (XVIe-XXe siècles)*, Gallimard, Paris 1975; André Burguière, 'The Marriage Ritual in France: Ecclesiastical Practices and Popular Practices', in *Ritual, Religion and the Sacred*, Baltimore 1982. 'Bundling' was courting a girl in bed, in the dark, partially unclothed. Although most authors refer to the custom, Alan Macfarlane casts strong doubt on its existence in England in his work *Marriage and Love in England, 1300-1840*, p. 306.

120. John Gillis, p. 39: a ritual ceremony used in some regions to mark official recognition of a love relationship by the couple's families and friends.

121. FH.

122. FH.

123. FH.

124. FH.

125. FH.

126. FH.

127. FH.

128. FH.

129. FH.

130. FH.

131. FH.

132. FH.

133. FH.

134. Christopher N was about 50 and Susan T 29.

135. FH.

136. FH.

137. FH.

138. FH.

139. FH.

140. FH.

141. FH.

142. FH.

143. FH.

144. FH.

145. FH.

146. FH.
147. FH.
148. FH.
149. A statement made in a number of petitions.
150. FH.
151. FH.
152. FH.
153. FH.
154. FH.
155. FH.
156. FH.
157. 'The Muslin', in Crampton, p. 197.
158. Peter Laslett, p. 143.
159. Lawrence Stone, p. 609.
160. Ibid.
161. For confirmation, see notably *The Autobiography of Francis Place, 1771–1854*, ed. Mary Thrale, Cambridge University Press 1972, pp. 73–82.
162. 'Keeping company' could be both prolonged and sporadic, and was strongly influenced by the couple's employment. Sarah P, a housemaid, in 1859 met John E, a carpenter working on a Notting Hill development close to her master's house. Then she left to work in Brighton, and they did not see each other for two years although she returned to the capital and worked in Kensington Park Terrace. The couple resumed their courtship when she went to work for a Mr E in Lansdowne Road, then for a woman living nearby, staying in this job for six months. John E visited her at the houses of both these employers. This went on for fifteen months, until she found yet another job at a house in Chilworth Street. It was at this point that the seduction took place in a 'house of ill fame'.
163. The speaker is Esther in *Mary Barton*.
164. FH.
165. FH.
166. FH.
167. FH.
168. FH.
169. FH.
170. FH.
171. FH.
172. FH.
173. FH.
174. FH.
175. FH.
176. FH.
177. FH.
178. FH.
179. FH.
180. Gillis, p. 282.
181. Only about fifty of the petitions give no details.
182. But the tone of sincerity is often manifest: 'CC took place at my lodgings under promise of marriage. CC was repeated a few days afterwards and once more at the same place. I soon found myself pregnant... and I told him I thought I was in the family way and he still promised marriage'.

183. FH.

184. FH.

185. 'The Muslin'.

186. 'Did You Ever Hear a Girl Say "No!" ', written and composed by Herbert Cole, sung by Herbert Campbell (undated).

187. FH.

188. Mary, who had been working as a chambermaid in the household of a peer, was unemployed when these events took place.

189. FH.

190. FH.

191. FH.

192. FH.

193. FH.

194. FH.

195. FH.

196. FH.

197. FH.

198. Chloroform was invented in 1834. Queen Victoria was the first woman to use it to achieve painless childbirth. It was both miracle cure and absolute weapon.

199. Anon., *The Work Girls of London, Their Trials, and Temptations, Two Tales and Two Numbers Every Week*, London 1866, p. 207.

200. G.W.M. Reynolds, *The Mysteries of London*, London 1845–48, vol. 1, p. 151.

201. FH.

202. FH.

203. FH.

204. FH.

205. FH.

206. FH.

207. FH.

208. FH.

209. FH.

210. FH.

211. FH.

212. FH.

213. 'You Know', written and performed by Arthur Lloyd, 1882.

214. FH.

215. FH.

216. Lord Byron, *Don Juan*, 1819–24, part 1, lines 935–6.

217. 'Going to Chelsea To Buy a Bun', in Crampton, p. 55.

218. FH.

219. FH.

220. FH.

221. FH.

222. FH.

223. FH.

224. FH.

225. FH.

226. FH.

227. It seems probable that the Hospital committee no longer asked this question in every

case.
228. FH.
229. FH.
230. FH.
231. FH.
232. Many of the letters have shaky grammar, spelling and handwriting. I have retained the original grammar and spelling.
233. FH.
234. FH.
235. FH.
236. FH.
237. FH.
238. FH.
239. FH.
240. FH.
241. FH.
242. FH.
243. FH.
244. FH.
245. FH.
246. FH.
247. FH.
248. A Dickens character embodying blissful Victorian conformism.
249. FH.
250. FH.
251. FH.
252. FH.
253. FH.
254. FH.
255. FH.
256. FH.
257. In Vivian de Sola Pinto and Allan Edwin Rodway, eds, *The Common Muse, An Anthology of British Ballad Poetry from the 15th to the 20th Cntury*, Penguin Books, Harmondsworth 1965.
258. FH.
259. FH.
260. FH.
261. FH.
262. FH.
263. FH.
264. FH.
265. FH.
266. FH.
267. Oliver Goldsmith, *The Deserted Village*, 1764, line 331.
268. See chapters XI and XII on impure women in Françoise Basch, *Relative Creatures: Victorian Women in Society and the Novel*.
269. FH.
270. FH.
271. 'The Muslin', in Crampton, p. 197.

272. FH.
273. FH.
274. FH.
275. FH.
276. FH.
277. FH.
278. FH.
279. FH.
280. The tracts of Francis Place were widely diffused in the 1820s, and works by neo-Malthusians like Richard Carlile, Charles Knowlton, Robert Dale Owen and William Thompson were very popular. There was also a good deal of advertising aimed at the labouring classes promoting mechanical methods of contraception.
281. Patricia Knight says that the least fertile moment was believed to be midway between two menstruations, something which helps to explain the quite extraordinary ineffectiveness of this particular pattern of abstinence (Patricia Knight, 'Women and Abortion in Victorian and Edwardian England', *History Workshop Journal*, no. 4, Autumn 1977, p. 59).
282. FH.
283. FH.
284. FH.
285. FH.
286. FH.
287. James Simpson, *A Probationary Essay on Infanticide, Edinburgh, 1825*, cited in Angus McLaren, 'Women's Work and Family Size', *History Workshop Journal*, no. 4, Autumn 1977, p. 73. It was observed pragmatically that women working in factories using lead had a high incidence of miscarriages.
288. FH.
289. FH.
290. FH.
291. The opinion is that of the Foundling Hospital's inquirer.
292. FH.
293. FH.
294. FH.
295. FH.
296. FH.
297. FH.
298. FH.
299. FH.
300. FH.
301. FH.
302. FH.
303. FH.
304. FH.
305. FH.
306. FH.
307. FH.
308. FH.
309. FH.
310. FH.
311. FH.

312. FH.
313. FH.
314. FH.
315. FH.
316. FH.
317. FH.
318. FH.
319. FH.
320. As workers' purchasing power increased, fewer women were continuing to work after marriage; in the 1890s Booth noted that the wives of skilled workers spent all their time doing housework (Charles Booth, *Life and Labour of the People in London*, Series I, vol. I, pp. 50–51). Even if not all the Foundling Hospital applicants had this ambition, women's wages were so low that women were especially anxious to have the support of a second wage to improve their standard of living. We might also mention the unsurprising wish to live with the man they loved. Finally, the unmarried state in women was seen negatively by Victorian society. 'Old maids' and women 'left on the shelf' are mocked in a number of ballads.
321. Flora Tristan. *Le Tour de France, Journal 1843–44*, , F.M. La Découverte, Paris 1980, vol. I, p. 138.
322. Engels, *The Condition of the Working Class in England*.
323. Charles Knight, *The Workingman's Companion or Year Book for 1839, containing informations especially calculated to advance the intelligence and better the condition of the Working Classes*, London 1839, p. 38.
324. Robert Tressell, *The Ragged Trousered Philanthropists*, Panther Books, London 1971 (1906), p. 27.
325. FH.
326. Knight, p. 7.
327. FH.
328. FH.
329. FH.
330. FH.
331. See, for example, Emile Zola's 1882 novel *Restless House (Pot-Bouille)*: 'The fact was, Adèle was nine months gone with child. For a long while she thought she was getting stouter, and this astonished her somewhat. Famished as she always was, it enraged her when Madame triumphantly pointed to her before all her guests, remarking that if anyone accused her of doling out food to her servant they might come and see what a great glutton she was, whose belly had never got as round as that by licking the walls, eh? When the dull-witted girl was, at last, aware of her misfortune, she was often within an ace of telling her mistress the whole truth, who thus took advantage of her condition to make all the neighbours believe that she was feeding her up, after all . . .' (transl. Percy Pinkerton, Weidenfeld Nicolson, London 1953).
332. 'She was a thoroughly respectable steady girl the very last we could have supposed likely to go astray – indeed so much so that not one of her fellow servants ever suspected her state, not even the Cook, a woman of nearly 40 who slept with her. Her stoutness was ascribed to some dropsical affection and some of her family died from this disease. . . .'
333. FH.
334. FH.
335. FH.
336. FH.
337. FH.

338. FH.
339. FH.
340. FH.
341. FH.
342. FH.
343. FH.
344. *General Lying-In Hospital Case Books, From March 1st 1854 to 15th December 1872*, 6 June 1854.
345. Ibid., 27 June 1858.
346. FH.
347. FH.
348. FH.
349. She was a waitress in a hotel.
351. Crampton, p. 78.
352. Ibid., p. 197.
353. FH, italics added.
354. FH.
355. FH.
356. FH.
357. FH.
358. FH.
359. FH.
360. FH.
361. Although strictly speaking this case does not concern Londoners – they were domestics who divided their time between London and Sussex – we quote it here for the clear light it throws on the seducer's attitudes.
362. FH.
363. FH.
364. FH.
365. FH.
366. FH.
367. FH.
368. FH.
369. FH.
370. FH.
371. FH.
372. FH.
373. FH.
374. FH.
375. FH.
376. FH.
377. FH.
378. FH.
379. FH.
380. FH.
381. FH.
382. FH.
383. FH.
384. FH.

385. FH.
386. FH.
387. FH.
388. 'The New Balow', in de Sola Pinto and Rodway, pp. 546–7.
389. Anna Davin, 'Imperialism and Motherhood', *History Workshop Journal,* no. 5, Spring 1978, p. 24.
390. Margaret Wynn Nevinson, *Life's Fitful Fever . . .* , London 1926, p. 94.
391. FH.
392. FH.
393. FH.
394. FH.
395. FH.
396. FH.
397. FH.
398. FH.
399. FH.
400. FH.
401. FH.
402. FH.
403. FH.
404. FH.
405. FH.
406. FH.
407. FH.
408. Alastair Reid, 'Intelligent Artisans and Aristocrats of Labour: The Essays of Thomas Wright', in Jay Winter, ed., *The Working Class in Modern British History, Essays in Honour of Henry Pelling, Cambridge University Press,* 1983.
409. FH.
410. FH.
411. Victor Hugo, 'Les Pauvres Gens', in *La Légende des siècles,* 1859, lines 235–7.
412. FH.
413. FH.
414. FH.
415. FH.
416. FH.
417. FH.
418. FH.
419. FH.
420. FH.
421. FH.
422. Mayhew, vol. IV, p. 258.
423. Ibid., p. 257.
424. William Acton, p. 207.
425. FH.
426. FH.
427. FH.
428. FH.
429. FH.
430. FH.

431. FH.
432. FH.
433. FH.
434. FH.
435. FH.
436. FH.
437. FH.
438. FH.
439. FH.
440. FH.
441. G.W.M. Reynolds, *The Mysteries of London*, p. 157.
442. Françoise Ducrocq, 'From Poor Law to Jungle Law: Sexual Relations and Marital Strategies', in Judith Friendlander *et al.*, eds, *Women in Culture and Politics, A Century of Change*, Indiana University Press, Bloomington 1986.

EPILOGUE

1. Françoise Ducrocq, 'Les Exclus de l'histoire', *Critique, numéro spécial: Victoria Station*, nos. 405–6, February–March 1981.
2. Peter Cominos, 'Innocent Feminina Sensualis in Unconscious Conflict', in Martha Vicinus, ed., *Suffer and Be Still*, Indiana University Press, Bloomington 1974, p. 167.

Bibliography

I MANUSCRIPT FILES

FOUNDLING HOSPITAL Collection, 1850–1880.
MUNBY, Arthur J.,
  Red Note-Books, 1860–1861.
Annual Reports of Medical Officers of Health in London Vestry Districts,
  1855–1893.

II REPORTS AND DOCUMENTATION OF PHILANTHROPIC AND OTHER ASSOCIATIONS

1 The London City Mission

Annual Reports of the London City Mission, London 1835–1845.
The City Mission Magazine; The London City Mission Magazine vol. I,
  1836–vol. XXII, London 1857.
VANDERKIST, R.W., Late London City Missionary,
  Notes and Narratives of a Six Years' Mission principally among the Dens of
  London, London 1852.
WEYLLAND, John Matthias,
  These Fifty Years, Being the Jubilee Volume of the London City Mission,
  London 1884.

2 The London Bible Women and Nurses Mission

The Book and Its Missions, Past and Present, a monthly magazine, London
  1859–1864.

The Missing Link Magazine, London 1865–1880.
'God's Message in Low London', Seven Missing Link Tracts, London 1871.
HILL, Octavia,
   Our Common Land and other short essays, London 1877.
MRS RANYARD (L.N.R.), WHITE, Ellen,
   The Missing Link; or Bible Women in the Homes of the London Poor, London
   1859
   The Missing Link Tracts, London 1871.
SELFE, Rose Emily,
   *Light amid London Shadows. A Record of 50 Years' Work in the London Bible
   Women and Nurses Mission*, London 1906.

3 The Salvation Army

Broken Fetters, Report of Women's Rescue and Social Work for 1894, London 1894.
Fitly Spoken, 1892–93, London 1893.
Quenched, Annual Report of the Women's Social Work for 1895, London 1895.
Ready to Perish, Report of Rescue and Women's Social Work for 1893, London
   1893.
*Saved in Time, Annual Report of the Salvation Army Women's Social Work,
   1892–93*, London 1893.
SWIFT, S.F.,
   *In the Slums! An Account of The Salvation Army Warfare in the Dark Courts and
   Alleys of Modern Babylon and Other Great Cities*, London 1889.
The Christian Mission Magazine, vol. II, 1870–vol. X, London 1878.
The Christian Mission Report (typed sheet), 1867.

4 The Moral Reform Union

Annual Reports, London 1882–1897.
BUTTER, Henry,
   *Is the Pleasure Worth the Penalty? A Commonsense View of the Leading Vice of
   the Age*, London 1865.
   What's the Harm of Fornication?, London 1865.
   Marriage for the Million for the Lads and Lasses of the Working Classes, London
   1872.
ENGSTRÖM, Rev. C. Lloyd,
   Purity Treated Purely, A Sermon Preached at the Foundling Hospital, Sunday

Morning, August 23, 1885, London 1885.

III PARLIAMENTARY PAPERS

Annual Report of the Registrar of Births, Deaths and Marriages in England, 1861, vol. XXIV.

Minutes of Evidence, Royal Commission on Divorce and Matrimonial Causes, 1912, vol. I.

Papers Relating to the Sanitary State of the People of England, 1857–1858, XXIII.

Report from the Committee on the Law Relating to the Protection of Young Girls, 1882, XIII.

Report from the Select Committee of the House of Lords on Poor Law Relief, 1861, IX.

Report from the Select Committee of the House of Lords on Poor Law Relief, 1888. XV.

Report of the Royal Commission on Divorce and Matrimonial Causes, 1912.

Royal Commission on the Housing of Working Classes, 1884–1885, XXX.

Tabulations of Statements Made by Men Living in Certain Selected Districts of London in March 1887, 1887, LXXXI.

The Select Committee of the House of Lords Appointed to Inquire into the Deficiency of Means of Spiritual Instruction and Places of Divine Worship in the Metropolis and other Populous Districts . . . 1857–1858, IX.

The Select Committee on Artisans' and Labourers' Dwellings Improvement, 1881, VII.

The Select Committee on Health, 1883, LXXXI.

IV NEWSPAPERS, JOURNALS AND PERIODICALS

Hackney Independent, 1863.

Hansard's Parliamentary Debates, Third Series,
    Vol. CXXXXVI, 1857.
    Vol. CXLVII, 1857.
    Vol. CLXI, 1861.
    Vol. CLXXXI, 1866.
    Vol. CCLXXXIV, 1884.

Journal of the Statistical Society, vol. I, 1838–vol. XLVI, 1883.

Journal of the Statistical Society, Subject Index, vols XXVIII, LVII, 1865–1894.

Knight's Penny Magazine, 2 vols., London 1846.
KNIGHT, Charles, ed.,
  The Working Man's Companion or Year Book Containing Information, calculated to advance the intelligence and better the condition of the working classes, London 1835–1840.
Lloyd's Illustrated London Newspaper, 1842–1843.
Lloyd's Weekly Newspaper, 1860–1861.
The Penny Magazine of the Society for the Diffusion of Useful Knowledge, vol. IV, 1835–vol. IX, 1840.
Reynolds' Newspaper, a Weekly Journal of Politics, History, Literature and General Intelligence, 1850–1867.
Reynolds' Miscellany, 1847–1869.
Times, 'Court for Divorce and Matrimonial Causes', 1838–1886.
Transactions of the Society of Medical Officers of Health, 1883–1884.

V CONTEMPORARY WRITINGS

1 Literature

ADCOCK, Arthur St John,
  East End Idylls, London 1897.
  In the Image of God, A Story of Lower London, London 1898.
  Love in London, London 1906.
BOOTH, Michael R.,
  English Melodrama, Herbert Jenkins, London 1965.
  English Plays of the Nineteenth Century, 5 vols, The Clarendon Press, Oxford 1969.
DICKENS, Charles,
  Sketches by Boz, J.M. Dent & Co., London/E.P. Dutton, New York 1907 (1837).
  Oliver Twist, J.M Dent, London/E.P. Dutton, New York 1907 (1839).
Life and Adventures of Nicholas Nickleby, Collins, London and Glasgow, 1953 (1839).
Bleak House, W.W. Norton & Co., New York and London 1977 (1853).
DICK'S
  Edition of Standard Plays, nos 1–305, John Dicks, London 1883.
DISRAELI, Benjamin,
  Sybil: or the Two Nations, Oxford University Press, London 1970 (1845).
ELIOT, George,

Adam Bede, Collins, London and Glasgow 1959 (1859).

The Mill on the Floss, Collins, London and Glasgow 1962 (1860).

FRAXI PISANUS (Henry Spencer Ashbee),

Index Librorum Prohibitorum: being Notes Bio-Biblio-Iconographical and Critical, on Curious and Uncommon Books, London 1877.

Centuria Librorum Absconditorum, London 1879.

Catena Librorum Tacendorum, London 1885.

GASKELL, Mrs,

Ruth, J.M. Dent, London/E.P. Dutton, New York 1967 (1853).

Mary Barton, J.M Dent, London/E.P. Dutton, New York 1967 (1848).

GISSING, George,

The Unclassed, Smith, Elder & Co., London 1884.

Thrysa, a Tale, The Harvester Press, Brighton 1974 (1887).

Demos, A Story of Socialist Life in England, Smith, Elder & Co., London 1886.

The Nether World, J.M. Dent, London/E.P. Dutton, New York 1973 (1889).

HARDY, Thomas,

Tess of the d'Urbervilles, Macmillan, London 1962 (1891).

Jude the Obscure, Macmillan, London 1964 (1895).

LAW, John,

A City Girl, A Realistic Story, London 1887.

Captain Lobe, A Story of the Salvation Army, London 1888.

MAUGHAM, W. Somerset,

Liza of Lambeth, Heinemann, London 1976 (1897).

MOORE, George,

Esther Waters, J.M. Dent & Sons, London 1962 (1894).

MORRISON, Arthur,

Tales of Mean Streets, London 1894.

A Child of the Jago, London 1907 (1896).

To London Town, London 1899.

REYNOLDS, G.W.M.,

The Mysteries of London, 2 vols, London 1845–1848.

SIMS, George Robert,

Rogues and Vagabonds, London 1900.

A Blind Marriage and other Stories, London 1901.

Biographs of Babylon, London 1902.

The Work Girls of London, their Trials and Temptations, two tales and two numbers every week, London 1866.

WRIGHT, Thomas (The Journeyman Engineer),

Johnny Robinson, The Story of the Childhood and Schooldays of an Intelligent

Artisan, 2 vols, London 1868.
The Bane of Life, 3 vols, London 1870.
Grainger's Thorn, 3 vols, London 1872.
ZOLA, Emile,
L'Assommoir, Penguin Books, Harmondsworth 1970 (1876).
Nana, Le Seuil, Paris 1970 (1878).
Pot-Bouille (Restless House), transl. Percy Pinkerton, Weidenfeld & Nicolson, London 1953 (1882).
Au bonheur des dames, Le Seuil, Paris 1970 (1883).
Germinal, transl. Leonard Tancock, Penguin Books, Harmondsworth 1954 (1885).
La Terre (Earth), transl. Ann Lindsay, Elek Books, London 1954.

2 Songs and ballads

ALBERT CHEVALIER'S,
5th Song Album, London 1890.
Humorous Songs, etc., London 1894.
ASHTON, John,
A Century of Ballads, London 1887.
Modern Street Ballads, London 1888.
BRATTON, J.S.,
The Victorian Popular Ballad, Macmillan, London 1975.
CAMPBELL, Herbert (sung by), written and composed by Herbert Cole,
'Did you Ever Hear A Girl Say "No"!' London.
CARTER, Harry and G.W. HUNTER,
'Kissing', London.
COMBES, Arthur (sung by), written by J.S. Evans,
'Angels are Hovering Round', London.
CRAMPTON, Thomas,
A Collection of Broadside Ballads Printed in London, 7 vols., London 1860.
D'ALCORN'S,
Musical Miracle, 120 Comic Songs Sung By Sam Cowell, London 1878.
DAVIDSON, P., ed.,
Songs of the British Music Hall, New York 1971.
DE SOLA PINTO, Vivian and Allan E. RODWAY,
The Common Muse, An Anthology of Popular British Ballad Poetry from the 15th to the 20th Century, Penguin Books, Harmondsworth 1965.
50 Favourite Songs and Ballads, Bossey & Co., London 1885.

HARDWICK, J.A.J.,
  Fourth Collection. Comic Songs. . . sung at Public Concerts, London 1854.
HINDLEY, Charles,
  The Canatch Press, etc., London 1869.
  ed., *Curiosities of Street Literature*, 2 vols., London 1871.
  A History of the Cries of London, Ancient and Modern, London 1881.
HOLLOWAY, John and John BLACK, eds,
  Later English Broadside Ballads, vol.I, Routledge & Kegan Paul, London
  1975; vol.II, Routledge & Kegan Paul, London 1979.
LEE Edward,
  Music of the People, Barrie & Jenkins, London 1970.
  McDermott's Comic Song Album, London.
PEARSALL, Ronald,
  Victorian Sheet Music Covers, David & Charles, London 1972.
  Victorian Popular Music, David & Charles, London 1973.
REEVES, James,
  The Idiom of the People, Heinemann, London 1958.
  The Everlasting Circle, Heinemann, London 1960.
RENDLE, Thomas McDonald,
  Swings and Roundabouts, A Yokel in London, etc., London 1919.

3 Autobiographies, biographies and personal diaries

ALLEN, Charles Grant B.,
  Biographies of Working Men, London 1884.
ANON. (Walter),
  My Secret Life, Grove Press, New York 1966.
CHURCH, Richard,
  Over the Bridge, an Essay in Autobiography, Heinemann, London 1955.
DAVIES, Margaret Llewellyn, ed.,
  Maternity: Letters from Working Women, London 1915.
  Life As We Have Known It, by Co-operative Working Women, Virago, London
  1977 (1931).
HARRIS, Frank,
  My Life and Loves, Five Volumes in One, Complete and Unexpurgated, Corgi
  Books, London 1967 (1925).
HUDSON, Derek,
  *Munby Man of Two Worlds, The Life and Diaries of Arthur J. Munby,
  1828–1910*, Abacus, London 1974.

HUGHES, Mary Vivian,
  A London Child of the 1870s, Oxford University Press, Oxford and London 1977 (1934).
  A London Home in the Nineties, Oxford University Press, London 1937.
  A London Girl of the 1880s, Oxford University Press, Oxford and London 1978 (1943).
NEVINSON, Margaret Wynn,
  Life's Fitful Fever: A Volume of Memories, A. & C. Black, London 1926.
ROBERTS, Robert,
  The Classic Slum, Salford Life in the First Quarter of the Century, Penguin Books, Harmondsworth 1977 (1971).
  A Ragged Schooling, Growing Up in the Classic Slum, Fontana/Collins, Glasgow 1978.
SAMUEL, Raphael,
  East End Underworld: Chapters in the Life of Arthur Harding, History Workshop Series, Routledge & Kegan Paul, London/Boston 1981.
TAYLOR, Shepard Thomas,
  The Diary of a Medical Student during the Mid-Victorian Period, 1860–1864, Norwich 1927.
WEBB, Beatrice,
  My Apprenticeship, Allen & Unwin, London 1926.
A WORKING MAN,
  Scenes from my Life, London 1858.
  Reminiscences of a Stonemason, London 1908.

4 Medical works

ACTON, William,
  The Functions and Disorders of the Reproductive Organs in Youth, in Adult Age and in Advanced Life Considered in their Physiological, Social and Moral Relations, London 1857.
BLACKWELL, Dr Elizabeth,
  The Moral Education of the Young in Relation to Sex, London 1882 (6th edn).
  The Human Element in Sex, being a Medical Enquiry into the Relation of Sexual Physiology to Christian Moralty, London 1885.
CAMPBELL, Harry,
  Differences in the Nervous Organisation of Man and Woman, London 1891.
DUNCAN, Dr John Matthews,
  On the Mortality of Childbed and Maternity Hospitals. Lectures on Midwifery and

Diseases of Women and Children in Surgeon's Hall Medical School, Clinical Lectures on Diseases of Women in Royal Infirmary, A. & C. Black, Edinburgh 1870.
Fecundity, Fertility, Sterility and Allied Topics, A. & C. Black, Edinburgh 1871.
On Sterility in Woman, being the Gulstonian Lectures delivered in the Royal College of Physicians in February 1883, London 1884.
ELLIS, Havelock,
  Studies in the Psychology of Sex, 3 vols., F.A. Davis Company, Philadelphia 1910 (1887).
WHITEHEAD, James,
  Studies on the Causes and Treatment of Abortion and Sterility, London 1847.

5 Surveys, inquiries and papers

(a) London

BESANT, Walter
  Fifty Years Ago, London 1888.
  South London, London 1899.
  East London, London 1901.
  Shoreditch and the East End, London 1908.
DORE, Gustave and W.B. JERROLD,
  London: a Pilgrimage, London 1872.
GARWOOD, Rev. John,
  The Million-Peopled City: or One-Half of the People in London Made Known to the Other Half, London 1853.
GRANT, James,
  Lights and Shadows of London, 2 vols., London 1842.
  The Great Metropolis, 2 vols., London 1837.
MAYHEW, Henry,
  1851: or the Adventures of Mr. and Mrs. Sandboys and Family who came up to London to 'enjoy themselves' and to see the Great Exhibition, London 1851.
PAYN, J.,
  Lights and Shadows of London Life, vol. I, London 1867 (in a serial form in 1862).
SALA, George Augustus H.,
  Gaslight and Daylight, With Some London Scenes they Shine Upon, London 1859.
  Living London: being 'Echoes' re-echoed, London 1883.

SHERWELL, Arthur,
  Life in West London, A Study and a Contrast, London 1897.
SIMS, George Robert, ed.,
  Living London, Its Works and Its Play, Its Humour and Its Pathos, Its Sights and Its Scenes, 3 vols, London 1902.
TRISTAN, Flora,
  Promenades dans Londres ou l'aristocratie & les prolétaires anglais, ed. and with a commentary by François Bédarida, Maspero, Paris 1978.
VALLES, Jules,
  La Rue à Londres, les Editeurs français réunis, Paris 1951 (1866).

(b) Housing

GAVIN, Hector,
  The Habitations of the Industrial Classes, Address delivered at Crosby Hall, Nov. 1850, London 1851.
GORE, Montague,
  On the Dwellings of the Poor and the Means of Improving Them, London 1851 (second edn).
HILL, Octavia,
  Homes of the London Poor, London 1875.
HOPKINS, Ellice,
  The Visitation of Dens, London 1874.
INGHAM, John Arthur,
  City Slums. Land Depression and Common Labour 'The Anomaly of Legislation'. A Policitical Thesis, London 1889.
TRIPE, J.W.,
  'Suggestions for the Amendement of the Artisans Dwellings Acts', *Transactions of the Society of Medical Officers of Health*, London 1883–1884.

(c) Health and hygiene

BATE, George,
  'Annual Report of the Medical Officer of Health and Bethnal Green for the Year 1878', in *Annual Reports of Medical Officers of Health*, London 1855–1893.
CANTLIE, Sir James,
  Degeneration amongst Londoners, London 1885.
CORNER, Matthew,
  'Report on the Sanitary Condition and Public Health of Mile End Old Town, 1873', in *Annual Reports of Medical Officers of Health*, London 1855–1893.

FLINN, M.W., ed.,
  Report on the Sanitary Condition of the Labouring Population of Great Britain, by
  E. Chadwick, Edinburgh University Press, Edinburgh 1965.
GAVIN, Hector,
  The Unhealthiness of London and the Necessity of Remedial Measures, London
  1847.
JEPHSON, Henry,
  Sanitary Evolution of London, London 1907.
POORE, George Vivian,
  London, Ancient and Modern, from the Sanitary and Medical Point of View,
  London 1889.
RENDLE, William,
  London Vestries and their Sanitary Work; are they willing and able to do it? etc.,
  London 1865.
SARVIC, Thomas,
  'Annual Report of the Medical Officer of Health of Bethnal Green, 1871', in
  Annual Reports of Medical Officers of Health, London 1855–1893.
SIMON, John,
  Sanitary Conditions of the City of London, London 1854.
  *Report on the Contagious Diseases Act, Showing the Expense in Policy, and
  General Inutility of Its Proposed Extension to the Civil Population*, London
  1871.
TRIPE, J.W.,
  'The Domestic Sanitary Arrangements of the Metropolitan Poor', *Trans-
  actions of the Society of Medical Officers of Health*, London 1883–1884.
WOODHULL, Victoria,
  The Rapid Multiplication of the Unfit, London 1891.

(d) The workers

BOOTH, Charles, ed.,
  Life and Labour of the People of London, 17 vols, London 1902.
ENGELS, Frederick,
  The Condition of the Working Class in England, Panther Books, London 1969
  (1845).
GIFFEN, R.,
  'The Progress of the Working Classes in the Last Half Century: being the
  Inaugural Address of R. Giffen, L.L.D., President of the Statistical
  Society', *Journal of the Statistical Society*, vol. XLVI, part IV, December
  1883.
LAYTON, W.T.,
  'Changes in the Wages of Domestic Servants during Fifty Years', *Journal of*

the Royal Statistical Society, 1908.
MEARNS, Andrew,
  London and Its Teeming Toilers, London 1886.
ROWE, Richard,
  How our Working People Live, London 1882.
'THE BRITISH WEEKLY' COMMISSIONERS,
  Toilers in London; Or, Inquiries Concerning Female Labour in the Metropolis,
  Hodder & Stoughton, London 1889.
THOMPSON, E.P. and Eileen YEO, eds,
  The Unknown Mayhew: Selections from the Morning Chronicle 1849–1850,
  Penguin Books, Harmondsworth 1973.
TWINING, Lousia,
  Workhouses and Women's Work, London 1858.
A JOURNEYMAN ENGINEER (Thomas Wright),
  Some Habits and Customs of the Working Classes, London 1867.
  The Great Unwashed, London 1868.
  Our New Masters, London 1873.

(e) Poverty

BOOTH, William,
  In Darkest England and the Way Out, Charles Knight, London 1970 (1890).
BOSANQUET, Helen,
  Rich and Poor, London 1898.
BURET, Emile,
  De la misère des classes laborieuses en Angleterre et en France, 2 vols, Paulin,
  Paris 1840.
GREENWOOD, James,
  A Night in a Workhouse, London 1866.
  The Seven Curses of London. Scenes from the Victorian Underworld, Basil
  Blackwell, Oxford 1981 (1869).
  In Strange Company, London 1873.
  Low Life Deeps, and an Account of the Strange Fish to be Found There, London
  1876.
HIGGS, Mary,
  Three Nights in Women's Lodging Houses, London 1905.
HILL, Octavia,
  District Visiting, London 1877.
HOLLINGSHEAD, John,
  Ragged London in 1861, Introduction and Notes by Anthony S. Whol, Dent,
  London and Melbourne 1986 (1861).
KEATING, Peter, ed.,

Into Unknown England 1866–1913, Selections from the Social Explorers, Fontana/Collins, Glasgow 1976.

LONDON, Jack,
The People of the Abyss, London 1903.

MASTERMAN, Charles Frederick G.,
From the Abyss, London 1902.
The Condition of England, London 1909.

MAYHEW, Henry,
London Labour and the London Poor, 4 vols, Dover Publications, New York 1968 (1861–1862).

MEARNS, Andrew,
The Bitter Cry of Outcast London. An Inquiry into the Condition of the Abject Poor, London 1883.

MEYRICK, F.,
The Outcast and Poor of London, London 1858.

SIMS, George Robert,
How the Poor Live, London 1883.
How the Poor Live and Horrible London, London 1889.

WOODS, Robert A., ed.,
The Poor in Great Cities, Their Problems and What is Being Done to Solve Them, London 1896.

(f) Morality and sexuality

ANON.,
The Servant Girl in London Showing the Dangers to which Young Country Girls are exposed on their Arrival in Town with Advice to Them, to their Parents, to their Masters, and to their Mistresses, Respectfully dedicated to all Heads of Families and Benevolent Socities, London 1840.

BARKER, Priscilla,
The Secret Book containing Private Information and Instruction for Women and Young Girls, London 1888 (1868).

BEETON, Isabella,
Mrs. Beeton's Book of Household Management, London 1861.

BLOCH, Ivan,
The Sexual Life of Our Time in its Relation to Modern Civilization, translated from the German, London 1908.

BRINDLEY, John,
The Immoralities of Socialisam: Being an Exposure of Mr. Owen's Attack upon Marriage . . . , Birmingham 1840.

BROWNLOW, John,
Thoughts and Suggestions Having Reference to Infanticide, London 1864.

BURNS, Jabez,
The Marriage Gift Book and Bridal Token, London 1863.
BUTLER, Josephine, ed.,
Can Women Regenerate Society?, London 1844.
CAIRD, Alice Mona,
The Morality of Marriage and other Essays on the Status and Destiny of Women,
London 1897.
CARLILE, Richard,
Every Woman's Book; or What is Love? Containing Most Important Instructions
for the Prudent Regulations of the Principle of Love and the Number of a Family,
London 1828.
CARPENTER, Edward,
Love's Coming of Age: A Series of Papers on the Relations of the Sexes,
Manchester 1896.
ELLIS, Mrs Sarah,
The Education of Character; with Hints on Moral Training, London 1856.
FRANCE, Hector,
En Police Court, Paris 1891.
JONES, Harry,
Courtship and Marriage, with a Few Plain Words about some Other Great
Matters, London 1890.
KELLY, Thomas,
Thoughts on the Marriage of the Labouring Poor, London 1806.
KNOWLTON, Charles,
The Fruits of Philosophy: or the Private Companion of Young Married People,
New York 1832.
LEA, John W.,
Christian Marriage: Its Open and Secret Enemies in England at the Present Day,
London 1881.
LUSHINGTON, G.,
The Law of Affiliation Bastardy, London 1897.
LYTTLETON, The Rev. The Hon. Edward,
Training of the Young in the Laws of Sex, London 1901.
MASSIE, Joseph,
Farther Observations concerning the Foundling-Hospital: Pointing out the Ill
Effects which such an Hospital is likely to have upon the Religion, Liberty, and
Domestic Happiness of the People of Great Britain . . . , London 1759.
MORRISON, Frances,
The Influence of the Present Marriage System Upon the Character and Interest of
Females Contrasted with that Proposed by Robert Owen, Esq., Manchester
1838.

NOEL, Baptist W.,
  Spiritual Claims of the Metropolis, London 1836.
OWEN, Robert,
  Lectures on the Marriages of the Priesthood in the Old Immoral World, delivered in the Year 1835, before the passing of the New Marriage Act, Leeds 1835.
OWEN, Robert Dale,
  Divorce: being a Correspondence between Horace Greeley and Robert Dale Owen, New York 1860.
STICKNEY (afterwards Ellis) Sarah,
  The Women of England, Their Social Duties and Domestic Habits, London 1839 (second edition).
  The Mothers of England, Their Influence and Responsibility, London 1843.
  The Wives of England, Their Relative Duties, Domestic Influence, and Social Obligations, London 1843.

(g) Prostitution

ACTON, William,
  Prostitution, Considered in Its Moral, Social and Sanitary Aspects in London and Other Large Cities and Garrison Towns with Proposals for the Mitigation and Prevention of its Attendant Evils, London 1857.
GREG, W.R.,
  'Prostitution', *Westminster Review*, vol. 53, July 1850.
LOGAN, William,
  An Exposure from Personal Observations of Female Prostitution in London, Leeds and Rochdale, and Especially in the City of Glasgow, Glasgow 1843.
PARENT-DUCHÂTELET, Dr Alex J.B.,
  De la prostitution dans la ville de Paris considérée sous le rapport de l'hygiène publique, de la morale et de l'administration, 2 vols, Paris 1836.
RYAN, Michael,
  Prostitution in London, with a Comparative View of That in Paris and New York, London 1839.
SANGER, William W.,
  History of Prostitution: Its Extent, Causes and Effect Throughout the World, New York 1897.

VI SECONDARY SOURCES

ALEXANDER, Sally,
  'Women's Work in Nineteenth-Century London', in Juliet Mitchell and

Ann Oakley, eds, *The Rights and Wrongs of Women*, Penguin Books, Harmondsworth 1976.

ANDERSON, Michael, ed.,
Sociology of the Family, Penguin Books, Harmondsworth 1971.

ANNALES E.S.C., numéro spécial: *Famille et société*, No. 4–5, July–October 1972.

ARIÈS, Philippe,
L'Enfant et la vie familiale sous l'Ancien Régime, Plon, Paris, 1960. (*Centuries of Childhood*, transl. R. Boldick, Penguin Books, Harmondsworth 1986).

BASCH, Françoise,
Relative Creatures: Victorian Women in Society and the Novel, Schocken, New York 1974.

BÉDARIDA, François,
'Londres au milieu du XIX^c siècle: une analyse de structure social', *Annales*, vol. XXII, no. 2, March–April 1968.

BENABOU, Erica-Marie,
introduced by Pierre Goubert, *La Prostitution et la police des mœurs au XVIIIe siècle*, Perrin, Paris 1987.

BRIGGS, Asa,
Victorian Cities, Pengiun Books, Harmondsworth 1968 (1963).

BROWNMILLER, Susan,
Against Our Will: Men, Women and Rape, Simon and Schuster, New York 1975.

BULLOUGH, Vern L.,
Sexual Variance in Society and History, John Wiley & Sons, New York 1976.

BURGIÈRE, André,
'Histoire et sexualité', *Annales E.S.C.*, July–August 1974.

BURGIÈRE, André,
'The Marriage Ritual in France: Ecclesiastical Practices and Popular Practices', in R. Forster and O. Ranum, eds, *Ritual, Religion and the Sacred*, Baltimore 1982.

BURN, W.L.,
The Age of the Equipoise, A Study of the Mid-Victorian Generation, Unwin University Books, London 1964.

COMFORT, Alex,
Sex in Society, Penguin Books, Harmondsworth 1964 (1950).

CORBIN, Alain,
Les Filles de noce, misère sexuelle et prostitution aux XIXe et XXe siècles, Aubier, Paris 1978.

CROSSICK, Geoffrey J.,
Social Structure and Working Class Behaviour: Kentish London 1840–1880,

Ph.D dissertation, University of London, February 1976 (unpublished).

DAVIDOFF, Leonore,
'Class and Gender in Victorian England: The Diaries of Arthur J. Munby and Hannah Cullwick', *Feminist Studies*, vol. 5, no. 1, Spring 1979.

DAVIN, Anna,
'Imperialism and Motherhood', *History Workshop Journal*, no. 5 Spring 1978.

DONZELOT, Jacques,
La Police des familles, Editions de Minuit, Paris 1977. (*The Policing of Familes: Welfare versus the State,* transl. Robert Hurley, Hutchinson, London 1980.)

DUCROCQ, Françoise,
'Les Exclues de l'histoire', *Critique, Victoria Station,* no. 405–6, February–March 1981.
'The London Biblewomen and Nurses Mission, 1857–1880: Class Relations/Women's Relations' in Barbara J. Harris and JoAnn McNamara eds, *Women and the Structure of Society*, Duke University Press, Durham, N.C. 1984.
'De la loi des pauvres à la loi de la jungle', in Marie-Claire Pasquier *et al.*, eds *Stratégies des femmes*, Editions Tierce, Paris 1984. ('From Poor Law to Jungle Law: Sexual Relations and Marital Strategies', in Judith Friend-lauder *et al.*, eds *Women in Culture and Politics, A Century of Change,* Indiana University Press, Bloomington 1986.)

DYOS, H.J. and Michael WOLF, eds,
The Victorian City: Images and Realities, 2 vols, Routledge & Kegan Paul, London 1973.

ENGELS, Frederick,
Origin of the Family, Private Property and the State, in Karl Marx and Frederick Engels, *Selected Works*, Lawrence & Wishart, London and New York 1976.

FAIRCHILDS, Cissie,
'Female Sexual Attitudes and Rise of Illegitimacy: A Case Study', *Journal of Interdisciplinary History*, vol. XIII, no. 4, Spring 1978.

FLANDRIN, Jean-Louis,
'Contraception, marriage et relations amoureuses dans l'Occident chrétien', *Annales E.S.C.*, November–December 1969.
Familles, parenté, maison, sexualité dans l'ancienne société, Hachette, Paris 1976. (*Families in Former Times: Kinship, Household and Sexuality,* transl. Richard Southern, Cambridge University Press, Cambridge 1979.)

FOUCAULT, Michel,
The History of Sexuality I, *An Introduction*, transl. Robert Hurley, Penguin Books (Peregrine), Harmondsworth 1984.

The History of Sexuality II, *The Uses of Pleasure*, Penguin Books, Harmondsworth 1988.

The History of Sexuality III, *Care of the Self*, Penguin Books, Harmondsworth 1990.

GAY, Peter,

The Bourgeois Experience, Victoria to Freud, vol. I, *Education of the Senses*, Oxford University Press, New York and Oxford 1984.

GILLIS, John R.,

Youth and History: Tradition and Change in European Age Relations, 1770 to Present, Academic Press, New York and London 1974.

'Servants, Sexual Relations, and the Risks of Illegitimacy in London, 1801–1900,, *Feminist Studies*, vol. V, no. 1, Spring 1979.

For Better, For Worse, British Marriages 1600 to the Present, Oxford University Press, New York and Oxford 1985.

GRISEWOOD, Harman, G.M. TREVELYAN, Bertrand RUSSELL, *et al.*, eds,

Ideas and Beliefs of the Victorians, An Historic Revaluation of the Victorian Age, E.P. Dutton & Co., New York 1966.

HAIR, P.E.H.,

'Bridal Pregnancy in Rural England in Earlier Centuries',

Population Studies, XX, part 2, November 1966.

HALL, Peter G.,

The Industries of London Since 1851, Hutchinson & Co., London 1962.

HARRISON, Fraser, ed.,

The Yellow Book, Sidgwick and Jackson, London 1974.

The Dark Angel, Aspects of Victorian Sexuality, Sheldon Press, London 1977.

HAVELOCK ELLIS,

La Prostitution. Ses causes, ses remèdes, Mercure de France, Paris 1929.

Sex in Relation to Society, Heinemann, London 1937.

Le Symbolisme érotique, le mécanisme de la détumescence, Tchou, Paris 1964.

HEATH, Stephen,

'Le Corps victorien anthologiquement', *in Critique, Victoria Station*, nos 405–406, February–March 1981.

HENRIQUES, Ursula R.Q.,

'Bastardy and the New Poor Law', *Past and Present*, no. 37, July 1967.

HENRIQUES, Dr Fernando,

Modern Sexuality, Prostitution and Society, vol. III, Panther, London 1969.

HOBSBAWM, Eric J.,

The Pelican Economic History of Britain, vol. III, *From 1750 to the Present Day*, *Industry and Empire*, Penguin Books, Harmondsworth 1969.

HOUGHTON, Walter E.,

The Victorian Frame of Mind, 1830–1870, Yale University Press, New Haven and London 1957.

KITSON CLARK, G.,
 The Making of Victorian England, Being the Ford Lectures Delivered before the University of Oxford, Methuen, London 1962.

KNIGHT, Patricia,
 'Women and Abortion in Victorian and Edwardian England', *History Workshop Journal*, no. 4, Autumn 1977.

LASLETT, Peter,
 The World We Have Lost, Methuen, London 1965.
 Family Life and Illicit Love in Earlier Generations, Essays in Historical Sociology, Cambridge University Press, Cambridge 1977.

MACFARLANE, Alan,
 Marriage and Love in England, 1300–1840, Basil Blackwell, Oxford 1986.

MARCUS, Steven,
 The Other Victorians: A Study of Sexuality and Pornography in Mid-Nineteenth Century England, Weidenfeld and Nicolson, London 1966.

NAVAILLES, Jean-Pierre,
 La Famille ouvrière dans l'Angleterre victorienne, Editions du Champ Vallon, Paris 1983.

PEARSALL, Ronald,
 The Worm in the Bud: The World of Victorian Sexuality, Weidenfeld and Nicolson, London 1969.

PERROT, Michèlle,
 'La Femme populaire rebelle', in *L'Histoire sans qualitiés*, Editions Galilée, Paris 1979.

PHAYER, J. Michael,
 Sexual Liberation and Religion in Nineteenth Century Europe, Croom Helm, London 1977.

PINCHBECK, Ivy,
 Women Workers and the Industrial Revolution 1750–1850, Frank Cass, London 1930.

QUINLAN, Maurice J.,
 Victorian Prelude: A History of English Manners 1770–1830, Archon Books, Hamden 1965.

RAPP, Rayna, Ellen Ross and Renate Bridenthal,
 'Examining Family History', *Feminist Studies*, vol.V, no. 1, Spring 1979.

RATTRAY, Taylor Gordon,
 Sex in History: The Story of Society's Changing Attitudes to Sex Throughout the Ages, Harper Torchbooks, New York 1973 (1954).

REICH, Wilhelm,
 La Révolution sexuelle, Plon, Paris 1968 (1930). (*The Sexual Revolution*, New

York 1969.)

REID, Alastair,
'Intelligent Artisans and Aristocrats of Labour: The Essays of Thomas Wright', in Jay Winter, ed. *The Working Class in Modern British History, Essays in Honour of Henry Pelling*, Cambridge University Press, Cambridge 1983.

RUGOFF, Milton,
Prudery and Passion, Rupert Hart-Davis, London 1971.

SHORTER, Edward,
'Illegitimacy, Sexual Revolution and Social Change in Europe, 1750–1900', *Journal of Interdisciplinary History*, no. 2, 1971
'Sexual Change and Illegitimacy: The European Experience', in Robert Bezucha, ed., *Modern European Social History*, Heath, London 1972.
The Making of the Modern Family, Fontana/Collins, Glasgow 1975.

SMITH, F. Barry,
'Sexuality in Britain, 1800–1990: Some Suggested Revisions', in Martha Vicinus, ed., *A Widening Sphere*, Indiana University Press, Bloomington 1977.

STEARNS, Peter N.,
'Working-Class Women in Britain, 1890–1914', in Martha Vicinus, ed., *Suffer and Be Still*, Indiana University Press, Bloomington 1972.

STEDMAN JONES, Gareth,
Outcast London: A Study in the Relationship between Classes in Victorian Society, Clarendon Press, Oxford 1971.
'Class Expression Versus Social Control? A Critique of Recent Trends in the Social History of "Leisure" ', *History Workshop Journal*, no. 4, 1977.
Languages of Class: Studies in English Working-Class History, 1832–1982, Cambridge University Press, Cambridge 1983.

STONE, Lawrence,
The Family, Sex and Marriage in England, 1500–1800, Weidenfeld and Nicolson, London 1977.

STRONG, Bryan,
'Towards a History of the Experimental Family: Sex and Incest in the Nineteenth Century Family', *Journal of Marriage and the Family*, vol. 33, no. 3, August 1973.

THANE, Pat,
'Women and the Poor Law in Victorian England', *History Workshop Journal*, no. 6, Autumn 1978,

TILLY, Louise A. and Joan W. Scott,
Women, Work and Family, Holt Rinehart and Winston, New York 1978.

TRUDGILL, Eric,

Madonnas and Magdalens: The Origins and Developments of Victorian Sexual Attitudes, Heinemann, London 1976

VICINUS, Martha,
Suffer and Be Still, Indiana University Press, Bloomington 1974.
The Industrial Muse: A Study of Nineteenth-Century British Working-Class Literature, Croom Helm, London 1974.
Independent Women, Work and Community for Single Women, 1850–1920, Virago Press, London 1985.

WALKOWITZ, Judith,
Prostitution and Victorian Society: Women, Class and the State, Cambridge University Press, Cambridge 1980.

WEBB, Sidney and Beatrice WEBB,
English Poor Law History, Part II, 2 vols., Longman, London 1929.

WEEKS, Jeffrey,
Sex, Politics and Society: The Regulation of Sexuality Since 1800, Longman, London and New York 1981.

YOUNG, G.M.,
Victorian England: Portrait of an Age, Oxford University Press, Oxford & New York 1983 (1936).

DATE DUE

DEC 2 0 1995

FEB 2 0 1997

FEB 2 4 1998

FEB 2 0 2000

DEMCO, INC. 38-2931